THE WALL STREET JOURNAL.

GUIDE TO UNDERSTANDING MONEY & INVESTING

KENNETH M. MORRIS

VIRGINIA B. MORRIS

LIGHTBULB

PRESS

LIGHTBULB PRESS
Project Team

Design Director Dave Wilder
Editors Sophie Forrester, Renée Ryerson
Copy Editor Sarah Norris
Production Thomas F. Trojan
Illustration Krista K. Glasser
Photography Danielle Berman, Andy Shen
Digital Output Quad Right, Inc.
Sales and Marketing Germaine Ma, Karen Meldrom

SPECIAL THANKS

DOW JONES

Dow Jones & Co. Dan Austin, Joan Wolf-Woolley, Lottie Lindberg and Elizabeth Yeh at The Wall Street Journal Library
The Wall Street Journal Tom Herman, Douglas Sease

PICTURE CREDITS
American Bank Note Company, American Stock Exchange, Bureau of Engraving and Printing, Chase Manhattan Archives, Chicago Board of Trade, CUC International, Museum of the City of New York, National Association of Securities Dealers, New York Stock Exchange, The Nasdaq Stock Market, T. Rowe Price Investment Services, United States Mint

Lightbulb Press, Inc., 112 Madison Avenue, New York, New York 10016, Tel. 917-256-4900, www.lightbulbpress.com
FIRESIDE and colophon are registered trademarks of Simon & Schuster Inc.
10 9 8 7 6
ISBN: 0-684-86902-0
Library of Congress Cataloging-in-Publication Data is available. No part of this book may be reproduced in any form or by any electronic or mechanical means, including photocopying or information storage and retrieval system, without written permission from the publisher, except by a reviewer who may quote brief passages in a review. This publication is sold with the understanding that the authors and publishers are not engaged in rendering financial, accounting or legal advice, and they assume no legal responsibility for the completeness or accuracy of the contents of this book. Some charts and graphs have been edited for illustrative purposes or reduced in size. The text is based on information available at time of publication. Distributed by Fireside, a division of Simon & Schuster. *The Wall Street Journal* is a registered trademark of Dow Jones & Company, Inc. and is used in the book pursuant to permission of *The Wall Street Journal*.

*W*hen *The Wall Street Journal Guide to Understanding Money & Investing* first appeared in 1993, we thought that the book, with its colorful graphics and clear language, would appeal to people who wanted to know about the often-baffling world of the financial markets.

But we had no idea that it would become an indispensable resource in brokerage firms, banks, financial advisors' offices and school classrooms, or that there would be over a million copies in print. Nor did we ever dream it would be recast for the Asian markets and translated into Chinese.

As popular as the guide remains, we felt it was time for a revised editon that recognizes the monumental changes in the financial markets in the 1990s: the increasing number of people who are investing, the longest bull market in history, the sometimes dizzying speed with which records have been smashed and the explosion of electronic trading fueled by access to the World Wide Web.

In updating *Money & Investing* we haven't lost sight of our original mission: to unravel the mysteries of the financial markets—the language, the players, the strategies and, above all, the risks and rewards of investing—in a straightforward but lighthearted way. We show (and tell) how the markets work, why money gains and loses value, and what you need to know to make the right investments and measure their performance.

In preparing this revision, we are deeply indebted to The Wall Street Journal for the use of their financial tables and charts, and for the vast information resources and financial expertise they made available to us. We are especially grateful to Douglas Sease for his unstinting editorial support.

Kenneth M. Morris
Virginia B. Morris

THE WALL STREET JOURNAL.

GUIDE TO UNDERSTANDING MONEY & INVESTING

MONEY

STOCKS

CONTENTS

BONDS

MUTUAL FUNDS

FUTURES & OPTIONS

The History of Money

Most money doesn't have any value of its own. It's worth what it can buy at any given time.

The history of money begins with people learning to trade the things they had for the things they wanted. If they wanted an ax, they had to find someone who had one and was willing to exchange it for something of theirs. The system works the same way today, with one variation: now you can give the seller **money** in exchange for the item you want, and the seller can use the money to buy something else.

IN THE BEGINNING WAS BARTER

Our earliest ancestors were self-sufficient, providing their own food, clothing and shelter from their surroundings. There was rarely anything extra—and nothing much to trade it for.

But as communities formed, hunting and gathering became more efficient. Occasionally there were surpluses of one commodity or another. A people with extra animal skins but not enough grain could exchange its surplus with another people with plenty of food but no skins. **Barter** was born.

As societies grew more complex, barter flourished. The most famous example may be Peter Minuit's swap in 1626 of $24 in beads and trinkets for the island of Manhattan. Its property value in 1998 was assessed at $23.4 billion.

MONEY FILLS THE BILL

It takes time and energy to find someone with exactly what you want who's also willing to take what you have to offer. And it isn't always easy to agree on what things are worth. How many skins is a basket of grain worth? What happens if the plow you want is worth a cow and a half?

As trade flourished, money came into use. Once buyers and sellers agreed what was acceptable as a means of payment, they could establish a system that assigned different values to coins or other durable and easily transportable items. The term **currency**, another word for money, means anything that's actually used as a means of exchange.

Using money also meant that buying and selling didn't have to happen at the same time. Sellers could wait until they were ready to make a purchase to spend the money they had received. What's more, they could accumulate money from a number of sales to give them more buying power.

Money has taken many different forms over the years. In Rome, for example, soldiers were often paid with sacks of salt—that's sal in Latin, the root of **salary**—and salt was also used in ancient China to pay for small purchases.

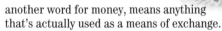

The expression "Don't take any wooden nickels" was a common warning for country boys headed for the big city in the 1800s. But there never were any—until 1932, when the bank closed in Tenino, WA, and left people without cash. The money they used was wooden coins worth 25¢, 50¢, and $1.

FOUR BITS

For small change, American colonists often cut up coins to make change on the spot. A half coin was considered four bits, and a quarter coin was two bits.

METAL BECOMES THE STANDARD

As early as 2500 B.C. various precious metals—gold, silver and copper—were used to pay for goods and services in Egypt and Asia Minor. By 700 B.C. the kingdom of Lydia was minting coins made of electrum, a pale yellow alloy of gold and silver. The coins were valuable, durable and portable. Better yet, they couldn't die or rot on the way to market. In addition, using coins permitted payments by **tale**, or counting out the right amount, rather than weighing it. That simplified the exchange process even more. For a long time, the relative value of currencies was measured against precious metals, usually gold or silver. That's where terms like **pound sterling** and **gold standard** originated. In modern times, though, national economies have moved away from basing their currency on metal reserves. Gold hasn't been a universal yardstick since 1971, when the U.S. stopped redeeming its paper currency with gold.

MONEY BY FIAT

When money was made of gold or silver—or could be exchanged for one of them—it was **commodity currency**. But money that has no intrinsic value and can't be redeemed for precious metal is **fiat currency**. Most currency circulating today is fiat money, created and authorized by various governments as their official currency.

FORMS OF PAYMENT

Stone Money
Yap Island

Salt
China

Ivory (Whale Tooth)
Fiji

Elephant Hair
Africa

Tobacco
Solomon Islands

Brick Tea Money
Siberia

East Indian Money Tree
Malay Peninsula

Copper Money
Alaskan Indian

Gold Stater
Turkey

Drachma
Thessaly

Owl Coin
Athens

Sestertius of Caesar Augustus
Rome

Pine Tree Shilling
Massachusetts

Yen, or Round Money
Japan

Piece of Eight (8 Reals)
Spain

5

Paper Money

Bills come in different sizes, colors and denominations, but their real value is based on the economic strength of the country that issues them.

THE ORIGINS OF PAPER MONEY

Although the idea of paper money can be found in bills and receipts recorded by the Babylonians as early as 2500 B.C., the earliest bills can be traced to China. In 1282, Kubla Khan issued paper notes made of mulberry bark bearing his seal and his treasurers' signatures. The **Kuan** is the oldest surviving paper money. The currency—about 8½x11 inches—was issued in China by the Ming dynasty between 1368 and 1399.

THE U.S. DOLLAR

The American **dollar** comes from a silver coin called the Joachimsthaler minted in 1519 in the valley (thal) of St. Joachim in Bohemia (Jachymov in Czech Republic). The coin was widely circulated and called the **daalder** in Holland, the **daler** in Scandinavia and the **dollar** in England.

Joachimsthaler
1519

More than two dozen countries besides the U.S. call their currency dollars.

The U.S. dollar's early history was chaotic until the National Banking Act of 1863 established a uniform currency. Before that, banks used paper money (called **scrip**), but they couldn't always meet their customers' demands for **hard currency** (gold or silver coins, or **specie**). Often the dollar could be exchanged for just a fraction of its stated value.

Dollars were once backed by gold and silver reserves. Until 1963, U.S. bills were called **silver certificates**. Today they are Federal Reserve notes, backed only by the economic integrity of the U.S. You can't exchange them for specie.

The first European bank notes were printed in Sweden in 1661, and France put paper money into wide circulation in the 18th century.

The first paper money in the British Empire was in the form of **promissory notes** given to Massachusetts soldiers in 1690, when their siege of Quebec failed and there was no booty to pay them with. The idea became popular with the other colonies, if not with the soldiers who were paid that way.

DOLLARS AROUND THE WORLD

Australia

Canada

Bermuda

Hong Kong

Antigua & Barbuda
Bahamas
Barbados
Belize
Brunei
Cayman Islands
Dominica
Fiji Islands
Grenada
Guyana
Jamaica
Liberia

Namibia
New Zealand
St. Kitts and Nevis
St. Lucia
St. Vincent
Singapore
Solomon Islands
Taiwan
Trinidad & Tobago
Zimbabwe

THE UPS AND DOWNS OF PAPER MONEY

Paper money has had its ups and downs because its value changes so quickly with changing economic conditions. When there's lots of money in circulation, prices go up and paper money buys less. That's known as **inflation**.

For example, during the American Revolution paper money dropped in value from $1 to just 2½¢. In Germany in 1923, you needed 726,000,000 marks to buy what you'd been able to get for 1 mark in 1918.

In 1923, a German housewife burned mark notes in her kitchen stove, since it was cheaper to burn marks than to use them to buy firewood.

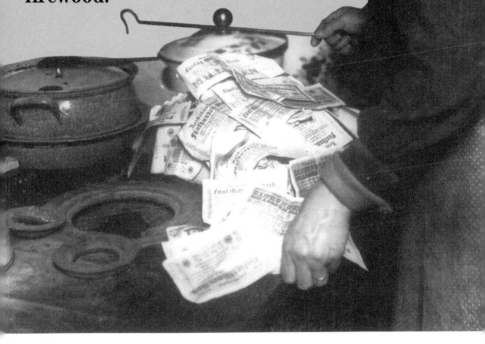

MAKING PAPER MONEY

The Bureau of Engraving and Printing prints money at plants in Washington, D.C., and Fort Worth, Texas. The money is printed in large sheets, stacked into piles of 100 and cut into bills that are bundled into bricks for shipping. The engraved plates, which can be used to produce up to three million impressions before they have to be replaced, are designed with intricate patterns of lines and curves to make the money hard to copy. As an added security measure, several different engravers work on each plate.

The Bureau makes the slightly magnetic ink itself from secret formulas. Special paper, made by Crane and Company, has been used for all U.S. currency since 1879.

The content of the paper is a closely guarded secret, although we know the sheets are now about 75% cotton and 25% linen and contain small, faintly colored nylon threads.

You can get back the full value of a torn bill from the Bureau of Engraving and Printing in Washington, D.C.—as long as you turn in at least 51% of the ripped one.

The U.S. Dollar

In 1862, the U.S. government issued its first paper money. The bills were called **greenbacks** because the backs were printed in green ink—to distinguish them from gold certificates.

Each U.S. banknote has a distinctively marked green-, black- and cream-colored face. On the dollar bill, a letter within a seal to the left of the portrait identifies the Federal Reserve bank that issued the bill. In this case, it's B for New York. A corresponding number—New York's is 2—appears four times on the face. On the redesigned bills, the seal of the Federal Reserve system itself appears. The back of each denomination is different. On the dollar, it's the **Great Seal of the United States**. Its reverse side, on the right of the bill, features the American eagle and the number 13, representing the country as a whole and the original 13 states. Symbols include: 13 stripes on the eagle's shield, the 13-star constellation above the eagle's head, 13 warlike arrows grasped in one of the eagle's claws and the olive branch of peace, with 13 leaves and 13 olives, grasped in the other.

Federal regulations require that any reproduction of U.S. currency be at least 1½ times larger than actual size (as it is here) or ¾ of actual size. No bills can be reproduced in color.

Greenbacks are created in three steps. The black front is printed the first day from the engraved plates. Then the green back is printed the second day, giving the ink time to dry. Finally, the green serial numbers and Treasury seal are added to the front using a process called COPE, or currency overprinting and processing equipment.

Legal tender is money a government creates that must—by law—be accepted as payment of debt. A $100 bill is legal tender, for example, but a $100 check isn't. That's because the check is issued by a bank, not the government.

Bills are numbered two ways. The **eight-digit serial number** is printed on the top right and lower left on the front. The number of every bill of the same denomination in the same series is different. The number begins with a letter (here B) identifying the issuing Federal Reserve Bank.

Each bill also has a **series identification number** engraved between the portrait and the signature of the Secretary of the Treasury. It gives the year the note's design was introduced, usually when a new Secretary or a new U.S. Treasurer has been appointed.

The front of the seal has a 13-letter Latin motto, **ANNUIT COEPTIS**, which means "He has favored our undertaking," a reference to the blessing of an all-seeing deity whose eye is at the apex of the pyramid. The pyramid itself suggests a strong base for future growth. Underneath, in Roman numerals, is the date 1776, the year the Declaration of Independence was signed. The second motto, **NOVUS ORDO SECLORUM**, means "New order of the ages."

DOLLARS BY ANY OTHER NAME...

boodle	clams	lettuce	simoleons
bread	dinero	long green	smackers
bucks	dough	loot	spondulics
	gelt	moolah	sugar
	gravy	rocks	the ready
	grease	sawbucks	wad
	jack	scratch	wampum
	juice	shekels	wangan

The Money Cycle

Money is a permanent fixture of modern society, but the bills and coins we use have a limited lifespan.

A major redesign of U.S. currency is underway. The first new bill, the $100, was introduced in 1996, followed by the $50 in 1997 and the $20 in 1998, with the others slated to follow. Their most noticeable features are larger, off-center portraits and even more intricate border designs—both calculated to make the bills more difficult to copy in an era of increasingly sophisticated computer and photocopying equipment.

Since paper bills wear out from changing hands, replacements are printed regularly to maintain a steady supply. Not surprisingly, dollar bills have the shortest life span, about 13 to 18 months. Other countries have successfully introduced durable coins with lifespans of 30 to 40 years to replace their small bills, though so far that approach hasn't worked in the U.S. A new $1 coin is scheduled for release in 2000 to replace the unpopular Susan B. Anthony dollar. Its design should resolve one of the existing coin's major drawbacks: It looks and feels so like the quarter that it's easy to confuse them.

The Money Cycle

Old money is taken out of circulation and replaced on a regular basis.

The Treasury ships new money to the Federal Reserve Banks.

U.S. TREASURY

FED BANKS

Federal Reserve banks return the old money to the Treasury. Paper money is shredded and burned into mulch. Coins are sent back to the Mint for melting and recasting.

THE LINCOLN PENNY

The first U.S. coin with the portrait of a president was the 1909 penny honoring Abraham Lincoln. The face of the penny is still the same today, though the back was redesigned in 1959 to include the Lincoln Memorial.

McKinley

Cleveland

Madison

Chase

Wilson

VANISHING AMERICANS

In 1969, bills over $100 in value were eliminated as currency because of declining demand. The faces that disappeared were McKinley on the $500, Cleveland on the $1,000, Madison on the $5,000, Chase on the $10,000 and Wilson on the largest of them all, the $100,000.

THE TWO-DOLLAR BILL

The Treasury from time to time issued $2 bills, but they've never been very popular with the public. The last ones were printed in 1976, but they faced all kinds of hurdles—including no place for them in cash register drawers. And a surprisingly large portion of the population is superstitious about using them.

Federal Reserve banks and branches distribute the new money to individual banks in their region.

The banks distribute the money to their customers, including businesses and individuals.

The money circulates through the economy and around the world, changing hands many times as people pay in cash and get change back.
Businesses and individuals deposit their cash, including old bills, in their bank accounts.

The banks separate the worn bills and coins they collect from the ones that can stay in circulation. They ship the worn (and very dirty) ones back to their Fed branch or bank.

HOW COINS COME TO LIFE

In the U.S., new coins are struck at three Bureau of the Mint branches, and each coin carries the mark of the branch where it was minted: **D** for Denver, **S** for San Francisco, and **P** (or no mark at all) for Philadelphia. The process of making coins is called **minting**, from the Latin word *moneta*.

The whole process is a modest profitmaker. For example, it costs about 9/10 of a cent to make a penny. That difference—about a dollar for every thousand pennies—is profit. The Mint prefers the term **seigniorage**. But whatever you call it, it amounts to more than $400 million annually.

Other Forms of Money

Money doesn't always change hands. It's often transferred from one account to another by written or electronic instructions.

Technology has revolutionized the way we use money. The form we're most familiar with—bills and coins—represents only about 8% of the trillions of dollars that circulate in the U.S. economy.

Before 1945, most people paid with cash. By 1990, about $30 trillion was transferred annually by check. Electronic transfers have increased the volume dramatically. In 1998, an average of $1.3 trillion was moved electronically every day through the Federal Reserve System.

NOT CASHLESS—YET

A society that gets along without cash still seems a long way off.

We haven't yet abandoned our pennies, let alone our bills. On the other hand, the money we move with a checkbook, an ATM card, a credit card and a debit card—or a program on a personal computer—suggests that the story of money is still being written.

Increasingly sophisticated **smart cards**, whose dollar value is imbedded in a microchip that can be debited and replenished electronically, are likely to be part of that tale. For example, they're already replacing tickets and tokens to pay for mass transit, highway and bridge tolls.

398

DEAN SCHARF
18 W. 81ST ST., APT. 8
NEW YORK, NY 10024

1–12/210

Oct 14 19 98

$ 43.00

THE OF

AT+T

Forty-three and no/100's

DOLLARS

FIRSTBANK
2219 BROADWAY, NEW YORK, NY 10024

Dean Scharf

⑈021000128⑈ 058⑈47539⑈7⑈ 0398 ⑈000000430⑈

HOW CHECKS MOVE MONEY

High-speed electronic equipment **reads** the sorting and payment instructions, called **MICR** (Magnetic Image Character Recognition) codes, printed in magnetic ink along the bottom of the check. The money is then **debited** (subtracted) from the writer's account and **credited** (added) to the receiver's.

Your bank account number, beginning with the branch number, identifies the account that money will be taken from to pay the check.

The check routing number identifies the bank, its location, and its Federal Reserve district and branch. The coded information explains the arrangement for collecting payment from the bank. The same information, in different format, appears in the upper right of the check, under the check number.

The check number and the amount of the check are printed by the first bank to receive the check when it is deposited or cashed. When you actually write the check, the space under your name is blank.

Information written and stamped on the back of the check shows the account the dollar value was credited to, the bank where it was cashed or deposited and the date, plus the payment stamp from your bank.

MAKING THE MOST OF CREDIT

In 1998, an estimated 70% of all U.S. households had one or more credit cards. And the majority used their cards regularly. But based on the number who pay their bills in full every month—about 86%, according to Veribanc—most people are taking advantage of credit to consolidate payment for their purchases or limit the amount of cash they have to carry around. Most sellers are happy to accept credit, too, despite the fee they pay the card issuer, because people tend to spend more when they're using a card than they do when they're laying out cash.

Due	New Balance	Minimum Payment	Enter Amount Enclosed
19	$456.90	$10.00	$ 456.90

MONEY 'ROUND THE CLOCK

With a **personal identification number (PIN)** or **personal identification code (PIC)** and a bank ATM card linked to one or more of your accounts, you can withdraw or deposit money, find out how much you have in an account, pay bills or choose from a growing list of other services—without ever entering a bank.

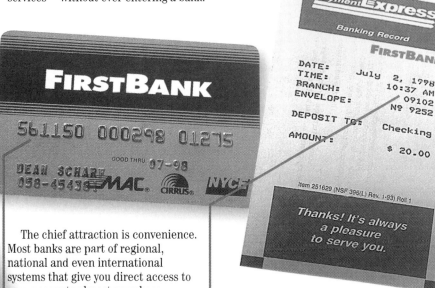

The chief attraction is convenience. Most banks are part of regional, national and even international systems that give you direct access to your accounts almost anywhere.

The card number is linked to your bank account, though it is not the same as your account number. The magnetic strip on the back identifies the bank and account when the card is inserted in a machine. The PIN number doesn't appear anywhere, for security reasons.

> **In the 1990s ATM fees have grown almost as fast as ATM use.**

Details of your transactions are printed on the receipt the ATM provides. **The date and location of the ATM** branch may be important if you question certain transactions. Cameras often record the activity at an ATM and can provide evidence in unresolved disputes. There's rarely a limit on the number of transactions you can make on any one visit, though there may be a daily limit on the total amount you can withdraw in one day.

ELECTRONIC TRANSFERS

You can use a telephone or computer to authorize movement of funds among your own accounts or to transfer amounts out of your accounts to pay bills. Other examples of electronic transfers are the direct deposit of paychecks and Social Security payments. Increasingly, mutual funds, brokerage firms, banks, utility companies and retail businesses are expanding your electronic options.

DEBIT AND CREDIT CARDS

Debit cards and credit cards look alike, but work differently. Credit cards let you charge a purchase and pay for it later because you've got a credit arrangement with a bank or other financial institution. Debit cards subtract the amount of your purchase directly from your bank account and credit it to the seller's account.

Usually you sign a credit card receipt after it's been verified by the seller's security system. When you use a debit card, you enter your PIN (or PIC) to authorize the transaction.

DEBIT

The Federal Reserve System

The Federal Reserve System is the guardian of the nation's money—banker, regulator, controller and watchdog all rolled into one.

Like other countries, the U.S. has a national bank to oversee its economic and monetary policies. But the Federal Reserve System, known informally as the Fed, isn't one bank. It's 12 separate district banks, with 25 regional branches, spread across the country, so that no one state, region or business group can exert too much control.

Each district bank has a president and board of directors, and the system itself is run by a seven-member board of governors. In addition, there's an Open Market Committee, whose responsibility is guiding day-to-day monetary decisions.

The Federal Reserve's Many Roles

The Fed plays many roles as part of its responsibility to keep the economy healthy.
The Fed handles the day-to-day banking business of the U.S. government. It gets deposits of corporate taxes for unemployment, withholding and income, and also of federal excise taxes on liquor, tobacco, gasoline and regulated services like phone systems. It also authorizes payment of government bills like Social Security and Medicare as well as interest payments on Treasury bills, notes and bonds.

REGULATOR

By authorizing buying and selling of government securities, the Fed tries to balance the money in circulation. When the economy is stable, the demand for goods and services is fairly constant, and so are prices. Achieving that stability supports the Fed's goals of keeping the economy healthy and maintaining the value of the dollar.

BANKER

The Fed maintains bank accounts for the U.S. Treasury and many government and quasi-government agencies. It deposits and withdraws funds the way you do at your own bank, but in bigger volume: Over 80 million Treasury checks are written every year.

LENDER

If a bank needs to borrow money, it can turn to a Federal Reserve bank. The interest the Fed charges banks is called the **discount rate**. Bankers don't like to borrow from the Fed, since it may suggest they have problems. And they can often borrow more cheaply from other banks.

Seattle
Helena
Portland
Salt Lake City
Denver
★ SAN FRANCISCO
Los Angeles
El Paso

MONEY

HOW THE FED WORKS

Technically a corporation owned by banks, the Fed works more like a government agency than a business. Under the direction of its chairman, it sets economic policy, supervises banking operations and has become a major factor in shaping the economy.

The governors are appointed to 14-year terms by the president and confirmed by Congress, which insulates them from political pressure to some extent. One term expires every two years. However, the chairman serves a four-year term and is often chosen by the president to achieve specific economic goals.

MEMBER BANKS

About half of all the banks in the country are members of the Federal Reserve System. All national banks must belong, and state-chartered banks are eligible if they meet the financial standards the Fed has established.

IT'S NOT THE FDIC!

The Fed is not the same as the **FDIC** (Federal Deposit Insurance Corporation). The FDIC insures bank depositors against losses if their bank gets into financial trouble. It doesn't regulate the banks.

AUDITOR	CONTROLLER	GUARDIAN	ADMINISTRATOR

The Fed monitors the business affairs and audits the records of all of the banks in its system. Its particular concerns are compliance with banking rules and the quality of loans.

When currency wears out or gets damaged, the Fed takes it out of circulation and authorizes its replacement. Then the Treasury has new bills printed and new coins minted.

Gold stored in the U.S. by foreign governments is held in the vault at the New York Federal Reserve Bank—some 10,000 tons of it. That's more gold in one place than anywhere else in the world, as far as anyone knows. Among its many tasks, the Fed administers the exchange of bullion between countries.

The Fed is also the national clearing house for checks. It facilitates quick and accurate transfer of funds in more than 15 billion transactions a year.

Controlling the Money Flow

The money that powers our economy is created essentially out of nothing by the Federal Reserve.

Keeping a modern economy running smoothly requires a pilot who'll keep it from stalling or overaccelerating.

The U.S., like most other countries, tries to control the amount of money in circulation. The process of injecting or withdrawing money reflects the monetary policy that the Federal Reserve adopts to regulate the economy.

Monetary policy isn't a fixed ideology. It's a constant juggling act to keep enough money in the economy so that it flourishes without growing too fast.

HOW IT WORKS

The Fed's Open Market Committee meets about every six weeks to evaluate the economy.

Then it tells the Federal Reserve Bank of New York—the city where the nation's biggest banks and brokerage firms have their headquarters—whether to speed up or slow down the creation of new money.

About 11:15 a.m. every day, the New York Fed decides whether to buy or sell government securities in order to implement the Open Market Committee's policy decisions.

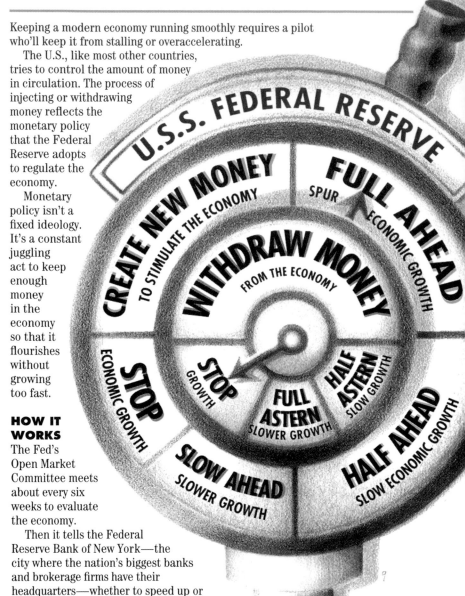

U.S.S. FEDERAL RESERVE

CREATE NEW MONEY
TO STIMULATE THE ECONOMY

FULL AHEAD
SPUR ECONOMIC GROWTH

WITHDRAW MONEY
FROM THE ECONOMY

STOP
GROWTH

FULL ASTERN
SLOWER GROWTH

HALF ASTERN
SLOW GROWTH

STOP
ECONOMIC GROWTH

SLOW AHEAD
SLOWER GROWTH

HALF AHEAD
SLOW ECONOMIC GROWTH

HOW FAST MONEY GOES

Money's velocity is the speed at which it changes hands. If a $1 bill is used by 20 different people in a year, its velocity is 20. An increase in either the quantity of money in circulation or its velocity makes prices go up—though if both increase they can cancel each other's effect.

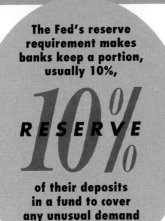

The Fed's reserve requirement makes banks keep a portion, usually 10%,

RESERVE 10%

of their deposits in a fund to cover any unusual demand from customers for cash.

REGULATION IS A TOUGH JOB

It isn't easy to regulate the money supply or control the rate of growth. That's because the economy doesn't always respond quickly or precisely when the Fed acts. Typically, it takes about six months for significant policy changes to affect the economy directly.

ADJUSTING THE RATE

Among the tools the Fed uses when it wants the economy to change direction is increasing or decreasing the discount rate, the rate it charges banks to borrow money. If the discount rate is increased, the banks tend to borrow less and have less money available to make loans to their clients. If the rate is decreased, banks tend to borrow more freely and lend money to their clients at attractive rates. The result is that changes in the discount rate have a ripple effect throughout the economy. And if the Fed isn't satisfied with the response, it can lower or raise the rate a second time or even a third.

CHANGING THE SUPPLY

The Fed regularly influences the amount of money in circulation when it chooses to buy or sell government securities in the open market.

To slow down an economy where too much money is in circulation, the New York Fed sells government securities, taking in the cash that would otherwise be available for lending. And to give the economy a shot in the arm, it creates money by buying securities.

For all practical purposes, there isn't any limit on the amount of money the Fed can create. The $100 million in the example to the right is only a modest increase in the money supply. In a typical month, the Fed might pump as much as $4 billion or as little as $1 billion into the economy.

CREATING MONEY

To create money, the New York Fed buys government securities from banks and brokerage houses. The money that pays for the securities hasn't existed before, but it has value, or worth, because the securities the Fed has bought with it are valuable.

More new money is created when the banks and brokerages lend the money they receive from selling the securities to clients who spend it on goods and services. These simplified steps illustrate how the process works.

1

The Fed writes a check for $100 million to buy the securities from a brokerage house. The brokerage house deposits the check in its own bank (A), increasing the bank's cash.

2

Bank A can lend its customers $90 million of that deposit after setting aside 10%. The Fed requires all banks to hold 10% of their deposits (in this example, $10 million) in reserve. A young couple borrows $100,000 from Bank A to buy a new house. The sellers deposit the money in their bank (B).

3

Now Bank B has $90,000 (the deposit minus the required reserve) to lend that it didn't have before. A woman borrows $10,000 from Bank B to buy a car, and the dealer deposits her check in Bank C.

4

Bank C can now loan $9,000.

This one series of transactions has created $190,099,000 in just four steps. Through a repetition of the loan process involving a wide range of banks and their customers, the $100 million that the Fed initially added to the money supply could theoretically become almost $900 million in new money.

The Money Supply

There's no ideal money supply. The Fed's goal is
to keep the economy running smoothly by keeping
an eye on the money that people have to spend.

The money supply measures
the amount of money that people
have available to spend—
including cash on hand and funds
that can be **liquidated**, or turned
into cash.

When the Federal Reserve
is following an easy money
policy—increasing the money
supply—the economy tends to
grow quickly, companies hire more
workers and consumer confidence
tends to increase, boosting spending.
But if the Fed adopts a tight money
policy—slowing the money supply to
combat inflation—the economy can
bog down, unemployment may increase and spending typically slows.

In a strong economy, demand for
currency increases without Federal
Reserve intervention, and the amount
of money in circulation goes up. In
the 1990s, for example, the supply of
dollars has grown steadily, reflecting
demand both in the U.S. and overseas.

MEASURING
THE MONEY SUPPLY

If you keep careful track of your personal
money supply, you know, for instance, how
much cash you have in your wallet and
how much money is in your checking
account. You also know how much salary
is coming in and which investments,
such as savings accounts and certificates
of deposit (CDs), can be turned into
cash quickly.

Similarly, economists and policy-
makers keep careful track of the public
money supply using measures called M1,
M2, M3 and L.

The three Ms are **monetary
aggregates**, or ways to group assets
that people use in roughly the same way.
M1, for instance, counts **liquid assets**,
like cash. The object is to separate money
that's being saved from money that's
being spent in order to predict impending
changes in the economy.

L is a measure of other highly liquid
assets, and adds a number of short-term
bonds, commercial paper and savings
bonds, for example, to M3.

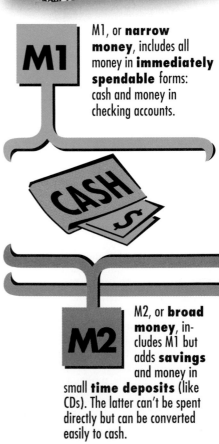

FEDERAL RESERVE DATA

RESERVE AGGREGATES
(daily average in millions)

	Two week Jan. 27
Total Reserves (sa)	45,072
Nonborrowed Reserves (sa)	45,004
Required Reserves (sa)	44,084
Excess Reserves (nsa)	988
Borrowings from Fed (nsa)-a	68
Free Reserves (nsa)	920
Monetary Base (sa)	515,876

a-Excluding extended credit. nsa-Not seasonal
sa-Seasonally adjusted.

	Feb. 3 Jar 1999
Reserve bank credit:	
U.S. Gov't securities:	
Bought outright	455,061 +
Held under repurch agreemt	3,674 —
Federal agency issues:	
Bought outright	336 —

M1, or **narrow
money**, includes all
money in **immediately
spendable** forms:
cash and money in
checking accounts.

M2, or **broad
money**, in-
cludes M1 but
adds **savings**
and money in
small **time deposits** (like
CDs). The latter can't be spent
directly but can be converted
easily to cash.

READING THE CHARTS

The Federal Reserve reports the financial details of the money supply every week. It's tracked in several different time periods to show both short-term changes and long-term trends. The average daily amounts—in billions of dollars—are provided for each component, M1, M2 and M3, and printed in The Wall Street Journal as Monetary Aggregates. The M3 figure, the most inclusive, is always the largest and the M1 the smallest. In addition, a summary of Reserve Aggregates appears every two weeks, providing additional financial statistics.

Seasonally adjusted (sa) amounts are always computed and compared with non-adjusted numbers (nsa). Seasonal adjustments reflect the varying flow of money into and out of bank accounts. In the spring, for instance, tax refunds tend to swell checking accounts that were depleted in the winter as consumers paid off holiday bills.

CHANGING YARDSTICK

In the early 1990s, the Federal Reserve stopped using its long-standing yardstick for measuring the economy— growth in the M2 money supply. Because people increasingly keep their cash in mutual fund money market accounts, which aren't included in M2, the Fed found that the figure wasn't a reliable indicator of economic growth.

So, instead of adjusting interest rates to control the money supply as a reaction to changes in M2, the new method is to set short-term real interest rates (the current interest rates minus the rate of inflation) at a level that the Fed believes will produce growth without inflation.

FEDERAL RESERVE DATA

MONETARY AGGREGATES
(daily average in billions)

	One week ended:	
	Jan. 25	Jan. 18
?y supply (M1) sa	1086.8	1087.2
?y supply (M1) nsa	1077.9	1090.0
?y supply (M2) sa	4434.0	4435.6
?y supply (M2) nsa	4407.9	4453.6
?y supply (M3) sa	6023.4	6031.9
?y supply (M3) nsa	6014.7	6060.6

	Four weeks ended:	
	Jan. 25	Dec. 28
?y supply (M1) sa	1091.6	1091.4
?y supply (M1) nsa	1106.3	1110.3
?y supply (M2) sa	4435.4	4412.0
Money supply (M2) nsa	4447.9	4428.0
Money supply (M3) sa	6031.4	6011.5
Money supply (M3) nsa	6041.7	6031.3

	Month	
	Dec.	Nov.
Money supply (M1) sa	1093.0	1088.8
Money supply (M2) sa	4412.9	4375.2
Money supply (M3) sa	6013.1	5954.7

nsa-Not seasonally adjusted. sa-Seasonally adjusted.

MEMBER BANK RESERVE CHANGES

M3 is the broadest measure of the money supply. It includes all of M1 and M2, plus the assets and liabilities of financial institutions, including long-term deposits, which can't be easily converted into spendable forms.

Measuring Economic Health

Economists keep their fingers on the pulse of the economy at all times, determined to cure what ails it.

Intensive care is a 24-hour business. Doctors and nurses measure vital signs, record changes in temperature and physical functions, conduct test after test. That gives you an idea of how thousands of experts—and countless more interested amateurs—watch the economy.

The biggest differences? The vigil never stops—even when the economy seems healthy. And there are usually multiple causes for any sign of weakness, often including a number that can't be cured by treating the U.S. economy alone.

The Index of Leading Economic Indicators is released every month by The Conference Board, a business research group. The numbers rarely surprise the experts, since many of the components are reported separately before the Index is released. But it does provide a simple way to keep an eye on the economy's overall health. Generally, three consecutive rises in the Index are considered a sign that the economy is growing—and three drops, a sign of decline and potential recession.

Ten leading indicators are averaged to produce the Index, with some carrying more weight than others. Taken together, they're designed to predict short-term economic conditions. Among them are the spread between the 10-year Treasury and the federal funds rate, the M2 money supply, the S&P 500-stock index and the four shown below.

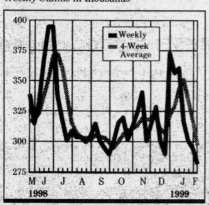

Jobless Claims

Weekly Claims in thousands

- Weekly
- 4-Week Average

400
375
350
325
300
275

M J J A S O N D J F
1998 — 1999

Unemployment Figures

New unemployment claims for state unemployment insurance give a sense of the number of people losing their jobs. A falling number is a sign the economy is growing. The chart here reports that initial claims fell dramatically in early 1999.

The flip side of low unemployment, however, is the fear of increasing inflation. In the past, at least, employers have increased wages to attract new workers when competition was tight. Whether that pattern will persist in what many experts consider a new economic environment remains unanswered.

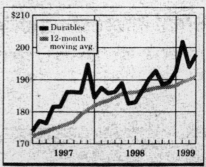

Durable Goods

In billions of dollars

- Durables
- 12-month moving avg.

$210
200
190
180
170

1997 1998 1999

NEW ORDERS received by manufacturers of durable goods rose in March to a

Durable Goods

A backlog of orders for a wide range of manufactured products, from machinery to transportation equipment, signals increasing demand that will keep the economy expanding.

Leading Indicators

Index (1992 = 100)

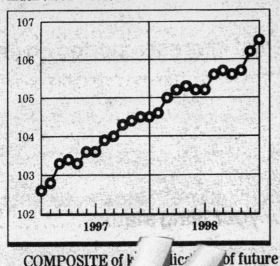

COMPOSITE of l...dic...f future

Housing Starts

Annual rate, in millions of dwelling units.

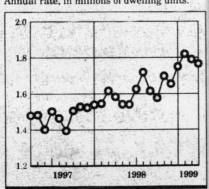

HOUSING STARTS in March fell to a seasonally adjusted annual rate of 1.766 –

Housing Starts
The number of housing permits being issued is a measure of economic health. A growing economy typically generates increased demand for new housing.

New Factory Orders

In billions of dollars.

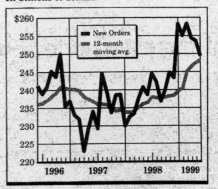

NEW ORDERS reported by manufacturers in May fell to a seasonally adjusted ...

New Factory Orders
Rising orders reported by manufacturers for consumer goods and materials affirms confidence in the economy and suggests continued growth.

Consumer Confidence

Consumers' attitudes toward the health of the economy are influenced by what they hear. And their confidence—or lack of it—affects how the economy fares.

If consumers feel good about their current situation and about the future, they tend to spend more freely, which boosts economic growth. If they're worried about things like job security, they tend to save more and spend less, slowing economic growth and the economy itself.

Consumers often respond slowly to news of an economic recovery if they don't see an immediate, positive financial impact on their own lives. Their reluctance to start spending helps keep the recovery slow.

The graphs shown on these pages illustrate how the complex information on the state of the economy that the government compiles each month is presented in The Wall Street Journal.

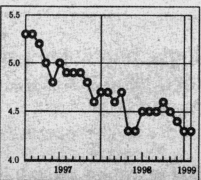

Unemployment Rate

In percent

UNEMPLOYMENT in January was unchanged from the previous month at 4.3%

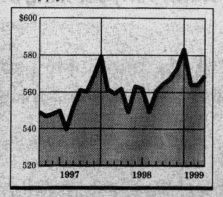

Weekly Earnings

Weekly pay, in dollars.

AVERAGE WEEKLY earnings of production workers in March rose

The Employment Report provides information on the unemployment rate, which industries were creating or losing jobs, and wage trends. In general, the higher the employment rate, the healthier the economy is and the more confident about spending consumers are.

Weekly Earnings, issued monthly by the Labor Department, tracks individual income. Individual spending is the largest single factor in economic growth.

MEASURING EMOTIONS

Consumer sentiment is measured in several different ways. Three of the principal guides that economists use are the monthly surveys done by the **University of Michigan Institute for Social Research**, the **Conference Board** and **Sindlinger & Co.** The results are intended for specific audiences, but it's only a matter of minutes before Wall Street's information networks make survey results public knowledge.

The surveys can produce different results because the organizations ask different questions.

● Michigan's poll asks if consumers are confident enough to take on debt for such big-ticket items as cars and appliances.

● The Conference Board focuses on consumer worries about job security.

● The Sindlinger Report measures consumers' income, sense of job security and business conditions.

The Sindlinger Report also looks at whether household income has risen or fallen in the past six months, and what consumers expect in the next six.

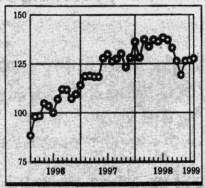

Consumer Confidence

Index (1985=100)

CONSUMER CONFIDENCE index rose to 127.6 in January from a ____ December, according ____

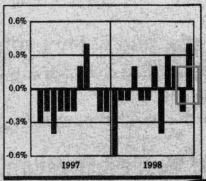

Producer Prices

Percentage change from previous month, seasonally adjusted

PRODUCER PRICES

The Producer Price Index measures the cost of raw materials. The PPI is a good indicator of what will be happening to prices: Consumer prices tend to rise a few months after production costs rise, as companies pass along their increased costs to consumers.

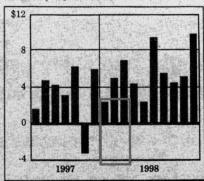

Consumer Credit

Seasonally adjusted, in billions

CONSUMER installment credit out-standing in the U.S. compared ____

Consumer credit, or the amount consumers are charging to pay for purchases, reflects consumer confidence—or lack of it. Increasing charges suggest people feel good about buying.

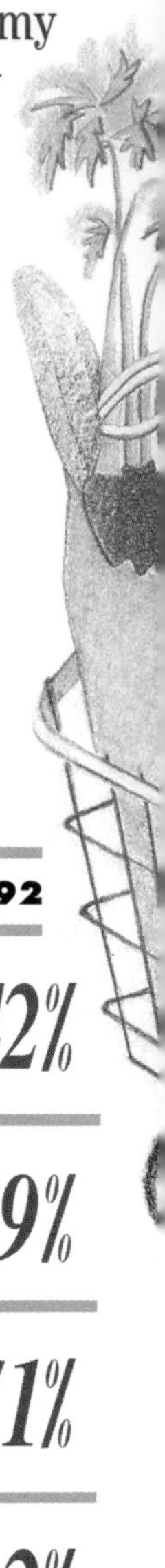

The Consumer Price Index

The Consumer Price Index (CPI) looks at the economy from your perspective: it reports what it costs to pay for food, housing and other basics.

The **Consumer Price Index (CPI)** serves the double role of reflecting economic trends and influencing economic policy decisions. Though its accuracy as well as its urban bias are sometimes questioned, it's the most widely used measure of inflation—and the basis for figuring adjustments to Social Security payments as well as determining cost-of-living increases in wages and pensions.

HOW THE CPI IS FIGURED

The Bureau of Labor Statistics compiles the CPI every month by recording prices for 80,000 goods and services that reflect the current lifestyle of the typical urban American consumer. It includes food, housing, clothing, transportation, health care, recreation and education as well as a catchall category called other. The Bureau reports changes from month to month and year to year, using the period 1982-1984 as the **basis**, or starting point, against which the numbers are measured.

The CPI components are adjusted periodically to reflect changes in lifestyle and in the relative cost of living.

CURRENT COMPONENTS OF THE CPI	1998	1992
 **HOUSING** • Shelter, rent and homeowners' equivalent of rent • Fuel, including oil, coal, bottled gas, gas, electricity	39.6%	42%
 **FOOD** • Eaten at home and away from home • Beverages	16.3%	17.9%
 **TRANSPORTATION** • Private cars, trucks, other • Public transportation	17.6%	17.1%
 **MEDICAL CARE**	5.6%	6.2%
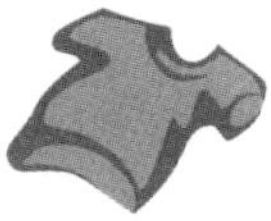 **CLOTHING**	4.1%	6.1%
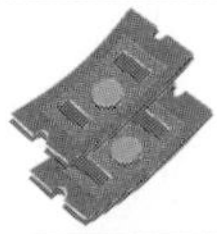 **RECREATION**	6.1%	4.4%
 **EDUCATION**	5.5%	*
OTHER	4.3%	6.3%

The cost of each component of this chart is used to figure the CPI. The relative weight of each item is calculated by using the percentage shown. *The category for education is the most recent addition to the list, covering elements previously grouped in the Other category.

THE CPI
Originally called the cost-of-living index, the CPI can't evaluate the changing quality of things you buy—which affects their price. An appliance that can do more things costs more—but perhaps doesn't last as long as an older, plainer model. And the CPI can't measure changing taste.

The Annual Change in the CPI

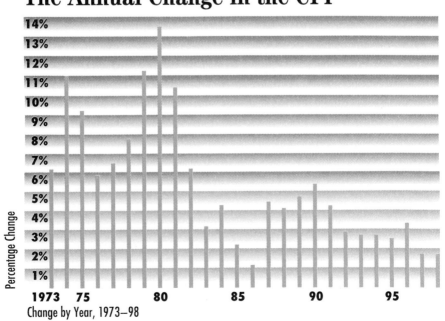

Percentage Change

1973 75 80 85 90 95

Change by Year, 1973–98

The Economic Cycle

Inflation and recession are recurring phases of a continuous economic cycle. Experts work hard to predict their timing and control their effects.

Inflation occurs when prices rise because there's too much money in circulation and not enough goods and services to spend it on. When prices go higher than people can—or will—pay, demand decreases and a downturn begins.

HIGH INFLATION

1 DEMAND INCREASES

2 WHICH MAKES PRICES INCREASE

WHEN DEMAND DECREASES 3

AND PRICES DECREASE 4

RECESSION

5 THE CYCLE BEGINS AGAIN

1
If ten people want new cars and only seven cars are available, the dealer can increase the price because some people will pay more to get what they want. Almost overnight car prices go up.

2
People—including the workers making the cars—demand higher wages so they can afford to buy a car. The cost of building the car goes up—so the selling price goes up.

3
When the car costs more than people can afford, they stop buying. Fewer cars are needed, and the factory lays off workers.

4
Unemployed people buy less of everything, so the economy slows down. This is known as a recession. Car dealers—desperate to sell their small but stagnant inventory—offer their cars at sale prices or with special deals.

5
So if ten people now want cars and only seven are available, the cycle begins again.

THE INFLATION STRUGGLE

Since inflation typically occurs in a growing economy that's creating jobs and reducing unemployment, politicians are willing to risk its problems. But the Federal Reserve prefers to cool down a potentially inflationary economy before it gets out of hand. So it sells government securities, which has the effect of raising interest rates and slowing borrowing. But since it also wants to prevent a long-term slowdown, it typically reverses its policy when the economy seems likely to shrink.

CONTROLLING THE CYCLE

Most developed economies try not to let the economic cycle run unchecked because the consequences could be a major worldwide **depression** like the one that followed the stock market crash of 1929. In a depression, money is so tight that the economy virtually grinds to a halt, unemployment escalates, businesses collapse and the general mood is grim.

Instead, most central banks adjust their monetary policy at the first sign of a slowdown, or recession, to ward off more trouble.

TIME AS MONEY

In 1800, you could travel from New York to Philadelphia in about 18 hours by stagecoach. The trip cost about $4.

Today the train costs about $35, but takes 75 minutes. While the trip's price has **inflated** about 775%, the travel time has **deflated** about 1,340%. So, if time is money, today's traveler comes out ahead.

EASY MONEY SPURS GROWTH—AND INFLATION

In a recession, the Fed can create new money to make borrowing easier. As the economy picks up, sellers sense rising demand for their products or services and begin to raise prices.

The rule of 72 is a reliable guide to the impact of inflation. Its formula has you divide 72 by the annual inflation rate to find out the number of years it will take prices to double. For example, when inflation is at 10%, prices will double in seven years ($72 \div 10 = 7$) and when it's 3%, they will double in 24 years ($72 \div 3 = 24$).

INFLATION DESTROYS VALUE

Most economists agree that inflation isn't good for the economy because, over time, it destroys value, including the value of money. If inflation is running at a 10% annual rate, for example, the book that cost $10 one year would cost $20 just seven years later. For comparison's sake, if inflation averaged 3% a year, the same book wouldn't cost $20 for 24 years.

Inflation may also prompt investors to buy things they can resell at huge profits—like art or real estate—rather than putting their money into companies that can create new products and jobs.

WHO GETS HURT?

The people hit the hardest by inflation are those living on fixed incomes. For example, if you're retired and have a pension that was determined by a salary you earned in less inflationary times, your income will buy less of what you need to live comfortably. Workers whose wages don't keep pace with inflation can also find their lifestyle slipping.

But inflation isn't bad for everyone. Debtors love it because the money they repay each year is worth less than it was when they borrowed it. If their own income keeps pace with inflation, the money they repay is also an increasingly smaller percentage of their budget.

WHEN THERE'S NO INFLATION

When the rate of inflation slows, it's described as **disinflation**. Several years of 1% annual increases in the cost of living are disinflationary after a period of more rapid growth. Employment and output can continue to be strong, and the economy can continue to grow.

Deflation, though, is a widespread decline in the prices of goods and services. But instead of stimulating employment and production, deflation has the potential to undermine them. As the economy contracts and people are out of work, they can't afford to buy even at cheaper prices.

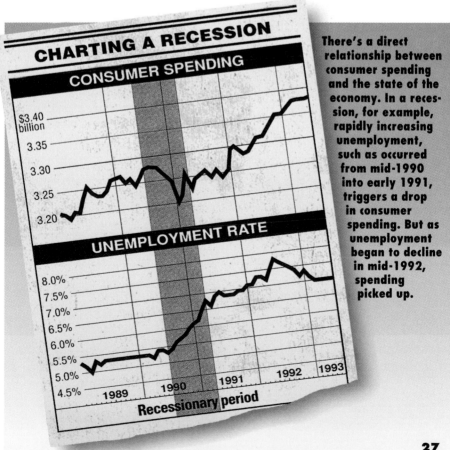

CHARTING A RECESSION

CONSUMER SPENDING

$3.40 billion
3.35
3.30
3.25
3.20

UNEMPLOYMENT RATE

8.0%
7.5%
7.0%
6.5%
6.0%
5.5%
5.0%
4.5%

1989   1990   1991   1992   1993

Recessionary period

There's a direct relationship between consumer spending and the state of the economy. In a recession, for example, rapidly increasing unemployment, such as occurred from mid-1990 into early 1991, triggers a drop in consumer spending. But as unemployment began to decline in mid-1992, spending picked up.

The World of Money

Currencies are **floated** against each other to measure their worth in the global marketplace.

A currency's value in the world marketplace reflects whether individuals and governments are interested in using it to make purchases or investments, or in holding it as a source of long-term security. If demand is high, its value increases in relation to the value of other currencies. If it's low, the reverse occurs.

Some currencies, like the U.S. dollar and the Swiss franc, are relatively stable in price, reflecting an underlying financial and political stability. Most experts expect the euro, introduced in 1999 as the currency of the European Union, to join that group of strong currencies.

Some other currencies experience wild or rapid changes in value, the sign of economies in turmoil as the result of runaway inflation, deflation, defaults on loan agreements, serious balance-of-trade deficits or economic policies that seem unlikely to resolve the problems.

Key Currency Cross Rates Late Ne

	Dollar	EURO	Pound	SFranc	Guilder	Peso	
Canada	1.5197	1.7898	2.5148	1.1095	.81133	.15520	
France	5.5755	6.5663	9.2263	4.0706	2.9766	.56939	
Germany	1.6625	1.9579	2.7511	1.2138	.88757	.16978	
Italy	1645.8	1938.3	2723.5	1201.6	878.65	168.08	
Japan	111.32	131.1	184.21	81.273	59.431	11.368	
Mexico	9.7920	11.532	16.204	7.1490	5.2277		
Netherlands	1.8731	2.2059	3.0996	1.3675		.19129	
Switzerland	1.3697	1.6131	2.2666		.73125	.13988	
U.K.	.60430	.71169		.44119	.32262	.06171	.0
EURO	.84911		1.4051	.61993	.45332	.08671	.0
U.S.		1.1777	1.6548	.73009	.53387	.10212	.0

Source: Telerate

NOTHING IS FIXED

Currency values of even the most stable economies change over time as traders are willing to pay more—or less—for dollars or pounds or euros or yen. For example, great demand for a nation's products means great demand for the currency needed to pay for those products.

If there's a big demand for the stocks or bonds of a particular country, its currency's value is likely to rise as overseas investors buy it to make investments. Similarly, a low inflation rate can boost a currency's value, since investors believe that the value of long-term purchases in that country won't erode over time.

HOW CURRENCY VALUES ARE SET

Between 1944 and 1971, major trading nations had a fixed, official rate of exchange tied to the U.S. dollar, which could be redeemed for gold at $35 an ounce. Since 1971, when the gold standard was abandoned, currencies have floated against each other, influenced by supply and demand and by various governments' efforts to manage their currency. Some countries, for example, have sought stability by pegging, or linking, their currency to the value of the U.S. dollar. In Europe, the European Union established the euro as a common currency for 11 participating member nations. At year's end, 1998, their currencies were permanently aligned with one another.

Lira	D-Mark	FFranc	CdnDlr
.00092	.91411	.27257	
.00339	3.3537		3.6688
.00101		.29818	1.0940
	989.95	295.18	1083.0
.06764	66.959	19.966	73.251
.00595	5.8899	1.7563	6.4434
.00114	1.1267	.33595	1.2325
.00083	.82388	.24566	.90130
.00037	.36349	.10839	.39765
.00052	.51074	.15229	.55874
.00061	.60150	.17936	.65802

CURRENCY CROSS RATES

Currency cross rates, reported as the late New York trading price of the basic units of 11 major currencies, including the euro, in relation to each other, are published daily in The Wall Street Journal. Since these exchange rates apply to bank trades of $1 million or more, they usually reflect a higher unit of foreign currency per dollar than you would get in a retail transaction, such as changing money at a bank.

To find the current exchange rate between two currencies, you find the place on the chart where one country's name (listed alphabetically in the vertical column) intersects with the other's currency value (in the horizontal column). Here, for example, the Mexican peso is trading at 9.7920 to the dollar.

The values of the U.S. dollar and the euro appear first and second, in recognition of the primary roles they play in international transactions. The chart has a global perspective, however, providing exchange information for a number of trading partners whose transactions may not be handled in dollars or euros—Japanese yen and U.K. pounds, for example, or yen and Canadian dollars.

STABILITY IS A GOAL

Governments usually want their currency to be **stable**, maintaining a constant relative worth with the currencies of their major trading partners. Sometimes they interfere with market forces—buying up large amounts of their own currency or agreeing with trading partners to lower interest rates—to achieve that goal.

If interest rates are lowered, however, fewer foreign investors will want to put money in the country's banks. They'll look for better return elsewhere.

Other times, a currency is deliberately **devalued** if a government decides to lower the value of its currency against those of other countries, often to make its exports more competitive.

EURODOLLARS

are U.S. dollars on deposit in non-U.S. banks. They can earn interest, be loaned or used to make investments in American or international companies. For example, U.S. banks borrow Eurodollars regularly.

The Value of Money

Exchanging dollars for euros, pounds for yen, or rupees for rubles is big business—to the tune of $1.5 trillion a day.

Some currencies are more widely traded than others, dominating world markets and setting standards of value. The U.S. dollar has held that position in recent years, along with the Japanese yen and the German mark. The euro, the currency of the European Union, is widely expected to be a major force in the world economy.

CURRENCY TRADING

Money flows across national borders all the time, so **foreign exchange**—changing one currency for another—flourishes. But there is no actual physical marketplace where the world's currencies are traded. The global foreign exchange market, or **forex**, is a network of interconnected telephones and computers that operate virtually around the clock. Traders working for big banks and other financial institutions buy and sell currencies in what is by far the largest single financial market in the world. On a typical day, roughly $1.5 trillion in currencies is traded electronically around the world.

GERMANY

17.40 marks*

JAPAN

1148.55 yen

AUSTRALIA

15.58*
dollars

TRADING FOR BUSINESS

Corporations that do business in more than one country depend on foreign exchange. If a corporation knows it needs Japanese yen to pay for a shipment of electronic equipment, it asks its bank to buy Japanese currency at the best exchange rate possible.

On a smaller scale, when a New York retailer buys sweaters from a Norwegian company, the New Yorker tells his bank to pay his bill. The bank either dips into its own reserves of kroners or buys them in the currency market. Then the bank calculates the current exchange rate between dollars and kroners, deducts the dollars from its client's account, and instructs the Norwegian company's bank in Oslo to credit the seller's account with the appropriate number of kroners.

ENGLAND

6 pounds*
15 pence

NORWAY

76.77 kroner*

FRANCE

50.27*
francs

*As of February 15, 1999

31

Trading Money

Everybody wants to do business at the best possible exchange rates.

You're unlikely to be involved in having to negotiate what a dollar is worth, since currency exchange is a huge business, handled by traders working for large commercial banks or through electronic brokering systems. But you are directly affected by the fact that its value is constantly changing, whether you're traveling abroad or buying imported goods. Basically, a strong dollar means more buying power.

World Value of the Dollar

The table below, compiled by Bank of America, gives the rates of exchange for the U.S. dollar a Friday February 12. Unless otherwise noted, all rates listed are middle rates of interbank bid a pressed in foreign currency units per one U.S. dollar. The rates are indicative and aren't based basis for particular transactions.

BankAmerica International doesn't trade in all the listed foreign currencies.

Country (Currency)	Value 2/12	Value 2/5
Afghanistan (Afghani -c)	4750.00	4750.00
Albania (Lek)	139.70	139.90
Algeria (Dinar)	63.4022	62.7906
Andorra (Peseta -7)	148.0303	146.9971
Andorra (Franc -8)	5.0269	4.9918
Angola (Readjust Kwanza)	257128.00	257128.00
Antigua (E Caribbean $)	2.70	2.70
Argentina (Peso)	0.9999	0.9999
Aruba (Florin)	1.79	1.79
Australia (Australia Dollar)	1.5576	1.5373
Austria (Schilling -14)	12.2423	12.1568
Azerbaijan (Manat)	3950.00	3950.00
Bahamas (Dollar)	1.00	1.00
Bahrain (Dinar)	0.38	0.38
Bangladesh (Taka)	48.50	48.50
Barbados (Dollar)	2.00	2.00
Belgium (Franc -9)	35.8896	35.6391
Belize (Dollar)	2.00	2.00
Benin (C.F.A. Franc)	502.6868	499.1784
Bermuda (Dollar)	1.00	1.00
Bhutan (Ngultrum)	42.4475	42.4675
Bolivia (Boliviano -o)	5.68	5.67
Bolivia (Boliviano -f)	5.69	5.68
Botswana (Pula)	4.5872	4.5455
Bouvet Island (Norwegian Krone)	7.6765	7.6925
Brazil (Real)	1.91	1.815
Brunei (Dollar)	1.6932	1.6874
Bulgaria (Lev)	1734.30	1726.40
Burkina Faso (C.F.A. Franc)	502.6868	499.1784
Burma (Kyat)	6.1047	6.0989
Burundi (Franc)	499.95	500.54
Cambodia (Riel)	3775.00	3775.00

Country (Currency)
Lebanon (Pound)
Lesotho (Maloti)
Liberia (Dollar)
Libya (Dinar -21)
Liechtenstein (Franc)
Lithuania (Litas)
Luxembourg (Lux.Franc -
Macao (Pataca)
Madagascar DR (Franc)
Malawi (Kwacha)
Malaysia (Ringgit)
Maldive (Rufiyaa)
Mali Rep (C.F.A. Franc)
Malta (Lira *)
Martinique (Franc -8)
Mauritania (Ouguiya)
Mauritius (Rupee)
Mexico (New Peso)
Monaco (Franc -8)
Mongolia (Tugrik -o-29)
Montserrat (E Caribbe
Morocco (Dirham)
Mozambique (Metical
Namibia (Rand -c)
Nauru Islands (Austr
Nepal (Rupee)
Netherlands (Guilder
Netherlands Ant'les
New Zealand (N.Z.D
Nicaragua (Gold Cor
Niger Rep (C.
Nigeria (N
Nigeria

WHAT A DOLLAR'S WORTH

A survey of the approximate rates of exchange for the U.S. dollar against various world currencies is reported every week in The Wall Street Journal. The figures give the amount of foreign currency a dollar would buy. Here, for example, a dollar was worth 1.79 Aruban florins and 35.8896 Belgian francs. A few countries with close tourist or political ties to the U.S., like Bermuda, set the value of their currency permanently at $1.

MONEY AWAY FROM HOME

Travelers exchanging money are very minor players in the currency market. But if they're savvy, they can benefit from banks' and credit card companies large-volume trading. The key is to get the most local currency for their own currency by exchanging where the rate is the best and the **commission**, or charge for the transaction, is the lowest.

BIG DEALS

Large-scale currency trading is done by telephone or electronically through a network controlled by banks or other financial institutions, in what's known as an **over-the-counter** market. The trades can be handled three different ways, as
- Spot transactions
- Forward transactions
- Swap contracts

TRADING ON THE SPOT

Spot transactions, in which the currency trade occurs immediately and is settled within two days, are big money deals, with minimum trades of $1 million. Trading goes on around the clock, through what is known as the global trading day, which begins when the New Zealand market opens and runs through the end of New York trading (see pages 74-75).

Exchange rates are updated constantly, and traders must pay careful attention, as a good deal typically depends on split-second timing and small price differences.

FORWARDS AND SWAPS

Companies doing business in more than one country need to protect themselves against sudden or dramatic changes in the relative value of currencies, so they hedge commitments to invest, sell or borrow with agreements that have predetermined **forex**, or foreign-exchange, rates. Conventional deals are described as plain vanilla, while others are complex, customized transactions.

Basically, swaps involve converting a cash flow or interest rate in one currency to a cash flow or interest rate in another. Forward transactions mean agreeing on an exchange rate that will apply when currency is traded on a set date in the future.

YOUR MONEY ABROAD

The near-universal popularity of credit cards and the growing use of globally linked electronic banking systems has made it easier to handle money matters when you travel.

In most places, you can pay for goods and services with a credit card. When the bills appear on your statement, the value of the transactions is converted to dollars, ususaly at favorable rates because the credit card companies do such a huge volume of international business.

With an ATM, American Express or Diner's Club card, you can withdraw cash in local currency directly from your checking account. There's a fee, typically $1 to $2 for each transaction, but the exchange rate is usually the best that you can get anywhere.

Origins of Currency Names

India
RUPEE
from the root meaning "silver"

Soviet Union
RUBLE
means "to cut"

Italy
LIRA
from Latin "libra" (pound)

Peru
SOL
means "the sun"

Brazil
CRUZADO
means "The Southern Cross"

Germany
MARK
from Old German meaning "to mark"—to keep a tally

France
FRANC
from Francorum Rex, a Latin inscription meaning "King of the Franks", found on medieval French coins

Japan
YEN
means "round", and originated when Japanese money changed from being square to round

England
POUND
a pound of silver

Spain
PESO
means "weight" (of a silver dollar)

33

Stocks: Sharing a Corporation

Stocks are pieces of the corporate pie.
When you buy stocks, or shares, you
own a slice of the company.

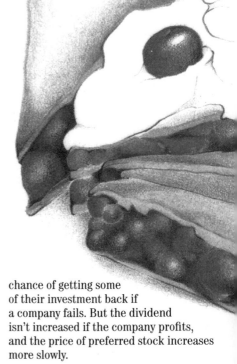

COMMON STOCK

- Owners share in success when company profits
- Owners at risk if company falters

Stocks are **equity** investments. If you buy stock in a corporation, you have an ownership share in that corporation and are described as a **stockholder** or **shareholder**. You buy stock because you expect it to increase in value, or because you expect the corporation to pay you dividend income, or a portion of its profits. In fact, many stocks provide both growth and income.

When a corporation issues stock, it gets the proceeds from that initial sale. After that, shares of the stock are **traded**, or bought and sold among investors, but the corporation gets no additional income. The price of the stock moves up or down depending on how much you and other investors are willing to pay for it at the time.

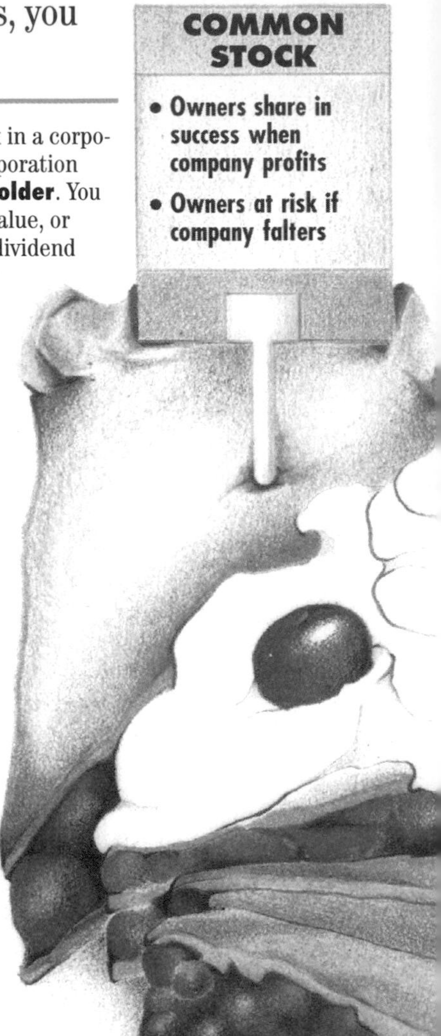

COMMON STOCK

Most stock in the U.S. is **common stock**. If you buy common stock, there are no guarantees you'll make money. You take the risk that the stock won't increase in value or pay dividends. In fact, it's possible that the value of the stock will drop, and you'll lose some or all of your investment if you sell at that point.

In exchange for the risk you take, however, you stand to make money if the company prospers—sometimes a lot of money. Over time, stocks in general, though not each individual stock, tend to increase in value.

PREFERRED STOCK

Preferred stocks are also ownership shares issued by a corporation and traded by investors. They differ from common stocks by reducing investor risk—but they may also limit reward. The amount of the dividend is guaranteed and paid before dividends on common stock. And preferred stockholders have a greater chance of getting some of their investment back if a company fails. But the dividend isn't increased if the company profits, and the price of preferred stock increases more slowly.

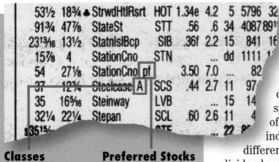

53½	18¾ ♦	StrwdHtlRsrt	HOT	1.34e	4.2	5	5796	32
91¾	47⅞	StateSt	STT	.56	.6	34	408789¹	
23¹³⁄₁₆	13½	StatnlslBcp	SIB	.36f	2.2	15	841	1€
15⅞	4	StationCno	STN	...	dd	1111	1	
54	27⅛	StationCno pf		3.50	7.0	...	82	
37	12¾	Steelcase A	SCS	.44	2.7	11	97	
35	16⁵⁄₁₆	Steinway	LVB	...	15	14		
32¼	22¼	Stepan	SCL	.60	2.6	11	4	
35¹⁵⁄			OTE		22			

Classes of Stock

Preferred Stocks

CLASSES OF STOCK

Companies may issue different classes of stock, label them differently and list them separately on a stock market. Sometimes a class indicates ownership in a specific division or subsidiary of the company. Other times it indicates shares that sell at different market prices, have different dividend policies, or impose voting or sales restrictions on ownership.

PREFERRED STOCK

- Dividend payment has priority over common stock dividends

- Dividends don't increase if company prospers

BLUE CHIPS

is a term borrowed from poker, where the blue chips are the most valuable. Blue chips refer to the stocks of the largest, most consistently profitable corporations. The list isn't official—and it does change.

SPLIT STOCK

- More shares created at lower price per share

- Stockholders profit if price goes up

STOCK SPLITS

When the price of a stock increases significantly, you and other investors may be reluctant to buy, either because you think the price has reached its peak or because it costs so much. Corporations have the option of splitting the stock to lower the price, which they expect to stimulate trading.

When a stock is split, there are more shares available, but the total market value is the same. Say a company's stock is trading at $100 a share. If the company declares a two-for-one split, it gives you two shares for each one you own. At the same time the price drops to $50 a share. If you owned 300 shares selling at $100 you now have 600 selling at $50—but the value is still $30,000.

The initial effect of a stock split is no different from getting change for a dollar. But the price may move up toward the presplit price, increasing the value of your stock.

Stocks can split three for one, three for two, ten for one or any other combination.

REVERSE SPLITS

In a **reverse split** the corporation exchanges more shares for fewer—say ten shares for five—and the price increases accordingly. Typically the motive is to boost the price so that it meets a stock market's minimum listing require-ment or makes the stock attractive to institutional investors, including mutual funds and pension funds, which may not buy very low-priced stocks.

AT&T

holds the record for the largest number of common shares. As of March 31, 1999, it had

2,098,000,000 shares

outstanding and

3,500,000 stockholders.

The Right to Vote

Owning stock gives you the right to vote on important company issues and policies.

As a stockholder, you have the right to vote on major policy decisions, such as whether a company should issue additional stock, sell itself to outside buyers or change the board of directors. In general, the more stock you own, the greater your voice in company decisions. But if you've held shares for more than a year, you may present a proposal to be voted on at the annual meeting, provided it meets the requirements of the Securities and Exchange Commission (SEC).

ALL STOCKS ARE NOT EQUAL

Usually, each share of stock gives you one vote. Some companies, however, issue different classes of stock with different voting privileges. When stocks carry extra votes, a small group of people can control a company's direction while owning fewer than 50% of the shares.

THE WAY YOU VOTE

You can attend the company's annual meeting and vote in person. Or you can cast your vote by mail using a ballot called a **proxy**, vote by telephone or sometimes online over the Internet.

Before the annual meeting you receive a **proxy statement**, a legal document that presents information on planned changes in company management that require shareholder approval. By law, it must also present shareholder proposals, even if they are at odds with company policy. The statement also identifies the nominees for the board of directors, and lists the major shareholders.

New SEC rules require proxies to show in chart form the total compensation of the company's top five executives. The proxy must also report stock performance in relation to comparable companies in the industry and to the S&P 500-stock index.

The proxy asks shareholders to elect a board of directors and vote on several issues. The directors oversee the operation of the company and set long-term policy goals. You can support them all, vote against them or vote for some but not others.

The proxy lets shareholders vote yes or no or abstain on shareholder proposals and other issues affecting the corporation. The directors want you to vote yes on the issues they support and no on the others. If you don't return your proxy, your votes aren't counted.

X	Please mark your votes as in this example.

Unless otherwise specified, proxies will be voted FOR the election of the nominees for directors, FOR proposals 2 and 3, and AGAINST proposals 4, 5 and 6.

The Board of Directors recommends a vote FOR election of directors and proposals 2 and 3.

1. Election of Directors (see reverse) — FOR [X]   WITHHELD [ ]
FOR, except vote withheld from the following nominee(s):
_____

2. Approval of Amendments to the 1987 Stock Option Plan — FOR [X]   AGAINST [ ]   ABSTAIN [ ]

3. Appointment of Independent Auditors — FOR [ ]   AGAINST [X]   ABSTAIN [ ]

The Board of Di... stockholder prop...

4. Stockholder proposal
5. Stockholder proposal
6. Stockholder proposal

SIGNATURE(S) _John Q. Investor_   DATE _9/17_

NOTE: Please sign exactly as name appears hereon. Joint owners should each sign. When signing as attorney, executor, administrator, trustee or guardian, please give full title as such.

CHANGING ATTITUDES

Institutional investors who own large blocks of stock are increasingly demanding a say in corporate affairs. For example, they may express concern about how effectively the board of directors sets policy and oversees the performance of the company's chief executive. They also want to confirm that current business practices provide an acceptable profit.

Similarly, socially and environmentally conscientious individual shareholders are becoming more involved in the voting process. Typically they want more information about corporate policies that touch on issues such as the environmental impact of company operations, the working conditions of employees and suppliers, and other ethical concerns. Although individuals may find it difficult to affect corporate policy directly, their inquiries, and their shareholder proposals, can force companies to explain and sometimes alter their business practices.

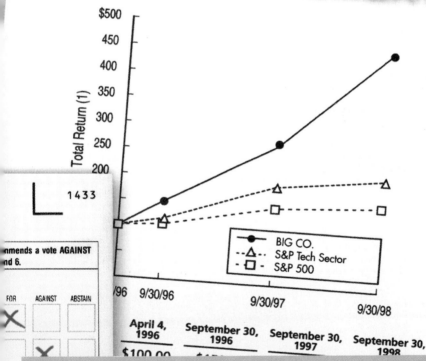

BIGCO.

NOTICE OF 1999 ANNUAL MEETING AND

PROXY STATEMENT

1433

nmends a vote AGAINST
nd 6.

	FOR	AGAINST	ABSTAIN
X		
X		

Total Return (1)

BIG CO.
S&P Tech Sector
S&P 500

/96   9/30/96   9/30/97   9/30/98

| April 4, 1996 | September 30, 1996 | September 30, 1997 | September 30, 1998 |

$100.00

CUMULATIVE VOTING

As a shareholder, you typically get one vote for each share of stock you own. But when you vote for the board of directors in some companies, you may have the opportunity to cast your votes in a nontraditional way. In traditional corporate voting—called statutory voting—you cast the same number of votes for each director running for election. In cumulative voting, on the other hand, you can combine your votes and cast different numbers of votes for different candidates.

For example, if you owned 100 shares and eight directors were running for election, in a statutory vote, you'd cast 100 votes for each of the candidates, for a total of 800 votes. In a cumulative vote, you could still do that, or you could distribute your 800 votes among some of the candidates, assigning no votes to others. You could even cast all 800 votes for a single candidate. The purpose of cumulative voting is to give small shareholders more voice in corporate governance.

The Value of Stock

A stock's value can change at any moment, depending on market conditions, investor perceptions, or a host of other issues.

A stock doesn't have a fixed value, as measured by its price. When investors are buying the stock enthusiastically because they believe it is a good investment, the stock increases in value. But if they think the company's outlook is poor, and either don't invest or sell shares they already own, the value of the stock will fall.

But price is only one measure of a stock's value. **Return on investment**— the amount you earn on the stock—is another. To assess the likelihood of a strong future return, you can look for a history of strong performance and steady growth.

THE BLUES AT BIGCO.

The peaks and valleys in the price of a stock dramatically illustrate how value changes.

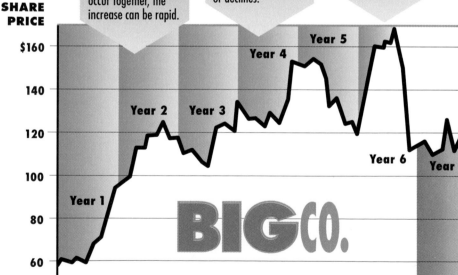

Usually a stock climbs in price when the overall stock market is strong, the company's products or services are in demand and its profits are rising. When the three factors occur together, the increase can be rapid.

A stock's price seldom moves in the same direction for more than a few days, though it may gain or lose a lot over a month or a year. A stock is most likely to decline when the market is weak, a competitor introduces a new product, or if profit growth slows or declines.

Nothing ultimately dictates the highest price a stock can sell for. As long as people are willing to pay more for it, it will climb in value. But when investors unload shares or the market falls, prices can drop rapidly.

STOCK SHARE PRICE

$160
140
120
100
80
60

Year 1
Year 2
Year 3
Year 4
Year 5
Year 6
Year

BIGCO.

CYCLICAL STOCKS

All stocks don't act alike. One difference is how closely a company's business is tied to the condition of the economy. **Cyclical stocks** are shares of companies that are highly dependent on the state of the economy. When things slow down, their earnings typically fall, and so does the stock price. But when the economy recovers, earnings rise and the stock price goes up. Airline and hotel stocks are typically cyclical: People tend to cut back on travel when the economy is slow. In contrast, stock prices for companies that provide necessary services and staples, such as food, tend to stay fairly stable.

TIMING IT RIGHT

The trick to making money, of course, is to buy a stock before others want it and sell

BETTING WITH THE ODDS

Investing is a gamble, but it's not like betting on horses. A long shot can always win the race even if everyone bets the favorite. In the stock market, the betting itself influences the outcome. If lots of investors bet on Atlas stock, Atlas's price will go up. The stock becomes more valuable because investors want it. The reverse is also true: If investors sell Zenon stock, it will fall in value. The more it falls, the more investors will sell.

MAKING MONEY WITH STOCKS

You can make money with stocks by selling your shares for more than you paid for them or by collecting dividends on the stocks—or both.

The profit you make on the sale of stock is known as a **capital gain**. Of course, it doesn't all go into your pocket. You owe taxes on the gain as well as a commission on the sale, but if you've owned the stock for a year or longer, it's a long-term gain.

If you're buying stocks for the quarterly income, you can figure out the **dividend yield**—the percentage of purchase price you get back through dividends each year. For example, if you buy stock for $100 a share and receive $4 per share, the stock has a dividend yield of 4%. But if you get $4 per share on stock you buy for $50 a share, your yield would be 8% ($4 is 8% of $50).

Purchase Price	Annual Dividend	Yield
$100	$4	4%
$ 50	$4	8%

That means you pay the tax at a lower rate than you pay on your earned income or on dividends and other investment income.

Dividends are the portion of the company's profit paid out to its shareholders. A company's board of directors decides how large a dividend the company will pay, or whether it will pay one at all. Usually only large, mature companies pay dividends, while smaller ones reinvest their profits to continue growing.

Following a price collapse, a stock can recoup its value or continue to decline, depending on its internal strength and what the markets are doing. In this example, the price moved up and down for several years at about $100, the level it had reached several years before.

If a company is out of favor with its shareholders, has serious management problems or is losing ground to competitors, its value can collapse quickly even if the rest of the market is highly valued. That's what happened here.

However, strong companies can cope with dramatic loss of value and can rebound if internal changes and external conditions create the right environment and investors respond with renewed interest.

Year 14   Year 15

Year 13

ar 8   Year 9   Year 10

Year 12

Year 11

before they decide to unload. Getting the timing right means you have to pay attention to:

- The rate at which the company's earnings are growing
- Competitiveness of its product or service
- The availability of new markets
- Management strengths and weaknesses
- The overall economic environment in which a company operates

Stocks that pay dividends regularly are known as **INCOME STOCKS**, while those that pay little or no dividend while reinvesting their profit are known as **GROWTH STOCKS**.

The Stock Certificate

The securities called stock certificates are traditional, and often elaborate, records of stock ownership—but they're increasingly rare.

Before the era of electronic record-keeping, written proofs of ownership, called **securities**, were needed to track investments. Today, you often don't get certificates—in fact, some brokerage houses charge a fee to issue them. Instead, the information is stored in computer files.

Like many investors, you may choose to have your stocks registered in a **street name**, which means in the name of your brokerage firm. That makes selling stock easier, since you don't have to deliver the certificate to your broker. It's also safer. Billions of dollars worth of security certificates are lost or stolen each year.

Still, the certificates have a charm of their own, and rather than abandoning them as outdated, many companies are redesigning them with new images of their identities.

Each corporation's stock certificate is distinctive, but they all share certain identifying features. **Registration numbers** are assigned to all stock certificates by the Securities and Exchange Commission

(SEC) as one way to establish their authenticity and ownership. Stock certificates are negotiable, but they're tracked in several ways to make stolen ones difficult to trade.

The **corporate seal** of the issuer, with the date and place of incorporation, appears along the bottom of the certificate.

Certificates are designed in several shades of color on specially made paper to ensure that they are difficult to forge. The intricate geometric designs that form the borders are created by machines programmed to specific settings to make them hard

The **name of the issuer** appears prominently on the certificate.

A **human figure** with clearly recognizable facial features must appear with at least a three-quarter frontal view on stocks traded on the New York Stock Exchange. It's these figures—and the scenes around or behind them—that are being updated to project new images for certain corporations. Belching smokestacks, for instance, are disappearing. The replacements often suggest environmental responsibility or contemporary lifestyles.

The **number of shares** the certificate represents appears several times.

1

COMMON

PAR VALUE $0.025

SEE REVERSE FOR CERTAIN DEFINITIONS

CUSIP 255555 55 5

INCORPORATED UNDER THE LAWS OF THE STATE OF DELAWARE
© 1986 The Walt Disney Company

ALT DISNEY COMPANY

THIS CERTIFICATE IS TRANSFERABLE IN THE CITY OF BURBANK OR NEW YORK

JANE INVESTOR

*****1**********
******1*********
*******1********
********1*******
*********1******

ONE

-PAID AND NON-ASSESSABLE SHARES OF THE COMMON STOCK OF

pany, transferable on the share register of the Corporation by the holder y authorized attorney upon surrender of this Certificate properly endorsed ...it countersigned by the Transfer Agent and registered by the Registrar the Corporation, and the signatures of its duly authorized officers.

Dated: MAY 22, 1992

COMPANY
Transfer Agent and Registrar,

Authorized Signature.
Secretary
Chairman of the Board

to copy. They're also printed on intaglio plates so that the image feels raised. Other printing methods can't reproduce the feel.

The **stockholder** is identified on the face of the certificate. To make any changes in the ownership or to sell the shares, the certificate has to be endorsed on the back and surrendered to the corporation or a broker.

A **CUSIP number** is a nine-digit identification number assigned to every security in the U.S. The Committee on Uniform Securities Identification Procedures was established by the American Bankers Association as a way to safeguard and track all traded securities.

Though the **par value** of a share of stock was once related to its investment value, today the issuing company sets it, typically at between 25 cents and $1 a share, strictly for accounting purposes.

In contrast, a bond's par value, also called its **face value**, is the amount that's repaid at maturity. The interest a bond pays is a percentage of its par value.

Selling New Stock

The first time a company issues stock, it's called **going public**.

Going public, or taking a company public, means making it possible for outside investors to buy the company's stock. To go public, the management registers the stock with the Securities and Exchange Commission (SEC) and makes an **initial public offering (IPO)**.

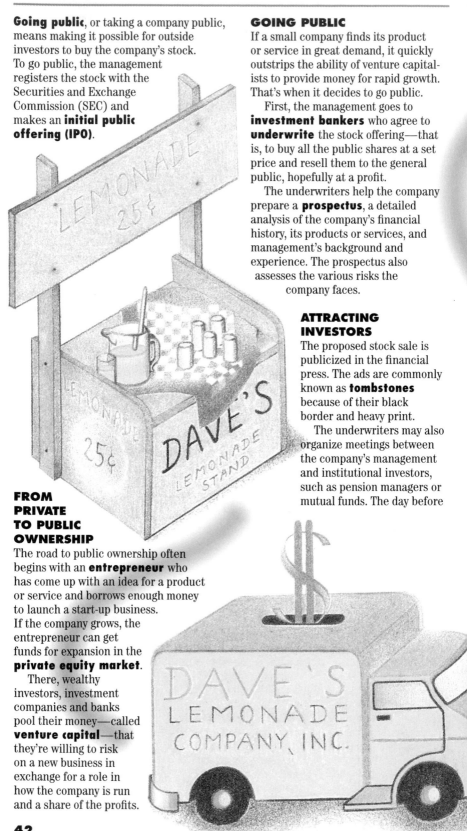

GOING PUBLIC

If a small company finds its product or service in great demand, it quickly outstrips the ability of venture capitalists to provide money for rapid growth. That's when it decides to go public.

First, the management goes to **investment bankers** who agree to **underwrite** the stock offering—that is, to buy all the public shares at a set price and resell them to the general public, hopefully at a profit.

The underwriters help the company prepare a **prospectus**, a detailed analysis of the company's financial history, its products or services, and management's background and experience. The prospectus also assesses the various risks the company faces.

ATTRACTING INVESTORS

The proposed stock sale is publicized in the financial press. The ads are commonly known as **tombstones** because of their black border and heavy print.

The underwriters may also organize meetings between the company's management and institutional investors, such as pension managers or mutual funds. The day before

FROM PRIVATE TO PUBLIC OWNERSHIP

The road to public ownership often begins with an **entrepreneur** who has come up with an idea for a product or service and borrows enough money to launch a start-up business. If the company grows, the entrepreneur can get funds for expansion in the **private equity market**.

There, wealthy investors, investment companies and banks pool their money—called **venture capital**—that they're willing to risk on a new business in exchange for a role in how the company is run and a share of the profits.

the actual sale, underwriters **price the issue**, or establish the price they will pay for each share.

When the stock begins trading the next day, the price can rise or fall, depending on whether investors agree or disagree with the underwriters' valuation of the new company.

SELLING DIRECT

Some companies are taking a shortcut to an IPO by making a direct offering to investors, or by selling shares on the Internet through an electronic brokerage firm. This type of do-it-yourself offering saves money by eliminating fees paid to underwriters. But the companies still must meet the SEC's filing rules.

One drawback of direct offerings that aren't listed on an exchange or followed by market analysts is that trading is often **thin**, or infrequent. That may limit investor interest in the stock.

SECONDARY OFFERINGS

If a company has already issued shares, but wants to raise additional **capital**, or money, through the sale of more stock, the process is called a **secondary offering**.

Companies are often wary of issuing more stock, since the larger the supply of stock outstanding, the less valuable each share already issued.

For this reason, a company typically issues new shares only if its stock price is high. To raise money, it may decide to issue bonds, or sometimes convertible bonds or preferred shares.

							Yld	Vol				Net
52 Weeks		Stock	Sym	Div	%	PE	100s	Hi	Lo	Close	Chg	
Hi	Lo							122	5¾	5½	5¾	+ ¼
6½	2⅛	AirMethod	ARF	...	...		17	1⅝	1½	1½	− ⅛
5⅞	1⅝	Cancer...	CTH	...	...		9	1¹⁵/₁₆	1¹⁵/₁₆	1¹⁵/₁₆	− ¹/₁₆
2¼	¼	DaveCo	DVCO	...	dd		113	7⅛	6⅞	7	...
n 13¾	6³/₁₆	Coltek	EDI	...	...		688	2¼	1¹⁵/₁₆	2³/₁₆	+ ⁵/₁₆
2½	1	Epigen	EPN	...	...		252	⅞	¾	⅞	+ ...
1¾	¼	Epigen wtA		...	...		50	⁷/₁₆	⁵/₁₆		
	...	Epigen wtB		...	...		121	6			

Stock Buyers

All investors buy stock for the same reason: to make money. But they do their buying differently.

An estimated 43% of adult Americans own stock, almost double the number invested in stocks in 1990. They own more than 80% of all stock in the U.S. marketplace, either directly or through mutual funds, pensions and insurers. And they account for 45% of the trading, as they buy and sell their directly held shares.

Almost 60% claim their investment is worth at least $10,000, or more than 20% of their total investment portfolio, compared to 10% in 1990. And for an increasing number, the value of their stock portfolio exceeds the value of their home, reversing a long-term trend.

INSTITUTIONAL INVESTORS

An institutional investor is an organization that invests its own assets or those it holds in trust for others. Typical institutional investors are investment companies (including mutual funds), pension systems, insurance companies, universities and banks.

For example, CalPERS, California's public pension fund, had $93 billion, or 67% of its assets, invested in stocks in early 1999. Because they have so much money to invest and are committed to making a profit, institutional investors trade regularly and in enormous volume.

A buy or sell order must be 10,000 shares or more to be considered an institutional trade—a small number for a big mutual fund eager to put its investors' money to work.

WHAT IS PROGRAM TRADING?

Some of the institutional investors speed up the trading process using computer programs to buy and sell large quantities of stock. The programs are sometimes triggered automatically when prices hit predetermined levels.

Such sudden buying or selling can cause abrupt price changes or even dramatic shifts in the entire market. The stock market crash of 1987 occurred, at least in part, because of program trading triggered by falling prices. Since then, the stock markets have put safeguards—called **circuit breakers**— in place to slow down or halt trading when markets fall too far or too fast.

SIZE MAKES A DIFFERENCE

Capitalization

LARGE-CAPS
(Companies with capitalizations of more than $5 billion)

MID-CAPS
(Companies with capitalizations of more than $1.5 billion)

SMALL-CAPS
(Companies with capitalizations of less than $1.5 billion)

BUYING STYLES

If you take a long-term view of investing, you may buy a stock and hold onto it until it rises substantially in price—sometimes over a period of years. Or you may look for quick profits in stocks whose prices you expect to increase dramatically in the short term. When the price goes up, you sell and buy something else. That approach is described as **day trading** or **market timing**.

Institutional investors and professional traders, using sophisticated analytical computer programs, have practiced market timing for years. But more recently, amateur investors with access, via the Internet, to volumes of information and nearly real-time stock quotes have been getting in on the action.

Increased day trading is making a number of radical changes in the market, among them an increased volatility, as more and more independent investors jump in and out of the market in an effort to realize a quick profit.

Many experts fear that the ease of online trading has lured many novice investors to try day trading. They warn that doing it successfully is hard in the best of circumstances, and it always magnifies the possibility of losing money.

INVESTMENT CLUBS

If you want to participate in the stock market but hesitate to get started on your own, you can join one of the more than 37,000 investment clubs in the U.S. or organize your own.

While investment clubs have many advantages— among them building confidence, sharing the burden of investment research and being able to build a diversified portfolio— joining a club doesn't necessarily guarantee stellar returns. One common problem is that investment decisions are typically made by consensus. That could mean agreeing to buy and sell decisions against your better judgment. Another is that many clubs buy small lots of stock, which can result in high commissions.

Most clubs follow guidelines from the National Association of Investment Clubs (NAIC). If you are interested, you can contact them at 877-275-6242 or visit their website (www.better-investing.org).

A company's size, or **market capitalization**, is one factor to consider when you decide which stocks to buy. Capitalization is calculated by multiplying a company's outstanding shares by its current stock price. For example, a company with 100 million outstanding shares at a current market value of $25 per share has a capitalization, or cap, of $2.5 billion. The chart below summarizes the differences between large-cap, mid-cap and small-cap stocks.

Where to Get Information	Volume of Trading	Ease of Trading	Risks and Rewards
Dow Jones Industrial Average, S&P 500-stock index	Large	Easy	Often high prices, though little risk of company failure
Extensive media and brokerage attention			Usually regular dividends
Companies provide information			Not always high growth potential
Some indexes	Large	Easy	Potential for growth greater than for larger companies
Some media and brokerage attention			
Companies provide information			
Little coverage until price has gone up dramatically	Small	Potentially difficult	Big gains possible
Companies provide information			Higher risk from company failure or poor management

Buying Stocks

Buying stocks isn't hard, but the process has its own rules, its own language and a special cast of characters.

To buy or sell a stock, you usually have to go through a **brokerage house**, an investment firm that is a member of a **stock exchange**. Your deal is handled by a **stockbroker** who has passed an exam on securities law and has registered with the Securities and Exchange Commission (SEC).

You may also be able to buy stock directly from the company that issues it through a **dividend reinvestment plan (DRIP)**. A number of large companies offer these plans and charge only a minimal fee to handle your transactions. If you sign up, your dividends are automatically reinvested to buy more shares, and you can make additional cash purchases as well.

WHAT'S IN A NAME?

Though you probably use the term broker to describe the professionals who buy and sell stocks, the financial markets use other, less widely recognized titles to describe the ways securities change hands.

Brokers handle buy and sell orders placed by individual and institutional clients in return for a commission.

Dealers buy and sell securities for their own accounts or the firm's account rather than for a client. Dealers make their money on the difference between what they pay to buy a security and the price they get for selling it. Dealers may also be called **broker-dealers**, since they can fill both roles.

Traders, also called registered or competitive traders, buy and sell securities for their own portfolios. The term traders also describes those employees of broker-dealers who handle the firms' securities trading.

CUSTOMER

PLACES ORDERS TO BUY AND SELL

When you tell your broker to buy or sell a stock at the current price, called the **market price**, you're giving a **market order**. The price you pay (or get) is usually the same as or close to the quote you're given when you place the order, depending on how quickly it's handled and how actively traded the stock is.

If you think the price of the stock you want to trade is going to change, you can place a **limit order**, which instructs your broker to buy or sell only when the stock is at the price you've named, or better.

A **stop order** instructs your broker to buy or sell at market price once the stock hits a specified target price, called the **stop price**. Stop orders are usually placed to limit losses or protect profits. Their downside is that they may be executed at a price higher or lower than the stop price (since the stock trades at the current market price after it hits the stop price).

When you give a stop order or a limit order, your broker will ask if you want a **good 'til canceled (GTC)** or **day order**. A GTC stands until it is either filled or you cancel it. A day order is canceled automatically if it isn't filled by the end of the trading day.

A **broker**, originally, was a wine seller who broached—broke open—wine casks. Today's broker has a less liquid but often heady job as a financial agent.

WHERE THE COMMISSION GOES
The commission you pay to buy and sell stocks is divided—by prearranged contract—between your broker and the brokerage firm. The commissions and any additional fees are set by the firm, but your broker may be able to give you a break if you trade often and in large volume. Generally, the higher the fee, the more room there is for negotiation.

BROKERAGE FIRM
HANDLES TRANSACTION

STOCK MARKET
REFLECTS ACTIVITY

Some brokers, usually called **full-service brokers**, provide a range of services beyond executing buy and sell orders for clients, such as researching investments and developing long- and short-term investment goals.

Discount brokers carry out transactions for clients but typically offer more limited services. Their fees, however, are usually much lower than full-service brokers'. And for experienced investors who trade often and in large blocks of stock, there are **deep-discount brokers**, whose commissions are even lower.

The cheapest way to trade securities, however, is with an **online brokerage firm**. Many established full-service and discount brokerage firms offer substantial discounts to their customers who buy and sell online.

ROUND LOTS
Usually you buy or sell stock in multiples of 100 shares, called a **round lot**. Small investors can buy just a single share, or any number they can afford. That's called an **odd lot**. Brokers often charge more to buy and sell odd lot orders.

Up-to-date information is the lifeblood of stock trading. It not only reflects current investment decisions but also influences what happens in the hours and days that follow.

Trading activity in individual stocks and the market as a whole is reported constantly online, on radio and television, and is summarized daily in The Wall Street Journal and other newspapers. Overall movement in the stock markets is tracked by a variety of indexes and averages, such as the Dow Jones Industrial Average and the S&P 500-stock index (see pp. 66-69).

Access to online information in particular is dramatically changing the way individuals invest. With just a little practice, you can research the financial history of a particular company, take advantage of online software that will help you choose an appropriate stock or access real-time stock quotes. Investors can also use this information to analyze the impact of their buy and sell decisions on their portfolios and plan their future trades.

Selling Short

Some stock investors take added risks in the hope of greater returns.

Not all stock trades are straightforward buys or sells. There are several strategies you can use to increase your gains, though they also increase your risk of incurring losses. Among these strategies are **selling short** and **buying warrants**. Both are based on a calculated wager that a particular stock will change in value, either dropping quickly in price—for a short sale—or increasing, for a warrant.

How Selling Short Works

While most investors buy stocks they think will increase in value, others invest when they think a stock's price is going to drop, perhaps substantially. What they do is described as **selling short**.

To sell short, you borrow shares you don't own from your broker, order them sold and pocket the money. Then you wait for the price of the stock to drop. If it does, you buy the shares at the lower price, turn them over to your broker (plus interest and commission) and keep the difference.

For example, you might sell short 100 shares of stock priced at $10 a share. When the price drops, you buy 100 shares at $7.50 a share, return them to your broker, and keep the $2.50-a-share difference—minus commission. Buying the shares back is called **covering the short position**. In this case, because you sold them for more than you paid to replace them, you made a profit. And you didn't have to lay out any money to do it.

YOU BORROW 100 SHARES AT $10 PER SHARE FROM YOUR BROKER	YOU SELL THE 100 SHARES AT THE $10 PRICE, GETTING $1,000
	Stock Value **$10**
SHARES YOU OWE YOUR BROKER	**100** Shares
YOUR COST TO PAY BACK THE SHARES	
YOUR PROFIT— OR LOSS	

SHORT INTEREST HIGHLIGHTS

Trading activity in stocks that have been sold short on the New York Stock Exchange and the American Stock Exchange and not yet repurchased is reported once a month in The Wall Street Journal. The volume of short interest gives you a sense of how many investors expect prices to fall and the stocks they expect to be affected.

Selling short often increases when the market is booming. Often, short sellers believe that a **correction**, or drop in market prices, has to come, especially if the overall economy does not seem to be growing as quickly as stock values are rising. But short selling is also considered a bullish sign, or a predictor of increased trading, since short positions have to be covered.

The average daily volume, which is the average number of shares sold short each trading day during the month, and the percentage change during the month are reported for each company that has had at least 550,000 shares sold short or a change of short interest of at least 250,000 in the month.

In addition, a graph tracks the recent history of short interest and a summary table provides the names of the companies with the largest short positions and the greatest change. There's also a graph and chart showing the short interest ratio. That's the number of days it would take to cover the short interest in selected stocks if trading continued at a consistent pace.

BUYING WARRANTS

Like a short sale, a warrant is a way to wager on the future price of a stock—though a warrant is definitely less risky. Warrants guarantee, for a small fee, the opportunity to buy stock at a fixed price during a specific period of time. Investors buy warrants if they think a stock's price is going up.

For example, you might pay $1 a share for the right to buy DaveCo stock at $10 within five years. If the price goes up to $14 and you **exercise**, or use, your warrant, you save $3 on every share you buy. You can then sell the shares at the higher price to make a profit ($14 − ($10 + $1) = $3), or $300 on 100 shares.

Companies sell warrants if they plan to raise money by issuing new stock or selling stocks they hold in reserve. After a warrant is issued, it can be listed in the stock columns and traded like other investments. A **wt** after a stock table entry means the quotation is for a warrant, not the stock itself.

If the price of the stock is below the set price when the warrant expires, the warrant is worthless. But since warrants are fairly cheap and have a relatively long life span, they are traded actively.

YOU PROFIT IF STOCK PRICE DROPS	YOU LOSE IF STOCK PRICE RISES
Stock Value **$7.50**	Stock Value **$12.50**
100 Shares	**100** Shares
$750	**$1,250**
$250 Profit	**$250** Loss

WHAT ARE THE RISKS?

The risks in selling short occur when the price of the stock goes up—not down—or when the drop in price takes a long time. The timing is important because you're paying your broker interest on the stocks you borrowed. The longer the process goes on, the more you pay and the more the interest expense erodes your eventual profit.

An increase in the stock's value is an even greater risk. If it goes up instead of down, you will be forced—sooner or later—to pay more to cover your short position than you made from selling the stock.

SQUEEZE PLAY

Sometimes short sellers are caught in a squeeze. That happens when a stock that has been heavily shorted begins to rise. The scramble among short sellers to cover their positions results in heavy buying, which drives the price even higher.

SHORT INTEREST HIGHLIGHTS

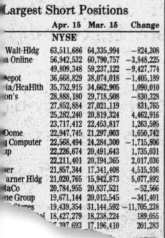

Largest Short Positions

	Apr. 15	Mar. 15	Change
	NYSE		
Walt-Hldg	63,511,686	64,335,994	−824,308
a Online	56,942,532	60,790,757	−3,848,225
	49,809,348	59,237,122	−9,427,774
epot	36,668,829	38,074,018	−1,405,189
ia/HcaHlth	35,752,915	34,662,905	1,090,010
on's	28,888,180	29,718,508	−830,328
	27,852,884	27,021,119	831,765
	25,282,240	20,819,324	4,462,916
	23,717,412	22,453,817	1,263,595
Dome	22,947,745	21,297,003	1,650,742
Computer	22,568,494	24,284,300	−1,715,806
p	22,226,674	20,491,643	1,735,031
	22,211,401	20,194,365	2,017,036
er	21,857,344	17,341,408	4,515,936
arner Hldg	21,020,765	15,942,873	5,077,892
aCo	20,784,955	20,837,521	−52,566
ne Group	19,671,144	20,012,545	−341,401
tores	19,439,354	31,144,592	−11,705,238
ol	18,427,279	18,238,224	189,055
	397,693	17,196,410	201,283

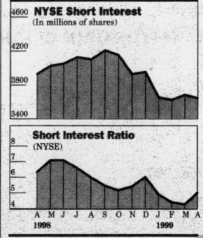

NYSE Short Interest (In millions of shares)

4600 — 4200 — 3800 — 3400

Short Interest Ratio (NYSE)

8 — 7 — 6 — 5 — 4

A M J J A S O N D J F M A
1998 · 1999

Largest % In

Rank		Apr
		NYSE
1	Met-Pro	29
2	CGI Group	28
3	CanadianImpBnkC	39
4	Midamr Enrgy Hldg	4,69
5	Newhall Land Farm	66
6	Enersis S.A. Ads	1,89
7	SummitProperties	1,15
8	CSK Auto	56
9	York Int'l	78
10	Empresa NacEl-Chile	89
11	SabreGroupHoldings	36
12	Toronto-DominionBk	32
13	BankofMontreal	31
14	CIT Group The	3,42
15	WatsonPhrmctcls	3,13
16	KansasCitySOInd	1,50
17	Jones ApparelGroup	2,59
18	Quaker Oats	78
19	PubSvcNewMexico	1,66
20	Fortune R	

Largest Short Int

Buying on Margin

Buying on margin lets investors borrow some of the money they need to buy stocks.

If you want to increase the potential return on a stock investment, you can **leverage** your purchase by **buying on margin**. That means borrowing up to half of the purchase price from your broker. If you can sell the stock at a higher price than it cost, you can repay the loan, plus interest and commission, and keep the profit. But if the stock drops in value, you still have to repay the loan. And if you must sell the shares for less than you paid, your losses could be larger than if you had owned the stock outright.

MARGIN ACCOUNTS

To buy on margin, you set up a **margin account** with a broker and transfer the required minimum in cash or securities to

How It Works

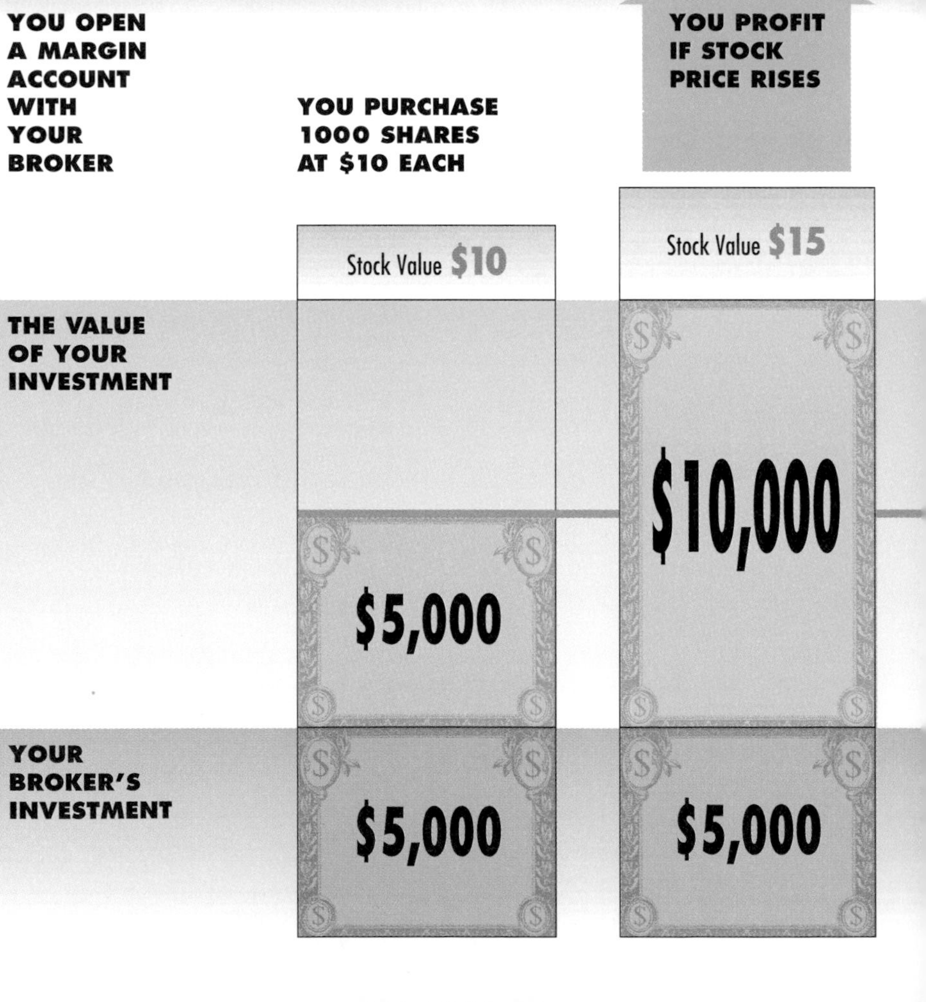

YOU OPEN A MARGIN ACCOUNT WITH YOUR BROKER

YOU PURCHASE 1000 SHARES AT $10 EACH

YOU PROFIT IF STOCK PRICE RISES

Stock Value **$10**

Stock Value **$15**

THE VALUE OF YOUR INVESTMENT

$5,000

$10,000

YOUR BROKER'S INVESTMENT

$5,000

$5,000

CLOSING THE BARN DOOR
The government and its regulatory agencies are good at figuring out ways to prevent financial disasters—after they happen. The rules and regulations that govern stock trading, for example, were devised in the wake of two major stock market crashes.

LEVERAGING YOUR STOCK INVESTMENT

Leverage is speculation. It means investing with money borrowed at a fixed rate of interest in the hope of earning a greater rate of return. Like the lever, the simple machine for which it is named, leverage lets the users exert a lot of financial power with a small amount of cash.

Companies use leverage—called **trading on equity**—when they issue both stocks and bonds. Their earnings per share may increase because they expand operations with the money raised by bonds. But they must use some of the earnings to repay the interest on the bonds.

the account. Then you can borrow up to 50% of a stock's price and buy with the combined funds.

For example, if you buy 1,000 shares at $10 a share, your total cost would be $10,000. But buying on margin, you put up $5,000 and borrow the remaining $5,000.

If you sell when the stock price rises to $15, you get $15,000. You repay the $5,000 and keep the $10,000 balance (minus interest and commissions). That's almost a 100% profit. Had you paid the full $10,000 with your own money, you would have made a 50% profit, or $5,000.

YOU LOSE IF STOCK PRICE DROPS

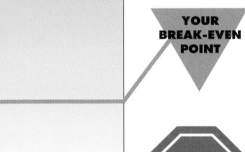

Stock Value **$6.50**

YOUR BREAK-EVEN POINT

MARGIN CALL

$1,500

$5,000

MARGIN MINIMUMS

To open a margin account, you must deposit a minimum of $2,000 in cash or eligible securities (securities your broker considers valuable). All margin trades have to be conducted through that account, combining your own money and money borrowed from your broker.

$2,000 MINIMUM

MARGIN CALLS

Despite its potential rewards, buying on margin can be very risky. For example, the value of the stock you buy could drop so much that selling it wouldn't raise enough to repay the loan.

To protect brokerage firms from losses, the New York Stock Exchange (NYSE) and the National Association of Securities Dealers (NASD) require you to maintain a margin account balance of at least 25% of the purchase price of any stock you buy long, to hold in your account.

Individual firms can require a higher margin level, say 30%, but not a lower one.

If the market value of your investment falls below its required minimum, the firm issues a **margin call**. You must either **meet the call** by adding money to your account to bring it up to the required minimum, or sell the stock, pay back your broker in full and take the loss.

For example, if shares you bought for $10,000 declined to $2,000, the shares would now be worth only 20% of their value at purchase. If your broker has a 30% margin requirement, you would have to add $1,000 to bring your margin account up to $3,000 (30% of $10,000).

During crashes, or dramatic price decreases in the market, investors who are heavily leveraged because they've bought on margin can't meet their margin calls. The result is panic selling to raise cash and further declines in the market. That's one reason the SEC instituted Regulation T, which limits the leveraged portion of any margin purchase to 50%.

Getting Stock Information

Up-to-date information is the lifeblood of stock trading. What was once reported on ticker tape is now completely electronic.

Investors—both individual and institutional—can follow the ups and downs of the stock market, and the minute-to-minute changes in a stock's price, all day long if they wish. That information is featured on dozens of broadcast and cable television programs, on business radio and increasingly on interactive websites with their frequently colorful combination of words, numbers and graphics.

While current trading information is only part of what you need to make long-term investment decisions, it is an example of the openness and accessibility of U.S. markets.

ONLINE RESEARCH

Much of the information you need to choose stocks and build a portfolio is available online—some of it for free and some of it when you open a brokerage account.

Thousands of corporate and financial websites, newsletters, FAQs and online forums provide comprehensive market information, from background reports on virtually every publicly traded stock to economic analyses and vital market statistics. Many online financial publishers will even send you a newsletter tailored to your exact specifications and interests, whether you want information on certain companies, particular market indices, or late-breaking news on the stocks in your portfolio.

One of the most reliable resources available for investors is the SEC's website (www.sec.gov).

In 1998, online trading accounted for 10% of all stock trades—both individual and institutional. By mid-1999, it was 25% and growing.

SEC filings for every publicly traded company are available from its EDGAR (Electronic Data Gathering, Analysis, and Retrieval system) database.

THE ROLE OF THE SEC

In the wake of the Great Depression and the stock-trading scandals that it exposed, the U.S. government created the **Securities and Exchange Commission (SEC)** in 1934. Its mission is to regulate the securities markets. When necessary, the SEC enforces securities law with various sanctions, from fines to prosecution. Simply put, the SEC's role is twofold:

- To see that investors are fully informed about securities being offered for sale
- To prevent misrepresentations, deceit and other types of fraud in securities transactions

The SEC also monitors **insider trading**, which occurs when corporate officers buy or sell stock in their own company. Their trading decisions are influenced by what they know about the company's inner workings and its prospects.

It is perfectly legal for officers to buy and sell their company's stock as long as they follow certain rules and report their trading activity. In fact, tracking legitimate insider trading can be a valuable indicator of which way a stock price is heading.

But corporate officers—or their legal or financial advisors—can be aware of potential problems or events that could affect the price of the company's stock. If they manipulate trading to profit from the information before it is released to the public, that trading is illegal. So are efforts to hide trading by having a third party—such as a relative—buy or sell for them.

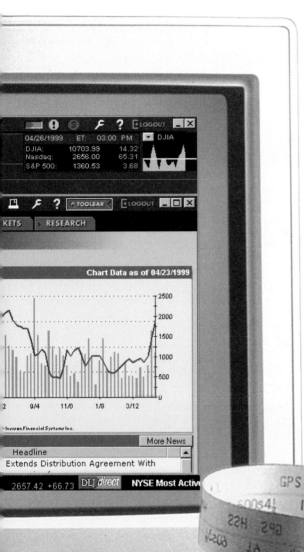

04/26/1999 ET: 03:00 PM DJIA
DJIA: 10703.99 14.32
Nasdaq: 2656.00 65.31
S&P 500: 1360.53 3.68

KETS RESEARCH

Chart Data as of 04/23/1999

Iverson Financial Systems Inc.

More News

Headline
Extends Distribution Agreement With

2657.42 +66.73 DLJ direct NYSE Most Active

TICKER TAPE

Before the development of computers and electronic media, the ticker tape was the broker's lifeline. (The first one was installed in 1867 and rented for $6 a week.) The tape listed the latest prices and the size of every stock transaction almost as quickly as prices changed. These days, it's tough to find actual ticker tape on Wall Street—or anywhere else—since the information is provided electronically. Even the ticker tape parades in lower Manhattan have crowds tossing shredded computer printouts and confetti.

Reading the Stock Tables

The stock tables keep investors up to date on what's happening in the market.

Highest and lowest prices for the past 52 weeks are reported daily. When there's a new high or low, it's indicated with an arrow in the margin like the one next to Kansas City Southern in the second column of this example. The range between the prices is a measure of the stock's volatility, or price movement. (The more volatile a stock is, the more you can make or lose in a relatively short time.) The stock with the most volatile price here is GaleyLord, whose range of movement is from 3½ to 28⅞, about 725%.

Percent yield is one way to evaluate the stock's current value. It tells you how much dividend you get as a percentage of the current price. For example, the yield on Gabelli Convertible is 7.6%.

Percent yield also lets you compare your earnings on a stock with earnings on other investments. But it doesn't tell you your total return, which is the sum of your dividends plus increases (or decreases) in stock price. When there's no dividend, yield can't be calculated, so the column is left blank.

NEW YORK STOCK EXCHANGE

| Net | | 52 Weeks | | | | | Yld | | Vol | | | | Ne |
Close	Chg	Hi	Lo	Stock	Sym	Div	%	PE	100s	Hi	Lo	Close	Chg
24	− 1/16	n 18¾	13 1/16	Gabelli A	GBL		...	...	541	14¾	14 7/16	14 7/16	+ 1/16
63 9/16	−1 13/16	11¾	9⅜	GabelliConv	GCV	.80	7.6	...	47	10⅝	10 9/16	10 9/16	− 1/
74 11/16	+1 15/16	28 11/16	25 7/16	GabelliConv pf		2.00	7.7	...	9	26 1/16	26	26	+ 1/
14 15/16	+ ⅜	12⅜	9½	GabelliTr	GAB	1.08	9.0	...	1294	12 1/16	11⅞	12	+ 1/
21	− 1/16	n 26⅜	24 9/16	GabelliTr pf		1.81	7.1	...	33	25 9/16	25½	25½	− 1/
72¾	− 2¾	▲ 12⅝	8	GabelliMlti	GGT	.80e	6.2	...	223	12 15/16	12 9/16	12⅛	+ 5/
23⅜	− ½	28 9/16	21 11/16	GblsRsdntl	GBP	2.04	9.0	20	267	22⅞	22½	22¾	+ 1/
18 3/16	− 3/16	25 3/16	22⅝	GblsRsdntl pfA		2.08	8.9	...	47	23 7/16	23 9/16	23 7/16	− 1/
84 13/16	−1 1/16	▼ 10	4¾	♣ Gainsco	GNA	.07	1.5	dd	131	4⅞	4⅝	4¾	
19⅞	+ ¼	28⅞	3½	♣ GaleyLord	GNL		...	4	324	4 7/16	4¼	4 7/16	+ 1/
31¾	+ ¼	57⅜	24¾	♣ GalileoInt	GLC	.30	.5	31	2076	57 9/16	56	57⅛	+ 7/
25 7/16	+ 1/16	50⅝	34⅞	Gallagr	AJG	1.60f	3.3	16	167	48½	47 13/16	48½	+1 5/
12	...	31¼	19½	GallaherGp	GLH	1.55e	6.5	...	1136	24⅝	24	24	− 1/
13 7/16	...	74 15/16	47⅝	♣ Gannett	GCI								−1 13/
9⅜	+ ⅜	s▲72 15/16	29½	Gap Inc									
2 9/16	...		29 13/										
66 9/													

Cash dividends per share is an estimate of the anticipated yearly dividend per share in dollars and cents. Notice that the prices of stocks that pay dividends tend to be less volatile than the prices of stocks with no dividends. Galileo International's yearly dividend is estimated at 30 cents a share. If you owned 100 shares, you'd receive $30 in dividends, probably in quarterly payments of $7.50.

Corporations are listed alphabetically—sometimes in shortened versions of the actual name—and followed by their trading symbol. Some symbols are easy to connect to their companies, like OAT for Quaker Oats, but others can be more cryptic. That often happens when companies have similar names or the logical abbreviation has already been used.

DECIMAL PRICING

Beginning in 2000, the New York Stock Exchange will quote stock prices in decimals rather than sixteenths. This is the final step in its conversion from trading in eighths, which had been in practice since the 16th century, when early settlers cut European coinage into eight pieces to be used as currency. Long favored by consumer advocates, decimal pricing will mean more efficient stock pricing, narrowing the gap, or **spread**, between the highest price offered by the buyer and the lowest price asked by the seller. For example, on the Toronto Stock Exchange, where decimal pricing has been in effect since 1996, spreads have narrowed by about 30%.

Price/earnings ratio (P/E) shows the relationship between a stock's price and the company's earnings for the last four quarters. It's figured by dividing the current price per share by the earnings per share—a number the stock table doesn't provide as a separate piece of information. Here, for example, Kaydon's P/E ratio of 13 means its price is 13 times its annual per share earnings.

Since stock investors are interested in earnings, they use P/E ratios to compare the relative value of different stocks. But the P/E ratio reported in this chart, called a trailing P/E, reports past earnings, not future potential. Two companies with the same P/E may face very different futures: one on its way to posting higher earnings and the other headed for a loss.

Those differences may be revealed in a **forward P/E**, which stock analysts compute by combining earnings reports for the two most recent quarters with the earnings they expect for the next two.

There's no perfect P/E ratio, though some investors avoid stocks if they think the ratio is too high. However, for others, a small, rapidly growing company can have a high P/E yet still be an attractive investment.

Volume refers to the number of shares traded the previous day. Unless a **Z** appears before the number in this column, multiply by 100 to get the number of shares. (The Z indicates the actual number traded.) An unusually large volume, indicated by underlining, usually means buyers and sellers are reacting to some new information.

COMPOSITE TRANSACTIONS

52 Weeks Hi	Lo	Stock	Sym	Div	Yld %	PE	Vol 100s	Hi	Lo	Close	Net Chg	52 Week Hi	L
1⅝	4⅝	KaiserAlum	KLU	...	...	cc	816	5⁷⁄₁₆	5³⁄₁₆	5⁷⁄₁₆	...	29⅝	21
37⅞	29⅜	KanPipLP	KPP	2.80f	8.5	...	100	33	32½	33	+ ⁹⁄₁₆	38¹⁵⁄₁₆	26
6⁷⁄₁₆	3½	KanebSvc	KAB	...	...	10	548	4³⁄₁₆	3¹⁵⁄₁₆	4³⁄₁₆ + ³⁄₁₆		11½	5
31¹³⁄₁₆	23½	KanCityP&L	KLT	1.66	7.0	12	980	23¹⁵⁄₁₆	23⅝	23¹¹⁄₁₆ − ¼		17¼	4
101¼	93	KanCtyP&L pfA		3.80	4.0	...	z130	95¼	95¼	95¼ − 1¾		28⁷⁄₁₆	4
66⅜	23	KanCitySo	KSU	.16	.2	40	13644	66⁷⁄₁₆	65⅛	65⅞ + ¼		77¹³⁄₁₆	53
18	14	KanCtySo pf		1.00	6.6	4	z110	15¼	15¼	15¼ + ¼		20¹¹⁄₁₆	8
21⁷⁄₁₆	13	Katylnd	KT	.30	2.1	9	64	14¹¹⁄₁₆	14½	14⁹⁄₁₆ + ¼		24¹⁵⁄₁₆	5
35	17⅛	KaufBrdHm	KBH	.30	1.3	9	853	22¹³⁄₁₆	22¼	22¾ + ⅛		18⅛	13
n 11⅛	6⅜	KaufBrdInc PRIDES		.83	11.0	...	11	7¾	7⁹⁄₁₆	7⁹⁄₁₆ − ¼		7¹¹⁄₁₆	2¹⁵
45¹⁵⁄₁₆	22¹³⁄₁₆	Kaydon	KDN	.40f	1.4	13	572	28¹³⁄₁₆	28	28¹¹⁄₁₆ + ½		39⅜	19
40½	23⅞	KeeblerFood	KBL	...	...	29	7050	33¹⁵⁄₁₆	31⁹⁄₁₆	32³⁄₁₆ − 1¹³⁄₁₆		11¹³⁄₁₆	9
9¹¹⁄₁₆	3¾	Keithlylnstr	KEI	.13	1.9	7	16	7	6⅞	7 + ⅛		14⅝	11
42¹¹⁄₁₆	28½	Kellogg	K	.94	2.8	27	3755	34⅝	33⅝	33¹³⁄₁₆ − 1		n 15⅛	11

High, low and **close** reports a stock's highest, lowest and closing price for the previous day. Usually the daily difference is small even if the 52-week spread is large. One of the largest spreads here is for Keebler Food, which was as high as 33¹⁵⁄₁₆ and as low as 31³⁄₁₆ before closing at 32³⁄₁₆.

Net change compares the closing price with the previous closing price. A minus (−) indicates that the price has fallen, and a plus (+) that it has risen. Here, Katy Industries closed at 14⁹⁄₁₆, up ¼ point from the day before. Prices that change 5% or more are in **boldface**, as Keebler Food is here.

The stock prices in this clipping are given in fractions of dollars, from ¹⁄₁₆ to ¹⁵⁄₁₆:

¹⁄₁₆	⅛	³⁄₁₆	¼	⁵⁄₁₆	⅜	⁷⁄₁₆	½	⁹⁄₁₆	⅝	¹¹⁄₁₆	¾	¹³⁄₁₆	⅞	¹⁵⁄₁₆
6¼¢	12½¢	18¾¢	25¢	31¼¢	37½¢	43¾¢	50¢	56¼¢	62½¢	68¾¢	75¢	81¼¢	87½¢	93¾¢

Sifting Stock Information

There are plenty of resources to help you make informed investment decisions.

Stock tables are a smart place to start if you're researching investments. But there is a lot of other information available that you can use to evaluate stocks and the companies that issue them.

WHAT THE NUMBERS TELL

The following figures are good indicators of the shape a company is in—and whether its stock is likely to be a good investment. They are reported regularly in the financial press, at financial websites and online brokerages, and are also available directly from brokers.

- **The book value** is the difference between the company's assets and liabilities. A small or low book value from too much debt, for example, means that the company's profits will be limited even if it does lots of business. However, a low book value may indicate that assets are underestimated, and that the stock is a good value for potential investors.

- **The earnings per share** are calculated by dividing the company's net profit by the number of its outstanding shares. If earnings increase each year, the company is growing.

- **The return on equity** is a percentage figured by dividing a company's earnings per share by its book value.

- **The payout ratio** is the percentage of net earnings a company uses to pay its dividend. The normal range is 25% to 50% of its net earnings. A higher ratio may mean that the company is struggling to meet its obligations.

DARTBOARD ANALYSIS

concludes that you make out just as well if you throw darts at the stock pages and buy what you hit. For several years The Wall Street Journal has carried a monthly column in which professional managers' stock picks are pitted against choices reporters make with darts. So far, the professionals are ahead, but sometimes the random darts come close to evening the score.

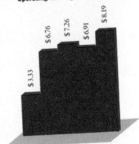

BIGCO.
Consolidated Financial Highlights

For the Year
Revenues
Operating earnings
Operating earnings per common share
Net income
Net income per common share
Dividends paid per common share

At Year-End
Total investments
Total assets
Common shareholders' equity
Book value per common share

Operating Earnings Per Common Share

$3.33 $6.76 $7.26 $6.91 $8.19

Return o

15.2%

Record per share 1996 operating earnings (excluding realized investment gains) exceeded the previous high year by 13%.

This r
dividi
(less
begin
comm

Contents

USING THE INFORMATION

Different investment professionals analyze stock in different ways. Those who do **fundamental analysis** study a company's financial condition, management and competitive position in its industry or sector. They may also look at features of the economy at large, such as unemployment and interest rates, in order to estimate the potential stock performance.

Those who do **technical analysis** chart the statistics of past market performance to identify price trends and cyclical movements of particular stocks, industries or the market as a whole.

	1999	1998	Percent Change
	$ 4,005,237,000	$ 3,788,648,000	5.7
	$ 385,458,000	$ 338,267,000	14.0
	$ 8.19	$ 6.91	18.5
	$ 391,270,000	$ 398,158,000	(1.7)
	$ 8.31	$ 8.12	2.3
	$ 2.35	$ 2.15	9.3
	$ 8,467,668,000	$ 8,106,756,000	4.5
	$12,203,990,000	$11,030,066,000	10.6
	$ 2,196,371,000	$ 2,349,254,000	(6.5)
	$ 52.00	$ 47.65	9.1

Dividends Paid Per Common Share

16.8% 16.1%

$1.50 $1.695 $1.94 $2.15 $2.35

ted by
earnings
dends) by
ear
ders' equity.

We have paid a common share dividend for 119 consecutive years.

A NOTE OF CAUTION:
Most annual reports are prepared by the company's public relations department and are intended to show the company in the best possible light.

WHAT THE COMPANY TELLS

Companies are required by law to keep shareholders up to date on how the business is doing. That information can be very valuable in keeping tabs on your investment. The most complete information the company provides is outlined in its **annual report**. You also get **quarterly reports**, which include concise summaries of the company's current performance.

An annual report summarizes the company's operations for the past year. Often quite elaborately designed and illustrated, it usually begins with a letter from the company's chairman touching on the year's highlights and offering some broad prediction for the coming one.

A typical annual report includes:
- A section outlining the company's **philosophy** of doing business.
- Detailed reports on each segment of the company's **operations**. This information can reveal weaknesses in the management structure, or the products or services the company offers.
- Financial information, including the profit-and-loss statement for the year, and the **balance sheet**, showing the company's assets and liabilities at the end of the year compared to previous years. Footnotes attached to the financial summaries can sometimes reveal problems, such as lawsuits against the company or proposed government regulations that might influence profitability.
- An **auditor's letter** reassuring shareholders that the company's financial statements are in order. Annual reports, along with other details about the company, are usually available from brokers, directly from companies, or increasingly at corporate websites on the Internet.

Evaluating Companies

A company's earnings and what it has paid in dividends can be a useful indicator of what's in store for a particular stock.

Earnings and dividend reports, along with feature stories on particular companies, various industry groups and the overall economy, give you the background you need to make informed buy and sell decisions. The information is available in the financial press—both in print and online—and on company home pages and the thousands of financial websites, forums, online newsletters and other resources that can provide new perspectives on your existing—and potential—investments.

DIGEST OF EARNINGS REPORTS

The rising prices and big dividends that make investors happy with a stock's performance are tied directly to the financial health of the company. When a company's earnings are up, investor confidence increases and the price of the stock usually rises. If the company is losing money—or not making as much as anticipated—the stock price usually falls, sometimes rapidly.

The Digest of Earnings Reports, printed regularly in The Wall Street Journal, is a scorecard of company quarterly, and sometimes annual, earnings and profits that covers different companies from day to day. **Losses** are indicated in parentheses.

The **name** of the company appears, followed by a **code** for the exchange where the company is traded: **N** for the New York Stock Exchange, **A** for the American Stock Exchange and **Nq** for the Nasdaq Stock Market.

Gross income is listed as **sales** for manufacturing companies and **revenues** for service companies.

Net income is the company's profit for the current quarter or year.

To find **share earnings**, or earnings per share, the **net income** is divided by the number of shares, with losses appearing in parentheses.

Shr earns (basic) are the primary earnings, or net earnings per common share.

Shr earns (diluted) are the net earnings per share assuming the exercise of all outstanding warrants and stock options, and the conversion of all preferred stocks and convertible bonds.

Year figures, including revenues and net income, are provided for companies reporting their cumulative second-, third- and fourth-quarter profits.

The Journal also publishes two earnings summaries regularly:

Highlights, a selection of the most important and noteworthy figures from the tables, and **Earnings Surprises**, reporting companies whose quarterly profits differed significantly from analysts' estimates.

DIGEST OF EARNINGS REPORTS

AASCHE TRANSPORT (Nq)   ASHE

Year Dec 31:	a1998	1997
Revenues	$113,431,000	$65,170,000
Net income.....	60,000	270,000
Shr earns (diluted):		
Net income ..	.01	.06

a-Includes the results of Specialty Transportation Services, Inc., acquired in January 1998.

ADVOCAT INC. (N)   AVC

Quar Dec 31:	1998	1997
Revenues	$49,656,000	$50,907,000
Net income.....	a(3,901,000)	97,000
Avg dil shs	5,399,000	5,384,000
Shr earns:		
Net income ..	(.72)	.02
Year:		
...ues	205,152,000	182,243,000
...3,000)	3,013,000
		5,373,000

BENTLEY PHARM (A)   BNT

Quar Dec 31:	1998	1997
Sales	$4,711,000	$3,374,000
Net income.....	(516,000)	(1,242,000)
Avg shares	8,439,000	6,110,000
Shr earns:		
Net income ..	(.06)	(.18)
Year:		
Sales	15,243,000	14,902,000
Net income.....	a(2,876,000)	(3,815,000)
Avg shares	8,431,000	4,072,000
Shr earns:		
Net income ..	(.35)	(.97)

a-Includes a nonrecurring charge of $1,176,000.

BIO-PLEXUS INC. (Nq)   BPLX

Year Dec 31:	1998	1997
Revenues	$9,307,000	$5,042,000
Net income.....	(2,960,000)	(12,312,000)
Avg shares	12,263,870	9,320,8..
Shr earns:		

THE INDEX TO BUSINESSES

appears every day in The Wall Street Journal. It lists all the businesses mentioned in that issue and the page on which the article begins. Scanning the list alerts investors to news stories and features on companies whose stock they own or are thinking of buying.

INDEX TO BUSINESSES

A		G	
Accor	B1	Gehl	C
Ahmanson H.F.	B4	General Electric	A3B,C
Alamco	B3	General Instrument	C
Albany Intl	C2	General Motors	C
Allied Irish Banks	A3A	Georgia-Pacific	
AlliedSignal	B1	Glenfed	
Allmerica Financial	B2		

CORPORATE DIVIDEND NEWS

Dividends, like earnings, often have a direct influence on stock prices. When dividends are increased, the message is that the company is prospering. That often stimulates added interest in the stock.

When dividends are cut, the opposite message is sent. Investors conclude that the company's future expectations have dimmed. One typical consequence is an immediate drop in the stock's price.

DIVIDEND NEWS

Dividends Reported April 6

Company	Period	Amt.	Payable date	Record date
REGULAR				
Brenton Banks	Q	.05½	4 –27 –99	4 –15
Claire's Stores	Q	.04	5 –19 –99	5 – 5
Cummins Engine	Q	.27½	6 –15 –99	6 – 1
First Finl Corp-RI	Q	.09	5 –17 –99	5 – 3
FrptMcMrnCop depSlvr	Q	.2137	5 – 1 –99	4 –16
FrptMcMrnCop depGld	Q	.2471	5 – 1 –99	4 –16
FrptMcMrnCop dpGldII	Q	.2294	5 – 1 –99	4 –16
FrptMcMrnCop depstp	Q	.43¾	5 – 1 –99	4 –16
Greenbrier Cos	Q	.06	5 –12 –99	4 –21
Hershey Foods Corp	Q	.24	6 –15 –99	5 –24
IllinoisPwr4.08%pf	Q	.51	5 – 1 –99	4 – 9
IllinoisPwr4.20%pf	Q	.52½	5 – 1 –99	4 – 9
IllinoisPwr4.26%pf	Q	.53¼	5 – 1 –99	4 – 9
IllinoisPwr4.42%pf	Q	.55¼	5 – 1 –99	4 – 9
IllinoisPwr4.70%pf	Q	.58¾	5 – 1 –99	4 – 9
Managed HiYield Plus	M	.12½	4 –30 –99	4 –19
Oxford Industries	Q	.21	5 –29 –99	5 –14
PNC Bank Corp pfC	Q	.40	7 – 1 –99	5 –28
PNC Bank Corp pfD	Q	.45	7 – 1 –99	5 –28
PugetSoundEnrgy7.45%pfI	Q	.465⅝	7 – 1 –99	6 –15
PugetSoundEnrgy8.50%pfII	Q	.53⅛	7 – 1 –99	6 –15
Puget Sound Energy Inc	Q	.46	5 –15 –99	4 –19
RPM Inc	Q	.11¾	4 –30 –99	4 –16

* * *

Stocks Ex-Dividend April 8

Company	Amount	Company	Amount
CNB Bancshares	.24	Mills Corp	.50¼
Carolina P&L	.50	Nevada Power	.25
Cmmnwlth Enrgy	.41½	Pep Boys ManMoe	k .06¾
Conectiv ClA	.80	Pilgrim Pr	
Conectiv	.38½		
France G			

The names of companies announcing dividends are listed in alphabetical order:

A **pf** following the name indicates a dividend on preferred stock, and a **clA** or **clB** shows different classes of stock.

Q indicates a quarterly dividend—the most common type.

M indicates a monthly dividend.

S indicates a semiannual dividend. A few stocks pay dividends irregularly.

The **period amount** is the amount of dividend per share, stated in cents. In this example, Hershey Foods is paying a quarterly dividend of 24 cents.

The **record date** is the date by which you must own shares in order to receive the dividend.

The **payable date** is the date the dividend will be paid.

Here Oxford Industries has declared a regular quarterly dividend of 21 cents per share, which will be paid on May 29 to shareholders of record as of May 14.

If a dividend has been announced but not yet paid, the stock is said to have gone **ex-dividend**. On most major exchanges, stocks go ex-dividend on the date of record, typically several days before the date on which the payment will be made. If you own the stock on the date of record, you receive the dividend. But if you buy stocks during the ex-dividend period, you don't receive a dividend until the next one is paid—usually three months later.

MOVING AVERAGE

A moving average is created by graphing 52 weeks of weekly average stock prices. It's moving because the chart is updated every week by dropping the oldest number and adding the newest one. The result is a smoother curve than you would get by recording the daily ups and downs of the market.

The Stock Market

Stocks change hands every trading day on traditional and electronic markets.

The first stock exchange in America was organized in Philadelphia in 1790. But by the time the traders who met every day under the buttonwood tree on Wall Street adopted the name **New York Stock Exchange** in 1817, New York had become the center of market action.

The rival **New York Curb Exchange** was founded in 1842. Its name said it all: Trading actually took place on the street until it moved indoors in 1921. In 1953, the Curb Exchange became the **American Stock Exchange**.

A STREET BY ANY OTHER NAME

Wall Street, which got its name from the stockade built by early settlers to protect New York from attacks from the north, was the scene of New York's first organized stock trading. Now it lends its name to the financial markets in general—though lots of traders never set foot on it.

WALL STREET AND BEYOND

As more and more trading is conducted by telephone and computer, the original stock exchanges that provide central-ized facilities for trading, such as the New York Stock Exchange and the American Stock Exchange, have come to be known as **traditional markets** to distinguish them from the newer elec-tronic markets that allow brokers to trade from their offices all over the country. In reality, however, traditional markets take full advantage of the latest technology to maximize the efficiency and volume of their trading.

OTHER U.S. MARKETS

Stocks listed on the NYSE or AMEX may also be traded in one of the smaller **regional exchanges**, including Chicago, Boston and the Pacific Exchange in Los Angeles. In addition, some smaller, regional companies are listed only on the exchange in their area. The most actively traded of those companies are listed in

the **U.S. Regional Markets** column of The Wall Street Journal.

Transactions handled on the regionals can be faster, and sometimes cheaper, than transactions on the larger exchanges, which encourages competition among the exchanges. However, trading results for all of the stocks listed on both the NYSE and the regional exchanges are combined daily into a single statistic in the NYSE **Composite Trading** table.

SEATS, AT A PRICE

The NYSE and AMEX are private associations that sell memberships, or seats, permitting brokers to trade on the exchange. The NYSE currently has 1,366 members, and the AMEX has 864. General-ly, the cost rises and falls with the market.

THE ELECTRONIC STOCK MARKET

Unlike traditional exchanges, the Nasdaq Stock Market has no central trading location and no exchange floor. Rather, it's an advanced telecommunications and

computer network run by the **National Association of Securities Dealers** that allows brokers to monitor stock prices, match orders and make trades from anywhere in the country. The Nasdaq is the country's largest market, listing nearly 5,000 companies, from small, emerging firms to corporate giants, such as Microsoft and Intel. It also trades more shares daily than any other U.S. market.

In 1998, the Nasdaq merged with the AMEX—the country's second-largest traditional exchange. Although they continue to operate as separate markets, the Nasdaq and the AMEX are united under a single management and are part of a technologically sophisticated network of worldwide markets.

Computer-based, rather than face-to-face, stock trading is assuming an increasingly important role, not only in the U.S. but around the world. Trading in London and Tokyo, for example, is exclusively electronic. The same is true of most of the stock markets in emerging nations.

OVER-THE-COUNTER TRADING

Stocks in more than 9,800 small and new companies aren't listed on either the Nasdaq or a traditional market. Instead, they're bought and sold **over the counter (OTC)**. The term originated at a time when U.S. investors actually bought stock over the counter at their local broker's office. Today, transactions are handled over the telephone or by computer.

Many OTC stocks are comparatively inexpensive and infrequently, or **thinly**, traded, and their prices aren't reported regularly. There are two quotation services for OTC stocks—the pink sheets, published by the National Quotation Bureau, and the OTC Bulletin Board (OTCBB). Both quotation services provide online real-time quotations for OTC stocks—the Bulletin Board for the approximately 6,500 OTC stocks that are registered with the SEC, and the National Quotation Bureau for the 3,300 stocks that are not registered.

REQUIREMENTS FOR STOCK MARKET LISTING

The major U.S. stock markets impose specific requirements that companies must meet before their stock can be listed, or traded on that market. If they qualify for all three, the companies can choose where they wish to be traded.

Exchange	Requirements*	Typical daily volume*	Number listed*
NYSE New York Stock Exchange	1.1 million publicly held shares minimum; $40 million minimum market capitalization	822.0 million shares	3,086
NASDAQ® The Nasdaq Stock Market	There are sets of quantitative and qualitative requirements for companies listed on the Nasdaq National Market and the Nasdaq Small-Cap Market	1.02 billion shares	4,934
AMEX American Stock Exchange	500,000 publicly held shares minimum; $3 million minimum market capitalization	29.7 million shares	765

*As of April 30, 1999

Trading on the New York Stock Exchange

A stock exchange is both the activity of buying and selling and the place where those transactions take place.

The New York Stock Exchange, like other traditional exchanges, provides the facilities for stock trading and rules under which the trading takes place. It has no responsibility for setting the price of a stock. That is the result of supply and demand, and the trading process.

Trading on the floor of the NYSE is **auction style**: In each transaction, stock is sold for the highest bid and bought for the lowest offer.

THE TRADING FLOOR
The NYSE's trading area is known as the **trading floor**.

1 The trading day begins (at 9:30 a.m. EST/EDT) and ends (at 4:00 p.m.) when the bell is rung from **the podium**.

8 **Confirmation** is made when the floor broker sends the successful trade details back to the branch office where the order originated.

7 After every deal, a reporter uses a digital scanning device to record the stock symbol, the price and the initiating broker. The scanner transmits the information within seconds to the Exchange's electronic tape. It also begins an **audit trail** in the event that something about the trade is suspicious.

COMPUTERIZED TRADING
Orders of fewer than 31,000 shares are filled using a computerized system called **Super DOT** (Designated Order Turnaround System).

6 **Post display units** show the day's activity at the post. They report the stocks traded, the last sale price and order size.

Action on the floor often occurs at a furious pace. People wear different colored jackets to indicate they're doing specific jobs:

light blue jackets with orange epaulets for messengers

green jackets for floor supervisors or traders

navy jackets for exchange reporters

2 The Exchange rents **booths** to brokerage houses. Each booth is home base for a firm's floor brokers. When an order is received from one of its brokerage offices, a floor broker takes the order to the appropriate **specialist** post to carry out the transaction.

3 The Exchange rents space to **specialist** firms—the brokers to the brokers. A specialist keeps a list of unfilled orders. As buy and sell orders move in response to price changes, the specialist processes the transactions.

The specialists' other job is to maintain an orderly market in a stock. If the **spread** between the **bid** and **asked** (the gap between the highest price offered by a buyer and the lowest price asked by a seller) becomes too wide, specialists turn into dealers themselves who buy and sell stock. This narrows the spread and stimulates trading—a good thing for the vitality of the Exchange and for the specialists as well, since the more they trade, the more commission they earn.

4 Various stocks or groups of stocks are traded at **trading posts** near the specialists' positions. Each company's stock trades at only one post on the floor of the Exchange so the trading can be tracked accurately. However, the stock of several different companies may be traded at the same post. The number of companies assigned depends on the combined volume of business they generate.

5 Floor brokers can use a specialist if they choose. But many trades actually occur between two floor brokers who show up at the post at the same time.

On a typical day a floor broker walks—or runs— an average of

12 MILES

in crisscrossing the floor.

Trading on the Nasdaq Market

Thousands of stocks are traded electronically—
using computers and telephones—on the
Nasdaq Stock Market.

The Nasdaq Stock Market was the world's first electronic market when it opened in 1971. Now dozens of markets around the world are screen based, including those in London, Paris, Tokyo and Hong Kong.

Trading on the Nasdaq is through an open market, multiple dealer system, with many market makers competing to handle transactions in each individual stock. That's a contrast to the system used on traditional exchanges, where all the buy and sell orders in a stock must go through a single specialist. And since there are a number of market makers, more transactions can take place at the same time.

The Nasdaq is working to build a global trading network featuring real-time trade reporting. Since 1992, its securities have

been traded in the early morning hours, when the London markets are open. And in 1997, an ECN, or electronic communications network, was introduced to let market makers and institutions around the world bid anonymously. The network checks for matches, which can be handled instantly. If none are found, the bid and asked prices are posted on the Nasdaq.

A 55-foot wall of 100 multimedia screens displays the most up-to-date information—from new data to live video.

TRADING SYMBOLS

All securities are represented by trading symbols—one-to-five letter abbreviations used to identify a stock in the market where it trades, and in stock quotations and tables. Originally developed in the 19th century, one-letter symbols were especially prestigious, since they were given to the most actively traded stocks. Nowadays, trading symbols are assigned according to availability. And no two symbols are alike—even in different markets.

READING NASDAQ TABLES

The largest and most actively traded Nasdaq stocks are listed in the **Nasdaq National Market Issues** and are published every trading day. National Market Issues uses a format similar to the listings for NYSE and AMEX stocks (see page 68). But the trading symbols in the Nasdaq lists have four or five letters, unlike the NYSE and AMEX exchanges, which use symbols of one to three letters. Because many of the Nasdaq companies are either small or start-up companies, which prefer to put earnings back into the business, few pay dividends.

In this example, Lycos (LCOS) had a high of 145⅜ and a low of 20 1/16 during the past 52 weeks. In other words, it was extremely volatile—with its high $125, or 625%, above its low. The company also declared a stock split during that period, as the **s** in the left-hand margin indicates.

The company paid no dividend, and the **dd** in the P/E (price/earnings ratio) column indicates it lost money in the past four quarters, typical of Internet stocks in the late 1990s. Nevertheless, trading was extremely active, at 1,108,100 shares, and the closing price of $101.50 (101½) was closer to its high than its low.

NASDAQ NATIONAL MARKET ISSUES

Close	Net Chg
27⅛	+ ⅛
4 5/32	− 5/32
5 5/16	+ 1/16
12¾	+ ½
9⅞	+2
4⅞	− ⅛
11¼	+ 3/16

	52 Weeks Hi	52 Weeks Lo	Stock	Sym	Div	Yld %	PE	Vol 100s	Hi	Lo	Close	Net Chg
s	145⅜	20 1/16	Lycos	LCOS		...	dd	11091	104⅝	101	101½	− 1⅛
	15	6¾	LynxThrptcs	LYNX		...	dd	464	10¼	9 9/16	9⅞	− ½
	14⅜	4 11/16 ♣	MFC Bcp g	MXBIF	.02e	...	...	34	6½	6⅛	6⅜	− ⅛
	8⅞	2¾ ♣	MFRI Inc	MFRI		...	9	10	3⅛	3⅛	3⅛	...
n♣	46	4	MGC Comm	MGCX		...	...	43697	49¼	41	46	+ 8½
	24	4⅝ ♣	MGI Pharma	MOGN		...	cc	241	9¼	8 7/16	9	+ ½
	21⅞	21/32	MH Meyersn	MHMY		...	...	17369	8¼	6¼	6 5/16	− 1 11/16
	6 7/16	2	MIM Cp	MIMS		...	8	1797	2⅜	2⅛	2⅜	+ ¼
								778	58¼	56 1/16	57½	− 5/16

	52 Weeks Hi	52 Weeks Lo
	20 15/16	10⅞
	18½	4 9/16
	8⅞	1½
	6	1⅜
	13 1/16	2¼
n	40	22
	8½	3
	25¾	19¼
	23	[illegible]

NASDAQ SMALL-CAP ISSUES

Vol 100s	Last	Chg
101	6⅜	− ½
48	2 9/16	...
227	1½	+ 5/16
28	13/16	...
1092	4¾	− 3/16
246	1½	...
297	1¼	− ⅛
	5/32	+ 1/32

Issue	Div	Vol 100s	Last	Chg
GoldRs		88	1 5/32	+ 1/32
GoldStd		12	1½	− ⅛
♣ GoldGen		407	1 7/16	+ 3/16
GoldIsl		4	9⅜	+ ⅜
GothicEn		1771	½	...
GrndAdv		38	1 15/16	+ 3/16
GrndCtrl n		30	10¼	...
GrndCSII		14	1¼	...

Issue	Div	Vol 100s	Last	Chg
IxysCp n		251	3 11/16	+ 1/16
JB Oxfrd		116868	12 7/16	− 2⅜
JLM Ctre		66	1 31/32	+ 1/32
JMC Gp h		12143	1⅜	+ 23/64
J2 Com		33		...
JksnvSB	.30	6	10⅞	...
JenkonI n		611	2¾	+ ⅜
JunipGrp		20	1 15/16	...

NASDAQ SMALL-CAP ISSUES

Smaller, emerging companies—the Nasdaq's specialty—are listed in the **Nasdaq Small-Cap Issues**. The table concentrates on current volume and price, since many of the companies are too new to have established a financial track record, including a P/E ratio.

Some of the companies do pay dividends, though, especially on preferred stock offerings, so that information is also reported immediately following the name.

Trading activity in the stocks varies. 177,100 shares of GothicEn changed hands at 50 cents (½) a share, but only 1200 of GoldStd, at $1.50 (1½).

Reading the Averages

Stock market activity is reported daily in averages and indexes designed to assess the state of the economy.

The change in price and the volume of sales of any single stock on any given day matters mostly to its shareholders. But what the market does as a whole—whether it climbs rapidly or slowly, stays flat or drops dramatically—is a gauge of what's happening in the economy. That activity is reported in several different averages and indexes designed to measure trends in the market.

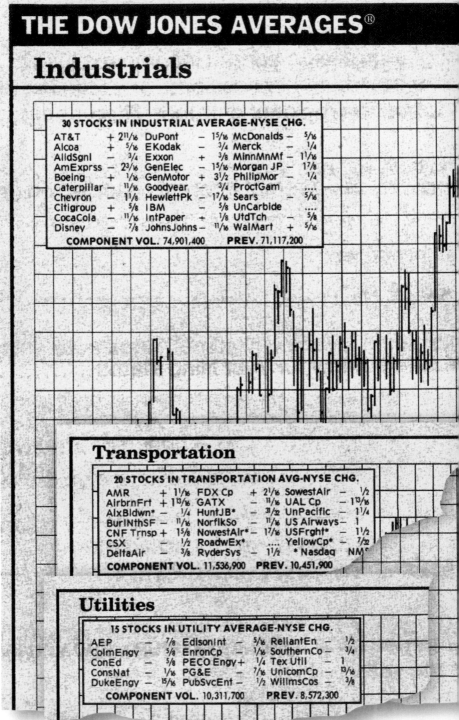

THE DOW JONES AVERAGES®

Industrials

30 STOCKS IN INDUSTRIAL AVERAGE-NYSE CHG.

AT&T	+ 2¹¹/₁₆	DuPont	− ¹⁵/₁₆	McDonalds	− ⁵/₁₆
Alcoa	+ ⁵/₁₆	EKodak	− ³/₄	Merck	− ¹/₄
AlldSgnl	− ³/₄	Exxon	+ ³/₈	MinnMnMf	− 1¹/₁₆
AmExprss	− 2³/₁₆	GenElec	− ¹⁵/₁₆	Morgan JP	− 1⁷/₈
Boeing	+ ¹/₁₆	GenMotor	+ 3¹/₂	PhilipMor	− ¹/₄
Caterpillar	− ¹¹/₁₆	Goodyear	− ³/₄	ProctGam	....
Chevron	− 1¹/₈	HewlettPk	− 1⁷/₁₆	Sears	− ⁵/₁₆
Citigroup	+ ⁵/₈	IBM	− ⁵/₈	UnCarbide	....
CocaCola	− ¹¹/₁₆	IntPaper	+ ¹/₈	UtdTch	− ⁵/₈
Disney	− ⁷/₈	JohnsJohns	− ¹¹/₁₆	WalMart	+ ⁵/₁₆

COMPONENT VOL. 74,901,400   **PREV. 71,117,200**

Transportation

20 STOCKS IN TRANSPORTATION AVG-NYSE CHG.

AMR	+ 1¹/₁₆	FDX Cp	+ 2¹/₁₆	SowestAir	− ¹/₂
AirbrnFrt	+ 1¹³/₁₆	GATX	− ¹¹/₁₆	UAL Cp	− 1¹³/₁₆
AlxBldwn*	− ¹/₄	HuntJB*	− ³/₃₂	UnPacific	− 1¹/₄
BurlNthSF	− ¹¹/₁₆	NorflkSo	− ¹¹/₁₆	US Airways	− 1
CNF Trnsp	+ 1⁵/₈	NowestAir*	− 1⁷/₁₆	USFrght*	− 1¹/₂
CSX	− ¹/₂	RoadWEx*	....	YellowCp*	− ⁷/₃₂
DeltaAir	− ³/₈	RyderSys	− 1¹/₂	* Nasdaq	NM*

COMPONENT VOL. 11,536,900   **PREV. 10,451,900**

Utilities

15 STOCKS IN UTILITY AVERAGE-NYSE CHG.

AEP	− ⁷/₈	EdisonInt	− ⁵/₁₆	ReliantEn	− ¹/₂
ColmEngy	− ⁵/₈	EnronCp	− ¹/₁₆	SouthernCo	− ³/₄
ConEd	− ⁵/₈	PECO Engy	+ ¹/₄	Tex Util	− 1
ConsNat	− ¹/₁₆	PG&E	− ⁷/₈	UnicomCp	− ¹³/₁₆
DukeEngy	− ¹⁵/₁₆	PubSvcEnt	− ¹/₂	WillmsCos	− ³/₈

COMPONENT VOL. 10,311,700   **PREV. 8,572,300**

THE DOW JONES AVERAGE

The **Dow Jones Industrial Average (DJIA)**—sometimes referred to as **the Dow**—is the best-known and most widely reported market indicator. In fact, when people say, "The market was up 15 points today," they typically mean that the DJIA rose 15 points.

Originally, the DJIA was a simple average of a group of stocks and was figured by dividing the total price by the number of stocks. Today, the DJIA is computed by adding the stock prices of 30 major industrial companies and dividing by a factor that adjusts for distortions caused by stock splits over the years or the impact of one company replacing another on the list. As a result, the DJIA is more like an **index** than an average.

WHY WATCH THE INDEX

The DJIA and other stock indexes, such as the New York Stock Exchange Composite Index and Standard & Poor's 500-stock index (S&P 500), serve as important tools for measuring the overall health of the stock market. By comparing current market performance with how stocks behaved in the past, you can draw better conclusions about when to buy and sell. The indexes also serve as benchmarks against which you can measure the performance of your own portfolio. For example, if all the indexes are going up, as the DJIA is in this example, and your portfolio is losing ground, it's probably time to reevaluate your holdings.

Actual High
Close
Actual Low

10200
10100
10000
9900
9800
9700
9600
9500
9400
9300
9200
9100
9000
8900
8800
8700
8600
8500
8400
8300
8200

MORE THAN ONE DOW

There are four Dow Jones Averages. Besides the DJIA, two monitor specific industries and the third is a composite, or combination of them all:

- **Dow Jones Industrial Average** monitors 30 industrial companies.
- **Dow Jones Transportation Average** monitors 20 airlines, railroads and trucking companies.
- **Dow Jones Utility Average** monitors 15 gas, electric and power companies.
- **Dow Jones 65 Composite Average** includes all 65 companies in the other three averages.

THE DOW'S RELIABILITY

The Dow accurately measures what it claims to measure: the performance of 30 key companies that are worth about 25% of the total value of all stocks listed on the NYSE. To the extent that those companies represent key sectors of the economy, their performance indicates how that part of the economy as a whole is doing. However, other sectors of the economy perform differently, and indexes that report on a broader range of companies sometimes give a clearer picture of the markets (see pages 68-69).

History of the Dow

In 1884, Charles Dow made a list of the average closing prices of 11 stocks he thought represented the economic strength of the country: nine railroads and two manufacturing firms. He published the list in the forerunner of the paper he later founded with his partner Edward Jones: The Wall Street Journal.

Charles Dow honed his list to create one comprising only industrial stocks. After 12 years of deletions, additions and substitutions, he published the first list of those stocks in 1896 and reported its average regularly. Only General Electric remains from the 1896 list.

The list was expanded to include 30 companies in 1928 and has been updated more than 20 times since. The editors of The Wall Street Journal decide which companies to list and when to make changes. Overall, the changes have not been dramatic—the list continues to be weighted with manufacturing and energy stocks. Some economists think a broader list would give a better picture of the economy.

Market Indexes

Because no single index can tell you everything you need—or want—to know about the stock market, there are indexes to track practically everything.

The stock market's every move is reported in 29 different indexes daily in The Wall Street Journal. Various indexes track market highs and lows, the changes from the previous trading day, and over the last year, plus the volume of trading and dozens of other details.

The NYSE Composite Index includes all stocks traded on the New York Stock Exchange. The NYSE also reports the activity in four sectors—industrial, utility, transportation and financial—in separate indexes.

This chart shows that the composite high during the last 12 months was 617.61 and its low was 477.20.

Standard & Poor's 500 Index incorporates a broad base of 500 stocks, including 400 industrial companies, 20 transportation companies, 40 utilities and 40 financial companies. It's widely considered the benchmark for large-stock investors. Some stocks have a greater influence on the direction of the market than others because of their market value, so the S&P 500 is calculated by giving greater weight to those stocks.

In this chart, the S&P 500 Index is up 9, or 0.68%, from the previous day.

The Nasdaq Stock Market Composite Index tracks the performance of stocks traded through its electronic system. The Nasdaq Composite often shows more volatility than the other indexes because of the kinds of companies it covers.

In addition, six other indexes track sectors that trade heavily on the market.

The AMEX Composite monitors the performance of the companies listed on the American Stock Exchange.

The Russell 2000 follows the smallest two-thirds of the 3,000 largest U.S. companies, including a great many of the initial public offerings of the last few years. It's widely considered the benchmark for small-company stocks.

Value-Line, an independent investment information service, tracks the performance of 1,700 common stocks in a geometric index.

The Wilshire 5000, the broadest index, includes nearly all stocks traded in U.S. markets.

THE GLOBAL-U.S. INDEX
The Dow Jones Global-U.S. index tracks more than 700 stocks traded in U.S. markets. Combined, they represent about 80% of the total U.S. market and are the U.S. portion of the DJ World Stock Index.

STOCK MARKET

MAJOR INDEXES

— ↑12-MO —		
HIGH	**LOW**	
DOW JONES AVERAGES		
10085.31	7539.07	30 **Industrials**
3686.02	2345.00	20 **Transportation**
320.51	271.67	15 **Utilities**
3070.99	2411.00	65 **Composite**
1255.67	900.71	**DJ Global-US**
NEW YORK STOCK EXCHANGE		
617.61	477.20	**Composite**
769.53	593.49	**Industrials**
460.50	354.33	**Utilities**
533.93	351.13	**Transportation**
599.15	399.19	**Finance**
STANDARD & POOR'S INDEXES		
1326.89	957.28	**500 Index**
1597.20	1134.73	**Industrials**
267.38	229.71	**Utilities**
395.13	275.93	**400 MidCap**
206.18	128.70	**600 SmallCap**
276.04	200.77	**1500 Index**
NASDAQ STOCK MARKET		
2563.17	1419.12	**Composite**
2219.64	1128.88	**Nasdaq 100**
1426.94	882.40	**Industrials**
2260.85	1346.58	**Insurance**
2297.71	1486.32	**Banks**
1381.92	690.19	**Computer**
645.49	310.74	**Telecommunications**
OTHERS		
754.74	563.75	**Amex Composite**
686.59	494.35	**Russell 1000**
491.41	318.28	**Russell 2000**
703.04	509.20	**Russell 3000**
508.39	346.66	**Value-Line (geom.)**
12005.20	8620.80	**Wilshire 5000**

READING THE INDEXES

Each index is tracked in three time frames: for the previous trading day, over the last 12 months and since the end of the previous December (or year-to-date). The high, low and close for the previous trading day are reported first, along with the net and percentage change from the trading day before that. Here, for example, the DJIA is up 121.82, or 1.22%. Next are change figures for the past 12 months and for the year to date. The increase over the past 12 months is 1193.83, or 13.43%, while the change since December 31 is comparatively stronger, at 903.88, or 9.84%.

SIMILARITIES IN THE DIFFERENCES

Although the indexes track different combinations of stock and produce very different numbers—from the Wilshire 5000 index of 12,005.29 down to S&P's SmallCap Index of 158.75—certain trends, or patterns, merge.

In this chart, for example, 17 of the 29 indexes are up for the day, 20 of them are up over the past 12 months, and all but seven are up since December 31. The rate of growth may be different, but generally, when the market is up over a period of time, it tends to be up for many types of stocks.

DATA BANK 4/7

HIGH	DAILY LOW	CLOSE	NET CHG	% CHG	†12-MO CHG	% CHG	FROM 12/31	% CHG
10089.75	9955.16	10085.31	+ 121.82	+ 1.22	+ 1193.83	+ 13.43	+ 903.88	+ 9.84
3352.36	3320.58	3338.87	+ 13.75	+ 0.41	− 167.70	− 4.78	+ 189.56	+ 6.02
294.62	290.54	292.37	− 1.20	− 0.41	+ 6.75	+ 2.36	− 19.93	− 6.38
3046.28	3018.31	3044.81	+ 23.34	+ 0.77	+ 181.99	+ 6.36	+ 173.98	+ 6.06
1259.23	1242.76	1255.67	+ 7.01	+ 0.56	+ 212.25	+ 20.34	+ 86.33	+ 7.38
616.70	611.70	616.23	+ 3.91	+ 0.64	+ 42.55	+ 7.42	+ 20.42	+ 3.43
767.61	760.75	765.83	+ 2.56	+ 0.34	+ 60.51	+ 8.58	+ 22.18	+ 2.98
454.39	448.97	453.34	+ 3.74	+ 0.83	+ 76.39	+ 20.27	+ 7.40	+ 1.66
511.39	505.18	511.29	+ 6.08	+ 1.20	− 6.19	− 1.20	+ 28.91	+ 5.99
553.49	544.25	553.03	+ 8.75	+ 1.61	− 8.39	− 1.49	+ 31.61	+ 6.06
1329.58	1312.59	1326.89	+ 9.00	+ 0.68	+ 225.24	+ 20.45	+ 97.66	+ 7.94
1604.24	1580.42	1597.20	+ 5.74	+ 0.36	+ 321.96	+ 25.25	+ 118.04	+ 7.98
235.16	232.87	233.97	− 0.61	− 0.26	− 10.51	− 4.30	− 25.65	− 9.88
367.89	361.57	362.46	− 4.74	− 1.29	− 4.32	− 1.18	− 29.85	− 7.61
160.57	158.46	158.75	− 1.22	− 0.76	− 39.31	− 19.85	− 18.62	− 10.50
276.80	273.33	276.04	+ 1.39	+ 0.51	+ 40.12	+ 17.01	+ 15.99	+ 6.15
2596.25	2511.39	2544.43	− 18.74	− 0.73	+ 737.42	+ 40.81	+ 351.74	+ 16.04
2251.29	2158.63	2192.29	− 26.54	− 1.20	+ 1001.23	+ 84.06	+ 356.28	+ 19.41
1439.71	1409.26	1411.58	− 13.46	− 0.94	+ 67.20	+ 5.00	+ 107.33	+ 8.23
1994.93	1930.94	1968.23	− 24.85	− 1.25	+ 56.87	+ 2.98	+ 171.44	+ 9.54
1743.30	1733.35	1742.75	+ 3.52	+ 0.20	− 492.26	− 22.02	− 95.25	− 5.18
1405.53	1346.59	1370.12	− 11.80	− 0.85	+ 615.57	+ 81.58	+ 235.93	+ 20.80
649.89	621.90	638.54	− 2.82	− 0.44	+ 256.15	+ 66.99	+ 137.63	+ 27.48
756.22	751.23	754.74	+ 39.53	+ 5.53	+ 17.24	+ 2.34	+ 65.75	+ 9.54
688.31	679.75	686.59	+ 3.87	+ 0.57	+ 106.52	+ 18.36	+ 43.72	+ 6.80
403.18	397.52	397.77	− 3.31	− 0.83	− 77.56	− 16.32	− 24.19	− 5.73
705.17	696.53	703.04	+ 3.31	+ 0.47	+ 92.16	+ 15.09	+ 38.77	+ 5.84
411.36	408.28	408.84	− 1.42	− 0.35	− 87.07	− 17.56	− 28.31	− 6
...	...	12005.29	+ 41.56	+ 0.35	+ 1518.57	+ 14.48		

Market Cycles

Stock market ups and downs can't be predicted accurately—though they often can be explained in hindsight.

The market goes up when investors put their money into stocks, and it falls when they take money out. A number of factors influence whether people buy or sell stocks—as well as when and why they make decisions.

Changing market direction doesn't always mirror the state of the economy. The crash of 1987 occurred in a period of economic growth. And the raging bull market of the 1990s survived a recession at home and economic turmoil abroad. But most of the time the strength or weakness of the stock market is directly related to economic and political forces.

WHEN PEOPLE INVEST

Economic, social and political factors affect investment. Some factors encourage it and others make investors unwilling to take the risk.

Positive factors	Negative factors
Ample money supply	Tight money
Tax cuts	Tax increases
Low interest rates	High interest rates offering better return in less risky investments
High employment rate	High unemployment rate
Political stability or expectation of stability	International conflicts
	Pending elections

MOVING WITH THE CYCLES

Pinpointing the bottom of a slow market or the top of a hot one is almost impossible—until after it has happened. But investors who buy stocks in companies that do well in growing economies—and buy them at the right time—can profit from their smart decisions (or their good luck).

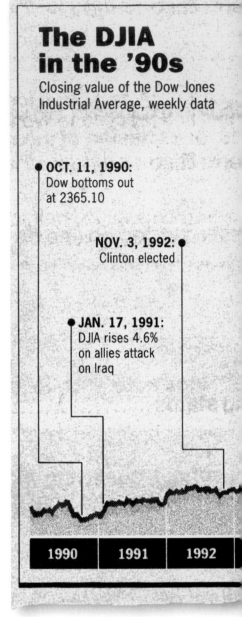

The DJIA in the '90s

Closing value of the Dow Jones Industrial Average, weekly data

OCT. 11, 1990: Dow bottoms out at 2365.10

NOV. 3, 1992: Clinton elected

JAN. 17, 1991: DJIA rises 4.6% on allies attack on Iraq

1990 | 1991 | 1992

One characteristic of expanding companies is their ability to raise prices as the demand for their products and services grows. Rising prices mean more profits for the company and increased dividends and higher stock prices for the investor.

But since no economic cycle repeats earlier ones exactly, it's impossible to predict with precision that what happened in one growth or recovery period will happen in another. And while some types of companies do poorly in a slump, it's hard to be certain which ones will take the biggest hits or find it hardest to recover. In that case, the strength of the company is probably as important to its performance as the state of the economy.

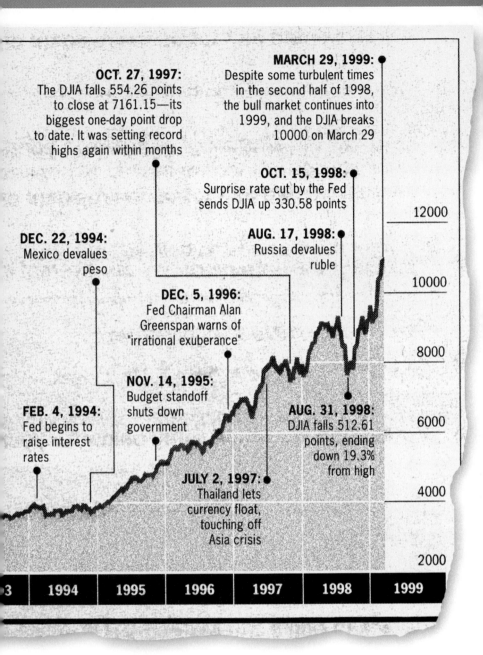

OCT. 27, 1997:
The DJIA falls 554.26 points to close at 7161.15—its biggest one-day point drop to date. It was setting record highs again within months

MARCH 29, 1999:
Despite some turbulent times in the second half of 1998, the bull market continues into 1999, and the DJIA breaks 10000 on March 29

DEC. 22, 1994:
Mexico devalues peso

OCT. 15, 1998:
Surprise rate cut by the Fed sends DJIA up 330.58 points

AUG. 17, 1998:
Russia devalues ruble

DEC. 5, 1996:
Fed Chairman Alan Greenspan warns of "irrational exuberance"

NOV. 14, 1995:
Budget standoff shuts down government

AUG. 31, 1998:
DJIA falls 512.61 points, ending down 19.3% from high

FEB. 4, 1994:
Fed begins to raise interest rates

JULY 2, 1997:
Thailand lets currency float, touching off Asia crisis

12000
10000
8000
6000
4000
2000

3 | 1994 | 1995 | 1996 | 1997 | 1998 | 1999

BULL AND BEAR MARKETS

The stock market moves up and down in recurring cycles, gaining ground for a period popularly known as a **bull market**. Then it reverses and falls for a time before heading up again. Generally, a falling market has to drop 20% before it's considered a **bear market**. Sometimes market trends last months, even years. Overall, bull markets usually last longer than bear markets.

Historically, the U.S. stock market has risen farther than it has fallen, producing a chain of record levels. But drops in the market tend to happen quickly, while rises tend to take a long time. It's much like the law of gravity: It takes a lot longer to climb 1,000 feet than it takes to fall that distance.

UP

The bear market of the early 1970s hit bottom in 1974. Prices that had fallen to 1960s levels started up again.

The October 1987 crash sent the Dow tumbling, but it was up again by year-end.

INVESTMENT ACTIVITY

When the DJIA closed above 1000 on November 14, 1972, it broke what had been considered a nearly absolute ceiling.

DOWN

Crash!

The bottom fell out of the stock market twice in the 20th century: in October 1929, and 60 years later in October 1987.

October is the cruelest month for the U.S. stock market. The two great market crashes of the 20th century—in 1929 and 1987—both came in October.

The crashes, or sudden collapses in the value of stocks that sent the DJIA into a tailspin, were triggered by too-high stock prices and inadequate controls on trading. Afraid of losing everything, investors rushed to sell, compounding the problem by driving the prices lower and lower. In 1987, the volume was intensified by the sell orders resulting from computerized **program trading** (see page 44).

WHICH WAS THE GREATER LOSS?

October 29, 1929

% Loss	**12.8%**
$ Loss	**$14 BILLION**

October 19, 1987

% Loss	**22.6%**
$ Loss	**$500 BILLION**

TRACKING THE COLLAPSE

The dramatic loss of value that characterized both market crashes is illustrated in these graphs, which index the weekly closing prices of the Dow Jones Industrial Average for 1929 and 1987. They use December 31 of 1928 and 1986 as the **index point**, or base, and show a parallel pattern of increasing prices and stunning drops—12.8% in 1929 and 22.6% in 1987.

Using an index, which gives figures in terms of an agreed-upon base, instead of the actual Dow Jones Industrial Average—which closed at 230.07 in 1929 and 1738.34 in 1987—makes it possible to compare the two events.

100

JAN FEB MAR APR MAY JUNE JULY

HOW BLUE CHIP COMPANIES FARED IN THE TWO GREAT CRASHES

1929	opening price	closing price	loss	% loss
AT&T	266	232	-34	12.7
Eastman Kodak	222⅞	181	-41⅞	18.7
Sears Roebuck	127	111	-16	12.5
1987	opening price	closing price	loss	% loss
AT&T	30	23⅝	-6⅜	21.2
Eastman Kodak	90⅛	62⅞	-27¼	30.2
Sears Roebuck	41½	31	-10½	25.3

LEARNING FROM THE PAST

In 1987, in part because of government regulations and trading limitations that had been put in place after 1929, the market recovered much more quickly, and the long-term effect on the economy was modest in comparison to the worldwide depression of the 1930s.

In the wake of '87, efforts to prevent yet another crash led to restrictions on computer-generated program trading and the introduction of shut-down mechanisms, called **circuit breakers**.

For example, trading on the New York Stock Exchange would be halted if the market, measured by the Dow Jones Industrial Average, dropped 10%. But trading could resume, depending on the time of day the drop occurred. If the DJIA dropped 20%, trading would end for the day. The actual number of points the Dow would need to drop is set twice a year (in January and June), based on the average value of the Dow in the previous month.

Circuit breakers have been set off only once, on October 27, 1997, when the Dow Jones Industrial Average fell 554 points, or 7.2%, and the trigger levels were lower. In fact, the market has dropped as much as 10% only three days since 1915.

That means a crash would almost certainly be drawn out over several days. Since investor panic makes any crash worse, slowing down the pace of the fall may help deter hasty sell decisions.

TRADING VOLUMES
On the day the stock market crashed in 1929, 16.4 million shares—a record—changed hands. In 1987, it was 604.3 million shares, another record. But in an average day in 1999, more than 700 million shares trade on the NYSE and more than 1 billion on the Nasdaq stock market.

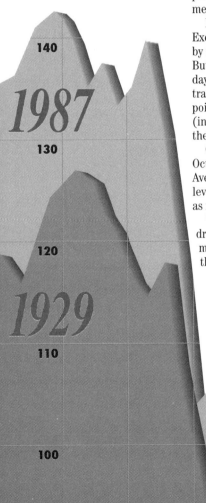

1987

1929

140
130
120
110
100
90
80

AUG   SEPT   OCT   NOV   DEC   JAN   FEB

Trading Around the Clock

Stock trading goes on around the world, around the clock, in an electronic global marketplace.

Stock trading goes on nearly 24 hours a day, on dozens of different exchanges on different continents in different time zones.

As the trading ends in one city, activity shifts to a market in another city, sweeping the changes in price around the world. The opening prices in Tokyo or Sydney are influenced by the closing prices in the U.S.—just as Asia's closing prices affect what happens in European trading, and what happens in Europe influences Wall Street. Just after the New York markets close, for example, trading begins in Wellington. Two and a half hours after Tokyo closes, London opens. And with two and a half hours to go in London, trading resumes in New York.

The global market explains why a stock can end trading one day at a specific price and open the next day at a different price.

What's still evolving is the extent to which the markets are interrelated. One reason is the growing number of multinational companies that trade on several exchanges. Another is the increasing tendency for investors to buy in many markets, not just their own.

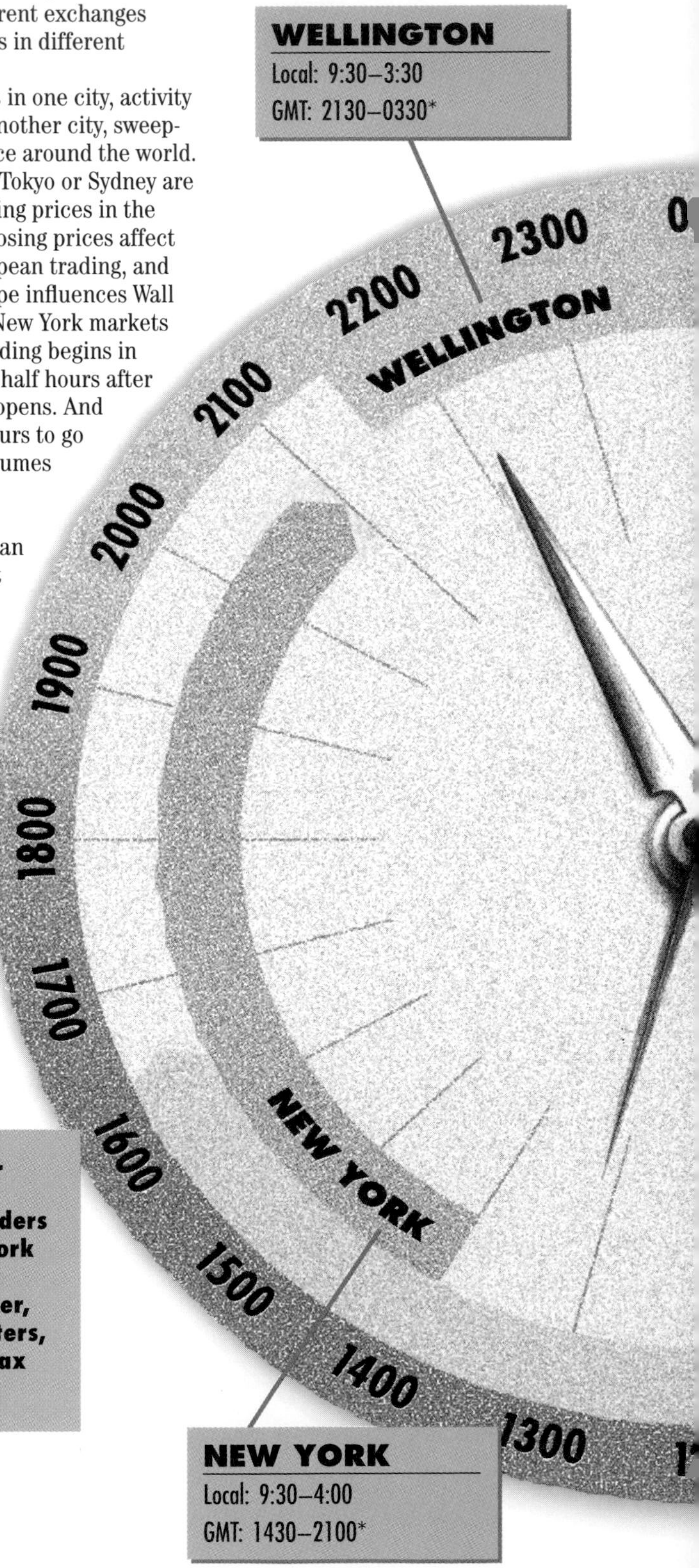

WELLINGTON
Local: 9:30–3:30
GMT: 2130–0330*

ZONING OUT— OR IN
International traders can—and do—work in one time zone and live in another, thanks to computers, telephones and fax machines.

NEW YORK
Local: 9:30–4:00
GMT: 1430–2100*

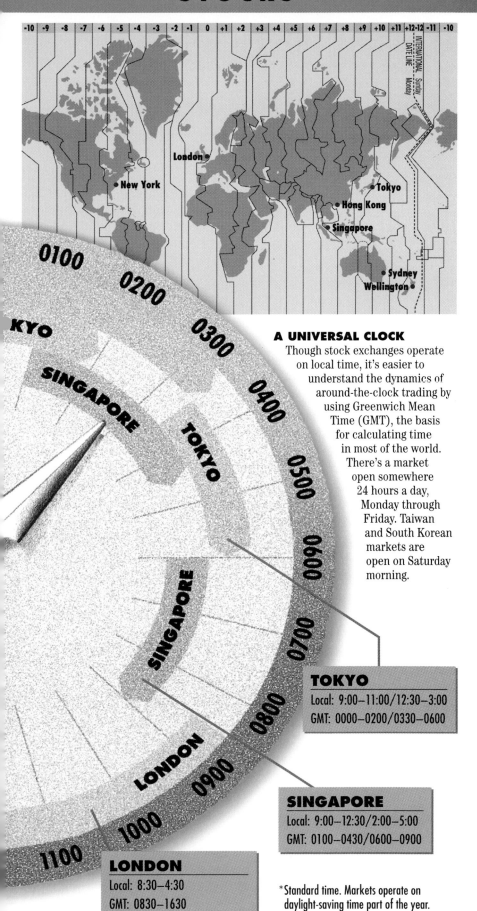

-10 | -9 | -8 | -7 | -6 | -5 | -4 | -3 | -2 | -1 | 0 | +1 | +2 | +3 | +4 | +5 | +6 | +7 | +8 | +9 | +10 | +11 | +12 -12 | -11 | -10

INTERNATIONAL DATE LINE

Sunday
Monday

London

New York

Tokyo

Hong Kong

Singapore

Sydney

Wellington

0100
0200
0300
0400
0500
0600
0700
0800
0900
1000
1100

KYO

SINGAPORE

TOKYO

SINGAPORE

LONDON

A UNIVERSAL CLOCK

Though stock exchanges operate on local time, it's easier to understand the dynamics of around-the-clock trading by using Greenwich Mean Time (GMT), the basis for calculating time in most of the world. There's a market open somewhere 24 hours a day, Monday through Friday. Taiwan and South Korean markets are open on Saturday morning.

TOKYO
Local: 9:00–11:00/12:30–3:00
GMT: 0000–0200/0330–0600

SINGAPORE
Local: 9:00–12:30/2:00–5:00
GMT: 0100–0430/0600–0900

LONDON
Local: 8:30–4:30
GMT: 0830–1630

*Standard time. Markets operate on daylight-saving time part of the year.

Tracking International Markets

As investors buy more global stocks, they want to know more about how those markets are doing.

With global markets increasingly open to all investors, and electronic media capable of providing up-to-the-minute reports on what's happening around the world, investors' appetites are being met with a steady stream of information.

The performances of 32 indexes tracking 24 national stock markets outside the U.S. and four Dow Jones indexes denominated in euros are reported daily in The Wall Street Journal. These statistical composites, which are similar to the S&P 500-stock Index, include the day's close and the net change from the previous day as well as the change expressed as a percentage.

Stock Market Indexes

EXCHANGE	INDEX	CLOSE	YTD PCT CHG
Australia	All Ordinaries	2893.80	+ 2.86
Belgium	Bel-20 Index	3411.59	− 2.93
Brazil	Sao Paulo Bovespa	8172.00	+ 20.46
Britain	London FT 100-share	5896.00	+ 0.23
Britain	London FT 250-share	5024.20	+ 3.49
Canada	Toronto 300 Comp.	6729.05	+ 3.75
Chile	Santiago IPSA	103.03	+ 3.03
China	Dow Jones China 88	120.76	− 0.36
Europe	DJ Stoxx (Euro)	288.31	+ 3.26
Europe	DJ Stoxx 50 (Euro)	3446.25	+ 3.79
Euro Zone	DJ Euro Stoxx (Euro)	308.97	+ 3.55
Euro Zone	DJ Euro Stoxx 50 (Euro)	3547.15	+ 6.13
France	Paris CAC 40	4251.80	+ 7.84
Germany	Frankfurt DAX	5159.96	+ 3.15
Germany	Frankfurt Xetra DAX	5180.29	+ 3.47
Hong Kong	Hang Seng	9506.90	− 5.39
Japan	Tokyo Nikkei 225	14499.25	+ 4.75
Japan	Tokyo Nikkei 300	224.58	+ 3.93
Japan	Tokyo Topix Index	1125.26	+ 3.52

(in Canadian)
13.1
6.1
37.2
31.7
12.5
37.5
2.1
30.7
62.3
43.7
9.3
64.1
31.5
28.3
8.4

DAILY NUMBERS
The daily numbers on a particular exchange have meaning only in relation to what has happened on that exchange in the past. For example, Japan's Nikkei 225 reports on only its market, as the Australian All Ordinaries, Canadian Toronto 300 Composite and French Paris CAC40 do on theirs.

COMPARATIVE PERFORMANCE
Worldwide stock market performance can be compared by looking at **percentage change**. Knowing that London's Financial Times 100-share index, or FTSE (pronounced *footsie*), is up 0.23% means more to investors than saying it was up 13.40 points.

About four times as many markets are up as down in this illustration, in various places around the world. That's because the political and economic situations at home still do have a major influence on stock performance despite what's happening in the world at large.

STOCKS

PICKING A MARKET

Financial analysts tend to evaluate overseas markets from a top-down perspective, focusing on a country's or a region's financial environment rather than on the prospects of individual companies. Among factors that make a country's stocks attractive to investors are the underlying strength and stability of its economy, the value of its currency and its current interest rate. Growing economies, strengthening currencies and flat or falling interest rates are generally good indicators of economic growth. Conversely, countries whose currencies are weak, interest rates high and economies in recession don't attract equity investors.

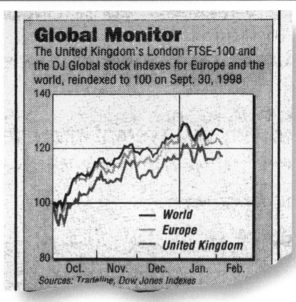

Global Monitor
The United Kingdom's London FTSE-100 and the DJ Global stock indexes for Europe and the world, reindexed to 100 on Sept. 30, 1998

— World
∼ Europe
— United Kingdom

Oct. Nov. Dec. Jan. Feb.
Sources: Tradeline, Dow Jones Indexes

The Wall Street Journal regularly tracks foreign markets in comparison with the benchmark Dow Jones indexes. For example, this chart shows the relative performance of the Dow Jones Global stock indexes for Europe and the world and the London FTSE-100.

FOREIGN MARKETS

MEXICO CITY in pesos			
Alfa A	24.25	+	0.25
Apasco A	37.40	—	1.10
Banacci B	11.02	—	0.32
Bimbo A	19.02	—	0.38
Cemex B	28.90	+	0.35
Cifra C	11.20	—	0.10
Cifra V	11.12	—	0.18
ComerciUBC	6.52	—	0.28
Femsa B	24.05	—	0.10
Gcarso A1	29.00	—	0.65
GModeloC	22.00		
Kimber A	29.50	—	0.50
Maseca B	8.24		....
Tamsa	73.50	—	0.50
Telecom A1	38.95	—	0.85
Televisa	130.50	—	2.70

FRANKFURT in euros			
Adidas Salmn	85.00	+	2.40
Allianz	287.70	—	16.30
BASF	31.06	—	0.89
Bayer	30.89	—	1.11
Beiersdorf	66.00	+	1.50
BMW	716.50	—	9.99
Byr Vereinsbk	54.96	+	0.77
Commerzbank	25.50	—	0.60
Continental	24.96	—	0.70
Daimler Chrysler	82.80	—	3.46
Degussa	35.85	—	0.20
Deutsche Bank	48.00	—	1.52
Deutsche Tel	36.10	—	2.35
Dresdner Bank	32.24	—	1.86
Gehe	52.00	—	1.00

TOKYO in yen			
Aiwa	2400	—	4
Ajinomoto	1245	—	1
Alps Elec	2040	—	3
Amada Co	567	—	2
ANA	343	—	
Ando Elec	690		...
Anritsu	944	—	
Asahi Chem	524	—	
Asahi Glass	685	+	
Banyu Pharm	2000		...
Bk of Yokohama	226	—	
Bridgestone	2490	—	1
Brother Ind	345	—	
Canon Inc	2275	—	

FOREIGN MARKETS

Some of the most actively traded stocks on overseas exchanges are listed in the Foreign Markets column. Their closing prices and their previous close are given in local currency. For example, on the Mexico City exchange, Cemex B shares closed at 28.90 pesos, up 0.35%.

For six of the European markets that are included in the chart, the local currency is the euro. Frankfurt is one example.

Many of the corporations whose stocks are listed on a home country's market are also traded on a U.S. stock market as **American Depositary Receipts (ADRs)**. Examples from this clipping include Daimler Chrysler on the Frankfurt market and Canon on the Tokyo market.

Because prices are quoted in different currencies, and the markets are influenced by different forces, there's no easy formula to compare the yields on international investments—with the exception of countries trading in the euro.

But stock market performances around the globe are increasingly interrelated, so that a boom or bust in one market affects what happens to prices in all markets. In fact, analysts regularly anticipate opening prices in New York based on prices in Tokyo and London.

The Global Indexes

The Dow Jones Global Indexes are barometers of stock market performance around the world.

The Dow Jones Global Indexes let you track the performance of almost three dozen global equity markets over the most recent 12-month period. You also find the countries grouped into three geographic regions—the Americas, Europe/Africa, and Asia/Pacific.

By looking at their percentage change, you can also compare the results for an individual country to behavior of other markets in its region and markets worldwide. You can also get a sense of the strength of regional markets in relation to each other, information that can be helpful in identifying attractive investment opportunities and those that seem to be in the doldrums.

Each country's index is computed in local currency and in four global currencies: U.S. dollars, British pounds, Japanese yen and euros. Each edition of

The Wall Street Journal uses a version of the index customized for its primary readers. For example, the U.S. edition—the one used here—gives the figures in dollars. Converting the indexes to global currencies lets you make comparisons that reflect the impact of currency exchange rates.

Each equity index, all the regional indexes and the overall World Stock Index are all capitalization weighted. That means that the stocks with larger capitalizations, figured by multiplying the number of shares times the current price per share, have greater influence on an individual index than shares with less capitalization. Similarly, countries with larger stock markets have more influence on regional indexes than countries with smaller stock markets.

DOW JONES GLOBAL INDEXES

REGION/ COUNTRY	DJ GLOBAL INDEXES, LOCAL CURRENCY	PCT. CHG.	IN U.S. DOLLARS				
			5:30 P.M. INDEX	CHG.	PCT. CHG.	12-MO CHG.	PCT. CHG.
Americas			294.51	+ 3.07	+ 1.05	+ 63.80	+ 27.65
Brazil†	827	+ 3.27	162.38	+ 1.02	+ 0.63	− 244.61	− 60.10
Canada	204.72	+ 1.15	156.53	+ 2.38	+ 1.54	+ 4.25	+ 2.79
Mexico	290.71	− 0.12	87.73	+ 0.11	+ 0.13	− 32.86	− 27.25
U.S.	1215.79	+ 1.05	1215.79	+ 12.62	+ 1.05	+ 286.82	+ 30.88
Venezuela	320.89	+ 1.85	34.50	+ 0.58	+ 1.71	− 40.90	− 54.25
Latin America			108.43	+ 0.26	+ 0.24	− 82.90	− 43.33
Europe/Africa			235.59	+ 0.71	+ 0.30	+ 39.95	+ 20.42
Austria	111.57	+ 1.10	98.36	+ 0.57	+ 0.58	− 12.51	− 11.29
Belgium	315.40	+ 0.14	278.30	− 1.01	− 0.36	+ 92.26	+ 49.59
France	257.38	+ 1.25	230.79	+ 1.71	+ 0.75	+ 67.52	+ 41.36
Germany	289.64	+ 2.29	254.75	+ 4.45	+ 1.78	+ 57.00	+ 28.83
United Kingdom	223.82	+ 0.38	197.01	+ 0.16	+ 0.08	+ 15.38	+ 8.47
Europe/Africa (ex. South Africa)			244.80	+ 0.72	+ 0.29	+ 44.21	+ 22.04
Europe/Africa (ex. U.K. & S. Africa)			274.38	+ 1.05	+ 0.38	+ 60.86	+ 28.50
Asia/Pacific			81.69	+ 1.06	+ 1.31	− 1.55	− 1.86
Australia	182.05	+ 0.50	150.55	+ 1.20	+ 0.80	+ 8.44	+ 5.94
Hong Kong	189.91	+ 1.42	190.62	+ 2.68	+ 1.43	− 1.65	− 0.86
Japan	70.04	+ 1.52	75.14	+ 1.11	+ 1.50	− 2.13	− 2.76
DJ WORLD STOCK INDEX			206.68	+ 1.75	+ 0.85	+ 34.63	+ 20.13

DJ GLOBAL

COMPANION PIECES

A stock market's overall performance reflects the ups and downs of individual stocks and the strength or weakness of different market segments. **The Dow Jones Global Groups Biggest Movers** provides a daily glimpse of the industry groups that are currently strong and those that are lagging, plus the individual stocks helping to drive that performance.

In this example, two U.S. and three Japanese companies are the strongest stocks in Toys, the leading group, while Taiwanese companies dominate the lagging category described as Other Home Furnishings.

DJ GLOBAL GROUPS BIGGEST MOVERS

Groups Leading

Strongest Stocks	5:30 P.M.	CHG.		PCT. CHG.	
Toys	95.88	+ 4.31		+ 4.71	
Hasbro (US)	37.19	+ 2.75		+ 7.99	
Nintendo (JP)	10800.00	+ 650.00		+ 6.40	
Mattel (US)	22.69	+ 1.00		+ 4.61	
BandaiCo (JP)	1198.00	+ 8.00		+ 0.67	
SegaEntpr (JP)	2285.00	0.00		0.00	
Airlines	134.19	+ 5.59		+ 4.35	
NowestAir (US)	27.38	+ 4.13		+17.74	
USAirGp (US)	49.75	+ 4.25		+ 9.34	
DeltaAir (US)	54.56	+ 4.44		+ 8.85	
AMR (US)	58.75	+ 4.25		+ 7.80	
UALCp (US)	62.25	+ 3.88		+ 6.64	
Footwear	130.54	+ 4.79		+ 3.81	

Groups Lagging

Weakest Stocks	5:30 P.M.	CHG.		PCT. CHG.	
Othr Hom Furn	130.74	− 2.53		− 1.90	
MillerHrm (US)	18.94	− 5.06		− 21.1	
MasterHm (TW)	20.70	− 1.50		− 6.76	
MastrHmFurn (TW)	20.70	− 1.50		− 6.76	
TaiSakura (TW)	29.00	− 2.10		− 6.75	
Sampo (TW)	21.20	− 0.90		− 4.07	
Entertainment	389.33	− 6.25		− 1.58	
GrammyEnt (TH)	170.00	−11.00		− 6.08	
TimeWarner (US)	62.50	− 2.31		− 3.57	
Pathe (FR)	235.00	− 1.00		− 0.42	
KingWorld (US)	27.38	− 0.06		− 0.23	
Seagram (CA)	72.00	− 0.15		− 0.21	
Tobacco	169.29	− 1.95		− 1.14	
PhilipMor (US)	47.00	− 1.69		− 3.4
Panastratos (GC)	4350.00	− 50.00		− 1.1

FROM 12/31	PCT. CHG.
+ 10.73	+ 3.78
− 76.21	− 31.94
+ 10.29	+ 7.03
− 1.30	− 1.46
+ 46.45	+ 3.97
− 5.43	− 13.60
− 19.89	− 15.50
+ 0.60	+ 0.25
− 6.96	− 6.61
− 11.11	− 3.84
+ 9.78	+ 4.42
+ 6.73	+ 2.72
− 1.57	− 0.79
+ 0.41	+ 0.17
+ 1.49	+ 0.55
+ 0.66	+ 0.81
+ 9.53	+ 6.76
− 13.45	− 6.59
+ 0.95	+ 1.27
+ 3.89	+ 1.92

READING THE INDEX

In the **Dow Jones Global Index** the first column of numbers reports equity market level for the previous trading day and the percentage change from the day before, computed in local currency. Then the same information is provided in dollars, adding the amount of the change as well as the percentage change.

In France, for example, the closing index in francs is 257.38, up 1.25%. Computed in dollars for the benefit of U.S. investors, the index was 230.79, up 0.75%.

Each market is also tracked over the most recent 12 months, and since the beginning of the current year. In France, the markets were up 41.36% last year, and 4.42% since the beginning of this year.

In addition, there's a composite index for each of the three regional markets and one or more subgroups within them to provide a clearer picture of the influence of specific countries or groups of countries on regional performance. For example, the percentage change in Europe and Africa overall—20.42%—increases to 22.04% when South Africa is excluded and to 28.50% when both South Africa and the U.K. are excluded.

The last entry, the Dow Jones World Stock Index, is a composite of the individual country indexes. Since each of the three regions is up for the year, the world index is also up.

A FIXED MARK

Indexes are always measured against a **benchmark**, a fixed value—typically 100—established at a specific time. For the The Dow Jones Global Indexes, the starting date is December 31, 1991 (except the U.S., where the date is June 30, 1982).

The term benchmark originally referred to a surveyor's mark indicating a known height above sea level, but it has come to mean any standard that's used as a basis of comparison.

International Investing

In the new economy, investors looking for ways to diversify their portfolio have a world of opportunity.

If you want to balance some of the risks of investing in U.S. stocks, you can diversify your portfolio by putting some of your money into equities available on overseas markets. The assumption is that an economic downturn at home could be offset by stronger performances abroad, since the markets would be responding to different economic conditions.

As electronic trading makes investing in overseas markets easier, though, it also emphasizes their interaction. That means that strengths or weaknesses in one market or region tend to carry over into others.

THERE ARE REWARDS

Buying stocks abroad can produce rich returns. In the best of all possible worlds, investors win three ways, in what investment pros call the **triple whammy**:

- The stock rises in price, providing **capital gains**
- The investment pays **dividends**
- The country's **currency rises against the dollar**, so that when investors sell they get more dollars

BUT ALSO RISKS

Buying stocks abroad is no less risky than buying at home. Prices do fall and dividends get cut. Plus, there may be hidden traps that can catch unwary investors. Here are some of the common ones:

- Tax treatments of gains or losses differ from one country to another
- Accounting and trading rules may be different
- Converting dividends into dollars may add extra expense to the transaction
- Some international exchanges require less information about a company's financial condition than U.S. exchanges do, so investors need to be wary
- Giving buy and sell orders can be complicated by distance and language barriers
- Unexpected changes in overseas interest rates or currency values can cause major upheavals

ANOTHER PERSPECTIVE

Overseas investors make money in U.S. stocks when the dollar is strong against their currency and stock prices are climbing. If the dollar weakens, though, the value of their investment drops as well.

The Currency Risk—and Its Reward

The greatest variable in calculating the risks and rewards of international investing hinges on changes in currency values. If the dollar shrinks in value, U.S. investors make more when they sell at a profit. But just the opposite happens if the dollar gets stronger.

	STOCK PRICE IN MARKS
BUY • Dollar is stronger than euro	One Share EUR **50**
SELL • Stock rises • Dollar weak	One Share EUR **60**
SELL • Stock rises • Dollar unchanged	One Share EUR **60**
SELL • Stock drops • Dollar weak	One Share EUR **45**
SELL • Stock rises • Dollar very strong	One Share EUR **60**
SELL • Stock drops • Dollar very strong	One Share EUR **45**

WAYS TO INVEST

There are several ways for a U.S. investor to buy international stocks:

- Big U.S. brokerage firms with branch offices abroad can buy stocks directly
- Some international and multinational companies list their stocks directly on U.S. exchanges
- Multiple mutual fund firms offer international funds that invest overseas
- The stock of some of the largest companies is sold as **American Depositary Receipts (ADRs)** on U.S. exchanges.

Although trading information on ADRs, like Glaxo or Mitsubishi, is reported in U.S. stock tables, the ADRs are certificates representing a set number of shares held in trust for the investor by a bank. The bank converts the dividends it receives into dollars and takes care of withholding taxes, plus other paperwork. It's the method of choice for many investors.

In this example, a U.S. investor buys a German stock for 50 euros per share. A year later, the investor sells for 60 euros per share. Clearly that's a profit, but how much?

Since the price has gone up 10 euros per share, from 50 to 60, there's a gain of 20%. That's also what a German investor would have made on the deal. But the revaluation of the currency also affects the return. If the dollar were worth less—say 90 cents per euro instead of $1.10—an American investor would have a greater gain.

But if the dollar had gained ground against the euro and was worth $1.50, the U.S. investor would have a net loss despite selling the stock for a profit in euros.

To figure the stock price, divide the price per share by the exchange rate.

$$\frac{\text{Price per share}}{\text{Exchange rate}} = \text{Stock price}$$

To figure the gain or loss, divide the difference between the sale price and the initial cost by the initial cost.

$$\frac{\text{Sale price-initial cost}}{\text{Initial cost}} = \text{Gain or loss}$$

EXCHANGE RATE	STOCK VALUE IN DOLLARS
Dollar = EUR **1.10**	$**45.45**
Dollar = EUR **.90**	$**66.67**
Dollar = EUR **1.10**	$**54.55**
Dollar = EUR **.90**	$**50.00**
Dollar = EUR **1.50**	$**40.00**
Dollar = EUR **1.50**	$**30.00**

GAIN OR LOSS

47% GAIN The double advantage of a higher stock price and a lower dollar produced a $66.67 sale price, for a $21.22—or 47%—per-share profit.

20% GAIN Because the stock price increased and there was no change in the exchange rate, the $54.55 sale price was $9.10 more than the purchase price, a 20% gain.

10% GAIN Investors can make money on a dropping share price if the value of the dollar also drops. In this example the price drops to 45 but there's a $4.55, or 10%, profit.

12% LOSS American investors often lose money when the dollar increases in value if they bought when it was worth less. Here the 10 euro gain in price means a 12% loss.

34% LOSS The biggest losses occur when the value of the dollar increases and the share price drops. Here a loss of 5 euros a share represents a 34% loss in dollars.

Bonds: Financing the Future

Bonds are loans that investors make to corporations and governments. The lenders earn interest, and the borrowers get the cash they need.

A bond is a loan that pays interest over a fixed **term**, or period of time. When the bond **matures** at the end of the term, the **principal**, or investment amount, is repaid to the lender, or owner of the bond.

Typically, the rate at which interest is paid and the amount of each payment is fixed at the time the bond is offered for sale. That's why bonds are also known as **fixed-income securities**. That's one reason a bond seems less risky than an investment whose return might change dramatically in the short term.

A bond's interest rate is competitive, which means that the rate it pays is comparable to what other bonds being issued at the same time are paying. It's also related to the cost of borrowing in the economy at large, so when mortgage rates are down, for example, bond rates also tend to be lower.

TYPES OF BONDS

You can buy bonds issued by U.S. companies, by the U.S. Treasury, by various cities and states, and various federal, state and local government agencies. Many overseas companies and governments also sell bonds to U.S. investors. When those bonds are sold in dollars rather than the currency of the issuing country, they're sometimes known as **yankee bonds**. There is an advantage for individual investors: You don't have to worry about currency fluctuations in figuring the bond's worth.

ISSUERS PREFER BONDS

When companies need to raise money to invest in growth and development, they can issue stock or sell bonds. They often prefer bonds, in part because issuing more stock tends to **dilute**, or lessen, the value of shares investors already own. Bonds may also provide some income-tax advantages.

Unlike companies, governments aren't profit-making enterprises and can't issue stock. Bonds are the primary way they raise money to fund capital improvements like roads or airports. Money from bond issues also keeps everyday operations running when other revenues (like taxes, tolls and other fees) aren't available to cover current costs.

ISSUING A BOND

When a company or government wants to raise cash, it tests the waters by **floating a bond**. That is, it offers the public an opportunity to invest for a fixed period of time at a specific rate of interest. If investors think the rate justifies the risk and buy the bond, the issue floats.

THE INDIVIDUAL AS LENDER

INVESTORS WILLING TO LEND MONEY

INVESTOR GETS PAR VALUE AT MATURITY

INVESTOR GETS INTEREST PAYMENT AT SPECIFIC INTERVALS

THE LIFE OF A BOND

The life, or **term**, of any bond is fixed at the time of issue. It can range from **short-term** (usually a year or less), to **intermediate-term** (two to ten years), to **long-term** (30 years or more). Generally speaking, the longer the term, the higher the interest rate that's offered to make up for the additional risk of tying up your money for so long a time. The relationship between the interest rates paid on short-term and long-term bonds is called the **yield curve**.

BONDS

MAKING MONEY WITH BONDS

Conservative investors use bonds to provide a steady income. They buy a bond when it's issued and hold it, expecting to receive regular, fixed-interest payments until the bond matures. Then they get the principal back to reinvest.

Bonds that are issued when interest rates are high become increasingly valuable when interest rates fall. That's because investors are willing to pay more than the face value of a bond with a 8% interest rate if the current rate is 5%.

That means an increase in the price of a bond, or **capital appreciation**, can produce more profits for bond sellers than holding the bonds to maturity. More aggressive investors **trade** bonds, or buy and sell as they might with stocks, hoping to make money by selling a bond for more than they paid for it.

But there are risks in bond trading. If interest rates go up, you can lose money if you want to sell an older bond, which is paying a lower rate of interest. That's because potential buyers will typically pay less for the bond than you paid to buy it.

The other risk bondholders face is rising inflation (see pages 26–27). Since the dollar amount you earn on a bond investment doesn't change, the value of that money can be eroded by inflation. For example, if you have a 30-year bond paying $5,000 annual interest, the income will buy less at the end of the term than at the beginning.

THE INSTITUTION AS BORROWER

CORPORATE BONDS

Corporations use bonds:
- To raise capital to pay for expansion, modernization
- To cover operating expenses
- To finance corporate takeovers or other changes in management structure

U.S. TREASURY BONDS

The U.S. Treasury floats debt issues:
- To pay for a wide range of government activities
- To pay off the national debt

MUNICIPAL BONDS

States, cities, counties and towns issue bonds:
- To pay for a wide variety of public projects: schools, highways, stadiums, sewage systems, bridges
- To supplement their operating budgets

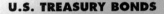

BOND MATURES

HOW BONDS ARE SOLD

For corporations, issuing a bond is a lot like making an initial public offering. An investment firm helps set the terms and underwrites the sale by buying up the issue. In cooperation with other companies, the investment firm then offers the bonds for sale to the public.

When bonds are issued, they are sold at **par**, or face value, usually in units of $1,000. The issuer absorbs whatever sales charges there are. After issue, bonds trade in the **secondary market**, which means they are bought and sold through brokers, similar to the way stocks are. The company gets no money from these secondary trades.

Government bonds (U.S. Treasury bills, notes and bonds) are available directly to investors through a Federal Reserve Bank program called Treasury Direct or through your broker. Most agency bonds and municipal bonds are sold through brokers, who often buy bonds in large denominations ($25,000 or more) and sell pieces of them to individual investors.

The Bond Certificate

A bond is an IOU, a record of the loan and the terms of repayment.

Unlike stockholders, who have **equity**, or part ownership, in a company, bondholders are **creditors**. The bond is an IOU, or a record of the money you lend and the terms on which it will be repaid.

Until 1983, all bondholders received certificates that provided the terms of the loan. Some of these **bearer bonds** had coupons attached to the certificate. When it was time to collect an interest payment, the investor (or bearer) detached the coupon and exchanged it for cash. That's why a bond's interest rate is known as its **coupon rate**.

Today most new bonds, known as **book-entry bonds**, are registered electronically, the way stock purchases are, rather than issued in certificate form. But there are still thousands of investors holding certificates that haven't yet matured.

BEARERS STILL
Eurobonds, which are bonds issued by borrowers outside their own country, are still bearer bonds. They're not registered with any regulatory authority, and the certificates can be traded or redeemed by whomever holds them.

You're not likely to own one, however, since they're sold in very large denominations. Typical buyers are corporations and governments.

WHAT THE CERTIFICATE TELLS
Issuers register bonds with an **identifying number** on the face of the bond. The bondholder's name also appears on the bond.

The **issuer** is the corporation, government or agency that sells the bond. It is identified by name and often by a symbol or logo. Its **official seal** authenticates the bond's validity. When a company issues bonds, the documents have the same design as the company's stock certificates. And they are protected against counterfeiting in the same way, with special paper, elaborate borders and intaglio printing (see page 40).

NUMBER
R

FOR FEDERAL INCOM
AMOUNT OF THE ORIGINAL
IS $55 PER $100 FACE AMOU
1989, THE TAX YIELD TO MAT
SEMI-ANNUALLY USING TH
SHOULD BE AWARE THAT
PURPOSES THIS NOTE IS
DISCOUNT AND THE AMO
DISCOUNT MUST BE RECE
HOLDER OVER A PERIOD BE
ENDING ON JUNE 6, 1996.
FOR PURPOSES OF T
BELOW, THE AMOUNT OF A
THE NOTE IS $55 PER $100
TO MATURITY IS 11.74%.

ZERO COUPO
SUBORDIN
DUI

DUE 1996

CUC INTERNATIONAL INC.
CORPORATE
SEAL
1974
DELAWARE

American Bank Note Company

at the Issuer's office or a
The principal of th
rate of 7% per annum (to
for. Such interest will be
office or agency of the
Reference is mad
full of all Senior Debt as
right to convert this Se
Indenture.
Such further pro
This Security sha

Dated:

CE
This is one
Indenture.
MORGAN GU

By

Interest rate is the fixed percentage of par value that is paid to the bondholder annually. For example, a $1,000 bond that pays 6.5% yields $65 a year. If the original buyer holds the bond to maturity, the **yield** (or return on investment) is also 6.5% a year. However, if the bond is traded, the yield could change even though the interest rate will stay the same. For example, if an investor buys the bond for $1,100 in the secondary market, the interest will still be $65 a year, but the yield will be reduced to 5.91% because the new owner paid more for the bond (see page 87, about figuring yield).

Par value, or the dollar amount of the bond at the time it was issued, appears several times on the face of the bond. Par value is the amount originally paid for the bond and the amount that will be repaid at maturity. Most bonds are sold in multiples of $1,000.

A **baby bond** has a par value of less than $1,000. Bonds of $500, or even less, can be issued by municipal governments to involve a larger number of people in the fund-raising process.

Maturity date is the date the bond comes due and must be repaid in full. A bond may be bought and sold in its lifetime and reregistered in the new owner's name. Whoever owns the bond at maturity is the one who gets par value back.

SES ONLY, THE
T ON THE NOTE
DATE IS JUNE 6,
COMPOUNDED
HOD. HOLDERS
L INCOME TAX
RIGINAL ISSUE
ICOME BY THE
JUNE 6, 1989 AND

E REFERRED TO
E DISCOUNT ON
AND THE YIELD

RTIBLE
TE

2 2 2 2 2
REGISTERED

CUSIP 121212 AA 0
SEE REVERSE FOR CERTAIN DEFINITIONS

CUC INTERNATIONAL INC.

...ational Inc., a Delaware corporation (the "Issuer"), for value received hereby promises to pay to

JOHN B. HOLDER

DUE 1996

DOLLARS

...rpose in New York, New York on June 6, 1996 in such coin or currency of the United States of America as at the time of payment shall be legal tender for the payment of public and private debts.
...not bear interest except in the case of a default in payment of principal upon acceleration, redemption or at maturity and in such case the overdue principal of this Security shall bear interest at the
...e payment of such interest shall be legally enforceable), which shall accrue from the date of such default in payment to the date payment of such overdue principal has been made or duly provided
...basis of a 360-day year of twelve 30-day months. Interest on any overdue principal shall be payable on demand. Payment of the principal of and any such interest on this Security will be made at the
...for that purpose in New York, New York.
...rvisions set forth on the reverse hereof including without limitation provisions subordinating the payment of principal of and interest on overdue principal, if any, on the Securities to the payment in
...denture dated as of May 25, 1989 (the "Indenture") between the Issuer and Morgan Guaranty Trust Company of New York, as Trustee (the "Trustee"), and provisions giving the holder hereof the
...on Stock, par value $.01 per share ("Common Stock"), of the Issuer on the terms and subject to the conditions and limitations referred to on the reverse hereof, as more fully specified in the

...l purposes have the same effect as though fully set forth at this place.
...obligatory until the certificate of authentication hereon shall have been duly signed by the Trustee acting under the Indenture.

In Whereof, the Issuer has caused this instrument to be duly executed under its corporate seal.

CUC International Inc.

AUTHENTICATION
described in the within-mentioned

T COMPANY OF NEW YORK,
as Trustee

Attest:

By:

Authorized Officer

Secretary

Chairman of the Board

The 30-year Treasury bond is popularly known as the long bond. But the longest bonds around are the 100-year corporate bonds that were introduced in 1993 by Disney Corporation. The first ones come due in 2093.

Figuring a Bond's Worth

The value of a bond is determined by the interest it pays and by what's happening in the economy.

A bond's interest rate never changes, even though other interest rates do. If the bond is paying more interest than is available elsewhere, you, as an investor, will be willing to pay more to own it. If the bond is paying less, the reverse is true.

Interest rates and bond prices fluctuate like two sides of a seesaw. As the table below illustrates, when interest rates drop, the value of existing bonds usually goes up. When rates climb, the value of existing bonds usually falls.

Several factors—including **yield** and **return**—affect whether or not a bond turns out to be a good investment.

PAR FOR THE COURSE

If you buy at par and hold the bond to maturity, **inflation**, or the shrinking value of the dollar, is your worst enemy. The further in the future the bond will mature, the greater the risk that at some point inflation will rise dramatically and

reduce the value of the money that you are repaid.

If the bond pays more than the rate of inflation, you come out ahead. For example, if a bond is paying 8% and the annual rate of inflation is 3%, the bond produces real earnings of 5%. But if inflation shoots up to 10%, the interest earnings won't buy what they once did. And the amount you have invested in the bond itself also shrinks in value.

UNDER (AND OVER) PAR

But many bonds, particularly those with maturities of five or more years, aren't held by one investor from the date of issue to the date of maturity. Rather, investors trade bonds in the secondary market. The prices fluctuate according to the interest rate the bond pays, the degree of certainty of repayment and overall economic conditions—especially the rate of inflation—which influence interest rates.

SELLERS	BUYERS

Original bond issuer is selling bond

AT PAR VALUE

Par value:	$1,000
Term:	10 years
Interest rate:	6%

6% Prevailing interest rate

At Issue

BUYING AT PAR VALUE
- Pay par value at issue and keep to maturity
- Receive 10 annual interest payments of $60
- Receive par value—$1,000—at maturity

If bondholder sells two years after issue when interest rates are high, the bond is

SELLING AT A DISCOUNT

Market value	$800
Interest (x2)	+ 120
	920
Less original cost	– 1000
LOSS	**$80**

8% Prevailing interest rate

2 Years Later

BUYING AT A DISCOUNT
- Pay $200 less than par value
- Receive 8 annual interest payments of $60
- Receive par value—$1,000—at maturity

If bondholder sells three years after issue when interest rates are low, the bond is

SELLING AT A PREMIUM

Market value	$1,200
Interest (x3)	+ 180
	1380
Less original cost	– 1000
RETURN	**$380**

3% Prevailing interest rate

3 Years Later

BUYING AT A PREMIUM
- Pay $200 more than par value
- Receive 7 annual interest payments of $60
- Receive par value—$1,000—at maturity

BONDS

HOW IT WORKS

Generally, when inflation is up, interest rates go up. And conversely, when inflation is low, so are interest rates. It's the change in market interest rates that causes bond prices to move up or down.

If DaveCo Corporation floats a new issue of bonds offering 6% interest, and it seems like a good investment, you buy some bonds at the full price, or par value, of $1,000 a bond.

Three years later, interest rates are up. If new bonds costing $1,000 are paying 8% interest, no buyer will pay you $1,000 for a bond paying 6%. To sell your bond you'll have to offer it at a **discount**, or less than you paid. If you must sell, you might have to settle for a price that wipes out most of the interest you've earned.

But consider the reverse situation. If new bonds selling for $1,000 offer only a 3% interest rate, you'll be able to sell your 6% bonds for more than you paid—since buyers will agree to pay more to get a higher interest rate. That **premium**, combined with the interest payments for the last three years, makes a tidy profit.

The fluctuations in interest rates, and therefore in bond prices, produce much of the trading that goes on in the bond market as investors try to sell low-interest-rate bonds or try to make a profit on high-interest-rate bonds.

CHANGING YIELD

Yield is what you actually earn. If you buy a 10-year $1,000 bond paying 6% and hold it until it matures, you'll earn $60 a year for ten years—an annual yield of 6%, or the same as the interest rate.

But if you buy in the secondary market, after the date of issue, the bond's yield may not be the same as its interest rate. That's because the price you pay affects the yield.

Most bond charts express current yield as a percentage. For example, if a bond's yield is given as 6%, it means your interest payments will be 6% of what you pay for the bond today—or 6% back on your investment. You can use the yield to compare the relative value of bonds.

Return, on the other hand, is what you make on the investment when the par value of the bond, your profit or loss from trading it, and the current yield are computed.

RETURN / YIELD

Original buyer gets	
Par value	$1,000
Interest (x10)	+ 600
	1,600
Less original cost	− 1,000
RETURN	**$600**

YIELD 6%

New buyer gets	
Par value	$1,000
Interest (x8)	+ 480
	1,480
Less original cost	− 800
RETURN	**$680**

YIELD 7.5%

New buyer gets	
Par value	$1,000
Interest (x7)	+ 420
	1,420
Less original cost	− 1,200
RETURN	**$220**

YIELD 5%

HOW TO FIGURE A BOND'S YIELD

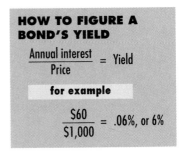

$$\frac{\text{Annual interest}}{\text{Price}} = \text{Yield}$$

for example

$$\frac{\$60}{\$1,000} = .06\%, \text{ or } 6\%$$

YIELD TO MATURITY

There's an even more precise measure of a bond's value called the **yield to maturity**. It takes into account:

- The interest rate in relation to the price
- The purchase price in relation to the par value
- The years remaining until the bond matures

Yield to maturity is a way to predict return over time, but it is calculated by a complicated formula—and it isn't often stated in bond tables. Brokers have access to the information, and some hand-held computers can be programmed to provide it.

Rating Bonds

Investors want to know the risks in buying a bond before they take the plunge. Rating services measure those risks.

As a bond investor you want to be reasonably sure that you'll get your interest payments on time and your principal back at maturity. It's almost impossible for an individual to do the necessary research. But rating services make a business of it.

The best-known services are **Standard & Poor's** and **Moody's** Investors Services, Inc. These companies carefully investigate the financial condition of a bond issuer rather than the market appeal of its bonds. They look at other debt the issuer has, how fast the company's revenues and profits are growing, the state of the economy and how well other companies in the same business (or municipal governments in the same general shape) are doing. Their primary concern is to alert investors to the risks of a particular issue.

Issuers rarely publicize their ratings unless they are top of the line. So you need to get the information from the rating services themselves, the financial press or your broker or financial advisor.

WHAT BONDS GET RATED?

The rating services pass judgment on municipal bonds, all kinds of corporate bonds and international bonds. U.S. Treasury bonds are not rated. The assumption is that they're absolutely solid, since they're obligations of the federal government, backed by its full faith and credit. This means the government has the authority to raise taxes to pay off its debts.

Rating a Bond: A Key to the Code

Moody's	Standard & Poor's
Aaa	AAA
Aa	AA
A	A
Baa	BBB
Ba	BB
B	B
Caa	CCC
Ca	CC
C	C
•	D

RANKINGS INFLUENCE RATES

As the chart to the left shows, credit ratings influence the interest rate an issuer must pay to attract investors. In comparing bonds with the same maturity, typically the higher the bond's rating, the lower the interest it pays and the lower its yield.

Similarly, lower-rated bonds must typically pay higher rates, providing higher yields, to entice investors who might be concerned about whether their interest will be paid on time or their principal repaid. That's why the lowest-rated bonds are sometimes described as high-yield bonds.

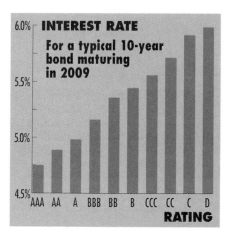

INTEREST RATE

For a typical 10-year bond maturing in 2009

6.0%
5.5%
5.0%
4.5%

AAA AA A BBB BB B CCC CC C D

RATING

THE RISK OF DOWNGRADING

One danger bondholders face—and one they can't anticipate—is that a rating service may **downgrade** its ratings of a company or municipal government during the life of a bond, creating a **fallen angel**. That happens if the issuer's financial condition deteriorates, or if the rating service feels a business decision might have poor results. If downgrading occurs, investors instantly demand a higher yield for the existing bonds. That means the price of the bond falls in the secondary market. It also means that if the issuer wants to float new bonds, the bonds will have to be offered at a higher interest rate to attract buyers.

The rating systems of the two major services are similar, but not identical, in the ways they label bond quality. Both services also make distinctions within categories Aa/AA and lower. Moody's uses a numerical system (1,2,3) and Standard & Poor's uses a + or − .

Meaning

Meaning		
Best quality, with the smallest risk. Issuers exceptionally stable and dependable		**Investment grade generally refers to any bonds rated Baa or higher by Moody's, or BBB or higher by Standard & Poor's.**
High quality, with slightly higher degree of long-term risk	**INVESTMENT GRADE BONDS**	
High-medium quality, with many strong attributes but somewhat vulnerable to changing economic conditions		
Medium quality, currently adequate but perhaps unreliable over long term		
Some speculative element, with moderate security but not well safeguarded		
Able to pay now but at risk of default in the future		
Poor quality, clear danger of default		
Highly speculative quality, often in default	**JUNK BONDS**	**Junk bonds are the lowest-rated corporate bonds. There's a greater-than-average chance that the issuer will fail to repay**
Lowest-rated, poor prospects of repayment though may still be paying		
In default		

its debt. The highly publicized mergers and acquisitions of the 1980s were financed with junk bonds. Investors were willing to take the risk because the yields were so much higher than on other, safer investments.

YIELD COMPARISONS

Based on Merrill Lynch Bond Indexes, priced as of afternoon Eastern time.

	8/12	8/11	−52 Week− High	Low
Agencies 1-10yr	5.34	5.34	6.22	5.24
10+ yr	6.79	6.78	8.01	6.78
Corporate				
1-10 yr High Qlty	5.79	5.82	7.00	5.72
Med Qlty	6.71	6.74	7.51	6.16
10+yr High Qlty	7.28	7.29	8.31	7.28
Med Qlty	7.64	7.66	8.74	7.64
Yankee bonds(1)	6.73	6.75	7.97	6.73
Current-coupon mortgages (2)				
GNMA 6.50%	6.57	6.61	7.97	6.51
FNMA 6.50%	6.57	6.58	7.98	6.53
FHLMC8.00%	6.25	6.22	7.95	6.14
High-yield corporates	9.81	9.81	11.43	9.80
New tax-exempts				4.65
10-yr G.O. (AA)	4.75	4.85	5.85	5.30
20-yr G.O. (AA)	5.35	5.45	6.60	5.75
30-yr revenue (A)	5.75	5.85	6.80	

quality rated AAA-AA; medium quality

TIME IS MONEY

When bonds have the same ranking but different terms, those with longer terms typically pay higher rates to encourage investors to commit their money for an extended period, which means greater potential for inflation risk.

Tracking Bond Performance

You can follow day-to-day changes in bond prices and yields.

Trading in corporate bonds listed on the New York Stock Exchange and on the American Stock Exchange is reported for every business day. The names of the companies issuing the bonds are listed alphabetically, usually in an abbreviated format.

The abbreviations can differ from those used for the same companies in the stock tables. Some are easy to decipher (like IBM or TVA) and some are fully spelled out (Hills). You may need help to figure out the others, including Bellso for Bell South.

The first number is the **interest rate**, expressed in points and fractions of points, or sometimes in points and decimals. This Bell South bond, for example, pays 6½% interest. Bonds issued at different times have different rates, as IBM's four different bonds maturing between 2000 and 2028 do. Bond interest always refers to a percentage of the **par value**, which is the amount the issuer will repay the bondholder when the bond comes due. The par value of most corporate bonds is $1,000. Thus, the annual interest payment on a 8½% bond will be $85.

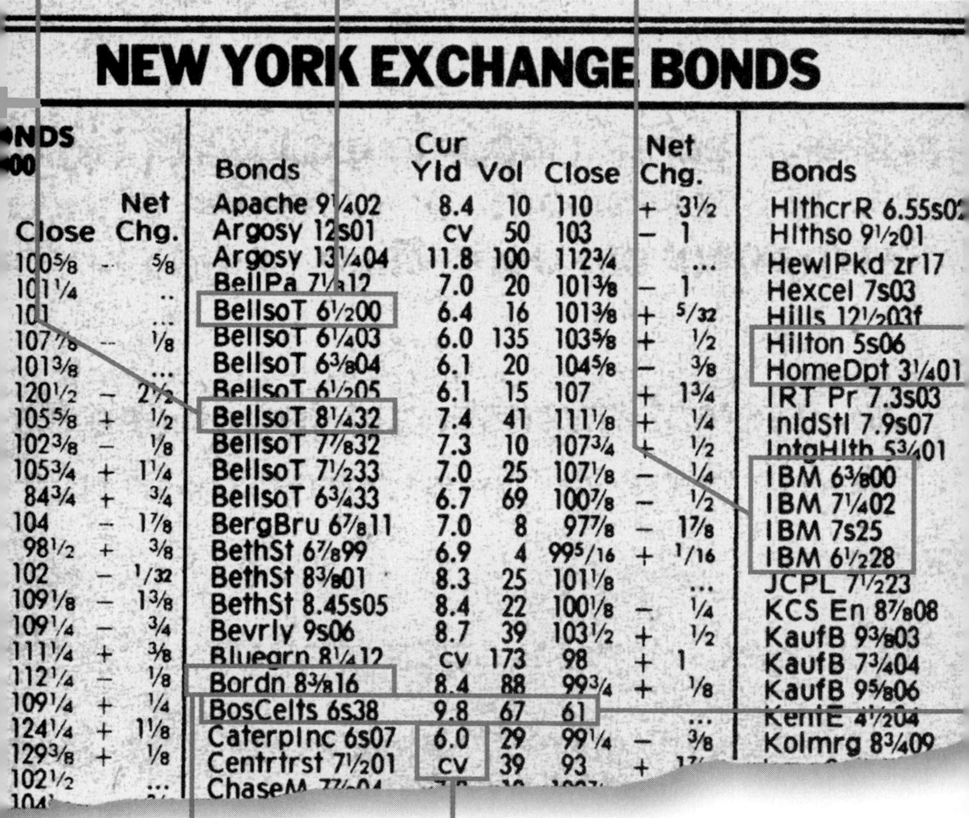

NEW YORK EXCHANGE BONDS

(Close)	(Chg.)	Bonds	Cur Yld	Vol	Close	Net Chg.	Bonds
100⅝	− ⅝	Apache 9¼02	8.4	10	110	+ 3½	HlthcrR 6.55s0?
101¼	..	Argosy 12s01	cv	50	103	− 1	Hlthso 9½201
101	..	Argosy 13¼04	11.8	100	112¾	...	HewlPkd zr17
107⅞	− ⅛	BellPa 7⅛12	7.0	20	101⅜	− 1	Hexcel 7s03
101⅜	...	BellsoT 6½200	6.4	16	101⅜	+ 5/32	Hills 12½203f
120½	− 2½	BellsoT 6¼03	6.0	135	103⅝	+ ½	Hilton 5s06
105⅝	+ ½	BellsoT 6⅜04	6.1	20	104⅝	− ⅜	HomeDpt 3¼01
102⅜	− ⅛	BellsoT 6½05	6.1	15	107	+ 1¾	IRT Pr 7.3s03
105¾	+ 1¼	BellsoT 8¼32	7.4	41	111⅛	+ ¼	InldStl 7.9s07
84¾	+ ¾	BellsoT 7⅞32	7.3	10	107¾	+ ½	IntgHlth 5¾01
104	− 1⅞	BellsoT 7½33	7.0	25	107⅛	− ¼	IBM 6⅜00
98½	+ ⅜	BellsoT 6¾33	6.7	69	100⅞	− ½	IBM 7¼02
102	− 1/32	BergBru 6⅞11	7.0	8	97⅞	− 1⅞	IBM 7s25
109⅛	− 1⅜	BethSt 6⅞99	6.9	4	99 5/16	+ 1/16	IBM 6½28
109¼	− ¾	BethSt 8⅜01	8.3	25	101⅛	...	JCPL 7½23
111¼	+ ⅜	BethSt 8.45s05	8.4	22	100⅛	− ¼	KCS En 8⅞08
112¼	− ⅛	Bevrly 9s06	8.7	39	103½	+ ½	KaufB 9⅜03
109¼	+ ¼	Bluegrn 8¼12	cv	173	98	+ 1	KaufB 7¾04
124¼	+ 1⅛	Bordn 8⅜16	8.4	88	99¾	+ ⅛	KaufB 9⅝06
129⅜	+ ⅛	BosCelts 6s38	9.8	67	61	...	KentE 4½204
102½	...	Caterplnc 6s07	6.0	29	99¼	− ⅜	Kolmrg 8¾09
104¹		Centrtrst 7½201	cv	39	93	+ 1?	
		ChaseM 7?-04					

The **last two digits** show the year in which the bond principal will **mature**, or be paid off. It's understood that the first two digits are either 19 or 20. For example, the Borden 8⅜% bond will mature in 2016.

The **current yield** is the percentage of interest an investor would earn if buying the bond at its current price. If the price is lower than par, the yield is higher than the stated rate. If the price is higher, the rate will be lower. A **cv** means a convertible bond.

Close is the price at which the bond closed on the previous trading day. When a bond is traded, it usually sells for more or less than its par value. The price moves in relation to the bond's interest rate, its yield to maturity and the bond's rating.

UNDERSTANDING BOND PRICES

Corporate bond prices are quoted in increments of points and eight fractions of a point, with a par of $1,000 as the base. The value of each point is $10, and of each fraction $1.25, as the chart shows:

$\frac{1}{8}$ = $1.25

$\frac{1}{4}$ = $2.50

$\frac{3}{8}$ = $3.75

$\frac{1}{2}$ = $5.00

$\frac{5}{8}$ = $6.25

$\frac{3}{4}$ = $7.50

$\frac{7}{8}$ = $8.75

So a bond quoted at 85½ would be selling for $855, and one quoted at 105⅞ would be selling for $1058.75.

Bond volumes report the dollar value of the previous day's trading, in thousands of dollars. To get the actual amount, add three zeroes. Thus, $5,000 of Home Depot bonds were traded—small in comparison to the $115,000 worth of Hilton bonds. The **s** which sometimes appears after the interest rate doesn't mean anything. It's used to separate the interest rate figure from the following numbers. Usually, it shows up when the interest rate doesn't include a fraction and may be confused with the maturity date. TVA's 6% bond maturing in 2000 is a typical example.

zr where the interest rate should be means that the bond is a zero-coupon bond like the Hewlett Packard bond maturing in 2017. Zero-coupons pay no periodic interest because interest accumulates until maturity.

	Cur Yld	Vol	Close	Net Chg.
	CV	35	90½	...
	9.3	15	102½	− 1
	...	15	56½	+ ¼
	CV	80	90	− 2
		10	95½	− 1
	CV	115	96⅝	...
	CV	5	236	− 1
	CV	15	98	− 1¾
	8.0	10	98⅝	− ¾
	CV	373	75½	− 6½
	6.3	5	101½	...
	6.9	10	105	− ¼
	6.5	5	107¼	+ ⅛
	6.1	15	106	+ 3
	7.2	10	104½	+ ½
	20.9	366	42½	− ½
	9.2	10	102¼	...
	7.8	92	100	− ⅜
	9.0	45	106⅞	− ⅜

Bonds	Cur Yld	Vol	Close	Net Chg.
TVA 6s00	6.0	10	100⅝	− ⅝
TVA 6⅛03	6.1	95	101¼	..
TVA 8.05s24	8.0	45	101	...
TVA 8⅝29	8.0	29	107⅞	− ⅛
TVA 8¼34	8.1	70	101⅜	...
TVA 8¼42	6.8	40	120½	− 2½
TVA 7¼43	6.9	130	105⅝	+ ½
TVA 6⅞43	6.7	270	102⅜	− ⅛
Tenet 8s03	7.6	10	105¾	+ 1¼
Tenet 05	CV	68	84¾	+ ¾
Tenet 8⅝07	8.3	10	104	− 1⅞
TxPac 5s00	5.1	5	98½	+ ⅜
TmeWar 7.95s00	7.8	14	102	− 1/32
TmeWar 7.98s04	7.3	11	109⅛	− 1¾
TmeWar 7¾05	7.1	10	109¼	− ¾
TmeWar 8.11s06	7.3	24	111½	+ ⅜
TmeWar 8.18s07	7.3	14	112¼	− ⅛
TmeWar 7.48s08	6.8	20	109¼	+ ¼
TmeWar 9⅛13	7.3	146	124¼	+ 1⅛
TmeWar 9.15s..				

Compare the Boston Celtics 6% bond yielding 9.8% (it's selling at a discount for $610, or $390 less than par) with IBM's 7% bond yielding only 6.5% (it's selling at a premium for $1,072.50, or $72.50 above par).

Net change is the difference between the closing price given here and the closing price given in the table the previous day. It's always stated as a fraction, and is based on the par value of the bond. For example, TVA's 7¼% bond was **up ½ point**, which means that the closing price is 0.5% of par value greater than the closing price on the previous day. To figure out the previous close, you subtract $5.00 (0.5% of its $1,000 par value) from this close of $1053.75 to get $1,048.75.

Net price changes almost always reflect interest rate changes. If bond prices are down from the previous day, you can conclude that interest rates rose or seemed likely to rise. When most bond prices are up, you can be fairly sure that interest rates fell or seemed likely to fall. When they're evenly split, as they are here, there's uncertainty about interest rates or other factors are influencing individual bond prices.

Municipal Bonds

The not-so-secret charm of municipal bonds is their tax-exempt status. You usually don't have to share your earnings with the IRS—or state taxing authorities.

The interest paid on most corporate bonds is taxed. To encourage investors to lend money to cities and states to pay for public projects—like highways and water systems—Congress exempts municipal bond interest from federal income taxes although it may be subject to the Alternative Minimum Tax.

If you were considering both a corporate bond and a municipal bond that paid 6% interest, the obvious choice would be the municipal bond. But the choices are seldom that simple. High-rated municipal bonds usually offer a lower rate than corporate bonds. That's why municipal

bonds, commonly called **munis**, usually appeal most to investors in the higher tax brackets, where the exemption can provide the biggest tax savings.

Municipal bond interest is also exempt from state tax (and city tax where it applies) if you live in the state where the bond is issued. An Ohioan, for example, would pay no Ohio income tax on bond interest earned on a Cincinnati bond. But someone from Kentucky who bought the Cincinnati bond would have to pay Kentucky tax on the interest income. Most investors, however, would not have to pay federal tax on the interest.

TAX-EXEMPT BONDS

Representative prices for several active tax-exempt revenue and refunding
Changes rounded to the nearest one-eighth. Yield is to maturity. n-New. Sourc

ISSUE	COUPON	MAT	PRICE	CHG	BID YLD	ISSUE
Alameda Corr TA Ca	4.750	10-01-25	95⅞	+ ⅛	5.03	Jefferson Parish Hs
Alameda Corr TA Ca	5.000	10-01-29	99	+ ¼	5.06	LA Stad & Expo Ho†
Alaska Intl Arpts	5.000	10-01-24	97⅛	+ ¼	5.21	MA Bay Trans Auth
Ca Hlth Fac Fin Auth	5.350	08-15-28	102½	+ ⅛	5.19	Mass Tpk Auth Ser
CA Hlth Fin Rev 98 Ser	5.000	10-01-20	97⅛	+ ⅛	5.22	Mo. Hlth & Ed Fac
California GO Ser 98	4.750	12-01-28	95⅝	+ ⅛	5.03	Monty BMC Spc Ca
Chgo III Sls Tx Rev	5.375	01-01-30	107⅞	+ ⅛	5.25	NJ Hlth Cr Rev Ser
Ctl Pgt Sd Transit WA	4.750	02-01-28	94⅜	...	5.12	NJ Hlth Fin Rev Ser
Denver Colo Arpt	5.000	11-15-25	97¼	...	5.19	NJ Trans Trust Fu‡
Denver Sch Dist #1	5.000	12-01-23	98¾	+ ⅛	5.08	No East Ind Sch Dis
Det Cty Sch Dist MI sch	4.750	05-01-28	94⅝	...	5.11	NYC Muni Wtr & Sw
Florida St Bd of Ed	4.500	06-01-23	92⅝	+ ⅛	5.02	Orge Co FL Trst De
Grpvn-Coly Sch TX	5.000	08-15-29	98	+ ⅛	5.13	Phil PA Go Ser 9‡
Highld Co Hlth FL	5.250	11-15-28	97⅜	+ ⅛	5.43	Phila Sch Dist Pਂ
Hono HI Wastewtr	5.000	07-01-23	98¼	...	5.12	Pub Hwy Auth Colo
Houstn Ind Sch Dis Tx	4.750	02-15-26	95	+ ⅛	5.09	Puerto Rico Pub Im
Houstn Ind Sch Dist Tx	5.000	02-15-24	98⅜	...	5.11	Sacramento Cty Fi‡
Huston Tx Airport Sys	5.000	07-01-25	97⅛	...	5.20	Wash Hlth Care
Ul Hlth Fac Auth19	5.000	01-01-05	97	+ ⅛	5.21	Wash Hl‡

READING MUNI STATISTICS

There are hundreds of thousands of munis in the market. The Wall Street Journal quotes price information for some of the largest bonds that are being actively traded.

The **name** of the issuing municipal government or government agency is listed, along with a series number, if it applies.

Coupon rate is the interest rate, given as a percentage of par value. The bond issued by the Denver School District pays 5% of par value in interest, or $50 per $1,000.

Maturity date is the date the bond matures and will be paid off. This Florida Board of Education bond comes due on June 1, 2023.

Munis are often long-term bonds, maturing in 20 to 40 years. All of the ones in this list mature between 2019 and 2038.

Price is the amount the bond sold for at the end of the previous trading day, given as a percentage of par. Massachusetts Bay Transit Authority's price of 97⅛ means it closed at $971.25.

MUNICIPAL BOND INDEXES

Each week The Wall Street Journal prints a Municipal Bond Index of the average interest issuers would have to pay to sell investment-quality long-term bonds. In the week ending January 26, for example, the average interest was 4.77%, down 0.05% from the week before.

Specific figures are given for the two main categories of municipal bonds.

Revenue bonds are backed by the revenues a specific project or agency generates. New York State Thruway revenue bonds, for example, are repaid by the money paid for tolls.

General obligation bonds are backed by the **full faith and credit**, meaning the taxing power, of the issuer. Because revenue bonds generally have longer terms and are somewhat riskier, they pay slightly higher rates overall.

Municipal Bond Index
Merrill Lynch Muni Master
Week ended Tuesday, January 26

The following index is based on major municipal issuers having bonds with amounts outstanding of at least $50 million, an investment grade rating and issuance within the last five years. The chart shown displays the market weighted average yield to worst* of each index. The index is calculated by Merrill Lynch, based on pricing obtained from Standard & Poor's J.J. Kenny Co.

— MUNI MASTER BOND INDEX —
4.77 −0.05

— REVENUE BONDS —
Sub-Index 4.91 −0.05

— 22-52 YEAR REVENUE BONDS —	01-26	Change In Week
AAA-Guaranteed.....		
Airport	4.86	− 0.05
Power....................	5.04	− 0.04
Hospital..................	4.86	− 0.05
Housing- Single Family	4.94	− 0.04
Housing- Multi Family	5.23	− 0.02
Miscellaneous..........	5.02	− 0.06
Pollution Control/ Ind. Dev.	n.a.	....
Transportation........	4.45	− 0.03
Water	4.88	− 0.05
Advance Refunded ..	4.91	− 0.05

— 12-22 YEAR GENERAL OBLIGATIONS —		
Sub-Index 4.63 −0.05		
Cities....................		3.93	− 0.06
Counties	4.68	− 0.05
States	3.67	− 0.05
Other Districts	4.59	− 0.05
The tra.....	n.a	

based on institutional trades.
Bond Buyer.

ON	MAT	PRICE	CHG	BID YLD
000	07-01-28	96¾	...	5.22
000	07-01-26	97⅞	...	5.14
000	03-01-28	97⅛	...	5.14
000	01-01-37	97	...	5.18
000	05-15-38	95⅜	...	5.28
000	11-15-29	97	+ ⅛	5.19
000	07-01-24	99	+ ⅛	5.07
750	07-01-28	95⅜	+ ⅛	5.05
500	06-15-19	94	+ ⅛	4.97
500	10-01-28	91⅜	+ ¼	5.0
750	06-15-31	94⅞	+ ⅛	5.07
750	10-01-24	95½	+ ⅛	5.
000	03-15-26	98⅛	+ ⅛	
750	04-01-27			
000				

Change is the difference between the price quoted here and the previous day's closing price. It is quoted as a fraction of par value, just as corporate bonds are. New Jersey's Transportation Trust Fund price was up ⅛ of a point, or $1.25. So, if this price is $940.00, the previous one was $938.75. You can use the table on page 91 to find the dollar value of each fraction, or multiply the fraction by 1 and then by $10.

Bid yield is the rate of return. It's figured using the interest, the amount paid for the bond, its redemption value and the time remaining until it matures.

BOND OFFERINGS

When states, cities or towns want to offer new bonds, there are two ways to get them to market. They can negotiate an arrangement with a securities firm to underwrite the bond, or they can ask for competitive bids.

A competitive bid means the issuer works with the lowest bidder to sell the bonds. A negotiated agreement takes other factors into account.

Since the mid-1980s, most offerings—up to 80% —have been negotiated. The main advantage is a guaranteed presale. The potential problems are the opportunity for manipulating the deal to the advantage of the underwriter at the expense of the taxpayer who foots the interest bills, and the possibility of political kickbacks. Competitive bids are free of those problems but may rule out developing a strong working relationship that could benefit the issuer.

U.S. Treasury Bonds, Notes and Bills

The U.S. government is a major force in the bond market.

The U.S. Treasury issues five types of debt securities. They differ from each other in their maturities, in the frequency with which they are offered, in the interest rates they pay and the way in which the interest is paid. But they share the reputation of being absolutely safe.

The most common issues are **bonds**, which have 30-year terms, **notes**, available with 2-, 5- or 10-year terms, and **bills**, available with 13-, 26- or 52-week terms. The others are Treasury **STRIPS**, which are government zero-coupon bonds, and cash management bills, which are infrequently issued short-term securities.

Bonds, sometimes called **long bonds** or **benchmark bonds**, are sold three times a year, in February, August and

November, and typically pay a higher rate of interest than the other issues. Notes with 5- and 10-year terms are available in those three months and also in May. The 2-year notes are available once a month, 52-week bills every four weeks, and the shorter-term bills weekly.

Treasury issues are sold in $1,000 increments, and you can invest as little as $1,000 or as much as $1 million. You can buy and sell directly, through a program known as Treasury Direct. But like other debt securities, Treasurys are traded in the secondary market after issue, and their prices and yield fluctuate as a reflection of changing demand. Details of those trades, in order of maturity date, are reported regularly in tables like the one below.

TREASURY BONDS,

GOVT. BONDS & NOTES

Rate	Maturity Mo/Yr	Bid	Asked	Chg.	Ask Yld.	Rate	Maturity Mo/Yr	Bid	Asked	Chg.	Ask Yld.
$7^{1}/8$	Sep 99n	101:15	101:17	-2	4.71	$5^{1}/2$	Jan 03n	102:17	102:19	-6	4.
6	Oct 99n	100:27	100:29	....	4.65	$6^{1}/4$	Feb 03n	105:09	105:11	-7	4.
$5^{7}/8$	Oct 99n	100:19	100:21	-1	4.70	$10^{3}/4$	Feb 03	121:11	121:17	-7	4.
$7^{1}/2$	Oct 99n	101:30	102:00	-1	4.69	$5^{1}/2$	Feb 03n	102:18	102:20	-6	4.
$5^{1}/8$	Nov 99n	100:26	100:28	-1	4.71	$5^{1}/2$	Mar 03n	102:19	102:21	-7	4.
$7^{7}/8$	Nov 99n	102:11	102:13	-1	4.68	$5^{3}/4$	Apr 03n	103:18	103:20	-8	4.
$5^{7}/8$	Nov 99n	100:22	100:24	-1	4.67	$10^{3}/4$	May 03	122:15	122:21	-8	4.
$7^{1}/4$	Nov 99n	102:12	102:14	-1	4.68	$5^{1}/2$	May 03n	102:23	102:25	-8	4.
$5^{7}/8$	Dec 99n	100:25	100:27	....	4.66	$5^{3}/8$	Jun 03n	102:11	102:13	-8	4.
$7^{1}/4$	Dec 99n	102:20	102:22	....	4.68	$5^{1}/4$	Aug 03n	102:01	102:02	-6	4.
$6^{3}/8$	Jan 00n	101:14	101:16	....	4.73	$5^{3}/4$	Aug 03n	103:29	103:31	-7	4.
$5^{3}/8$	Jan 00n	100:19	100:21	....	4.69	$11^{1}/8$	Aug 03	125:06	125:12	-9	4.
$7^{3}/4$	Jan 00n	102:27	102:29	-1	4.72	$4^{1}/4$	Nov 03n	98:04	98:05	-7	4.
$5^{7}/8$	Feb 00n	101:03	101:05	....	4.71	$11^{7}/8$	Nov 03	129:18	129:24	-6	4.
$8^{1}/2$	Feb 00n	103:23	103:25	-1	4.70	$5^{7}/8$	Feb 04n	105:00	105:02	-8	4.
$5^{1}/2$	Feb 00n	100:24	100:26	....	4.71	$7^{1}/4$	May 04n	111:12	111:16	-8	4.
$7^{1}/8$	Feb 00n	102:13	102:15	-1	4.72	$12^{3}/8$	May 04	134:14	134:20	-8	4.
$5^{1}/2$	Mar 00n	100:26	100:28	...	4.71	$7^{1}/4$	Aug 04n	111:23	111:27	-9	4.
$6^{7}/8$	Mar 00n	102:10	102:12	-1	4.73	$13^{3}/4$	Aug 04	142:14	142:20	-12	4.
$5^{1}/2$	Apr 00n	100:28	100:30	....	4.68	$7^{7}/8$	Nov 04n	115:04	115:08	-9	4.

Rate is the percentage of par value paid as annual interest. The note maturing in October 1999 pays 6% interest.

Maturity date is the month and year the bond or note comes due. An **n** after the date, which occurs in most entries, indicates that

the issue is a note. An * means the bond is callable before that date.

Prices for Treasury bonds and notes are measured in 32nds, rather than 100ths, of a point. Each $^{1}/32$ equals 31.25 cents, but the fractional part is dropped when the price is quoted.

For example, if a bond is selling at 100:02 (or 100 and $^{2}/32$), the price translates to $1,000.62.

Prices for Treasury issues are quoted as **bid** and **asked** instead of as a closing price. That's because Treasury issues are traded over the counter, in

FIGURING COUPON YIELD

$$\frac{\text{Dollar return on T-bill}}{\text{Cost of T-bill}} = \text{Coupon equivalent yield}$$

for example

$$\frac{\$40}{\$960} = 4.16\%$$

STRIPS AND BILLS

Trading in STRIPS and bills is also reported in separate sections of the table. STRIPS prices are always less than par, since they are issued at a **deep discount**. Those closer to maturity trade at higher prices, since they can be redeemed at par value when they come due. Compare the 95:10 bid price of the issue maturing in February 2000 with the 85:22 bid price for one maturing in May 2002. Those with later maturity dates are also more volatile, as the change figures shows.

T-bill bid and asked prices are stated as discount percents rather than price in relation to par value. The bills are sold originally at discount, and the difference between the price paid and par value is the interest. Full par value is repaid at maturity.

Dealers trade T-bills by bidding and asking discount percents. For example, the highest bid on the bill due March 25 was 4.45, meaning that the price offered was at a 4.45% discount. That is, the offer was to pay $955.50 to buy a $1,000 bill, yielding $44.50 interest.

Yield is the **yield to maturity**. As with bonds and notes, it represents the relative value of the issue. The figure that gives the most accurate sense of what an investor makes on a T-bill is the **coupon equivalent yield**, or the percentage return resulting from dividing the dollar return by the amount paid. For example, a $1,000 bill sold for $960 has a coupon equivalent yield of 4.16% (see box above).

NOTES & BILLS

U.S. TREASURY STRIPS

Mat.	Type	Bid	Asked	Chg.	Ask Yld.
00	np	95:10	95:11	+ 1	4.68
00	ci	94:08	94:08	+ 1	4.68
00	np	94:05	94:06	+ 1	4.74
00	ci	93:03	93:04	+ 1	4.71
00	np	93:01	93:02	+ 1	4.75
00	ci	92:01	92:02	+ 1	4.70
00	np	91:31	92:00	+ 1	4.74
01	ci	90:31	91:00	+ 1	4.70
01	np	90:31	91:00	+ 1	4.70
01	ci	89:29	89:30	+ 1	4.71
01	np	89:29	89:30	+ 1	4.71
01	ci	88:26	88:27	+ 1	4.72
01	np	88:26	88:27	+ 1	4.73
01	ci	87:25	87:26	+ 1	4.73
01	np	87:24	87:25	+ 1	4.74
02	ci	86:23	86:24	− 4	4.74
02	ci	85:22	85:24	− 4	4.75
02	np	85:20	85:22	− 4	4.78
02	ci	84:21	84:23	− 4	4.76

TREASURY BILLS

Maturity	Days to Mat.	Bid	Asked	Chg.	Ask Yld.
Mar 11 '99	36	4.47	4.43	− 0.03	4.51
Mar 18 '99	43	4.46	4.42	− 0.03	4.51
Mar 25 '99	50	4.45	4.41	− 0.01	4.50
Apr 01 '99	57	4.48	4.44	− 0.01	4.53
Apr 08 '99	64	4.47	4.45	+ 0.01	4.55
Apr 15 '99	71	4.49	4.47	+ 0.02	4.57
Apr 22 '99	78	4.51	4.49	+ 0.05	4.60
Apr 29 '99	85	8.74	8.72	....	9.03
May 13 '99	99	4.45	4.43	+ 0.03	4.55
May 20 '99	106	4.45	4.43	+ 0.04	4.55
May 27 '99	113	4.48	4.46	+ 0.06	4.59
Jun 03 '99	120	4.45	4.43	+ 0.06	4.54
Jun 10 '99	127	4.46	4.44	+ 0.05	
Jun 17 '99	134				
Jun 24 '99	141				
Jul 01 '99					
Jul 08 '99					
Jul					

thousands of telephone or electronic transactions instead of on the major exchanges. So it's not possible to determine the exact price of the last transaction. The best information that's available is the highest price being bid, or offered by buyers, and the lowest price being asked by sellers at 4:00 p.m. Eastern time.

For example, the bond paying 12⅜ that matures in May 2004 had a bid price of 134:14 and an asked price of 134:20. The :20 in the price refers to $\frac{20}{32}$ of a point, or $6.25 and :14 to $\frac{14}{32}$ or $4.38. So the bid price was $1,344.38 and the asked price was $1,346.25.

Bid change represents the change in the bid price given here and the bid price given in the tables for the previous trading day. The change is stated as a percent and preceded by a + if it is higher and a − if it is lower. For example, the bid price on the May 2004 bond is 8% of a point lower than on the previous day.

A Bond Vocabulary

The words that describe individual bonds have very specific meanings, which can influence your investment decisions.

Like the word **security**, which once meant the written record of an investment, the word **bond** once referred to the piece of paper that described the details of a loan transaction. Today the term is used more generally to describe a vast and varied market in debt securities.

The language of bonds tells potential investors the features of the loan: the time to maturity, how it's going to be repaid and whether it's likely to be **called**, or repaid ahead of schedule.

How Bonds Are Backed Up

Asset-backed bonds are secured, or backed up, by **accounts receivable**, or money owed to the issuers. An asset-backed bond can be created when a securities firm **bundles** some type of debt, like mortgages or credit card debt, and sells investors the right to receive the payments that consumers are making on those loans.

Debentures are the most common corporate bonds. They're backed by the credit of the issuer, rather than by any specific assets. Though they sound riskier, they're generally not. The debentures of reliable institutions are typically more highly rated than asset-backed bonds.

Pre-refunded bonds are corporate or municipal bonds, usually AAA rated, whose repayment is guaranteed by a second bond issue. Proceeds from the secondary issue are usually invested in safe U.S. Treasury issues.

Mortgage-backed bonds are backed by a pool of mortgage loans. They're sold to brokers by government agencies and private corporations, and the brokers resell them to investors. Mortgage-backed bonds are **self-amortizing**. That means each payment you get includes both principal and interest, so that there is no lump-sum repayment at maturity.

Collateralized mortgage obligations (CMOs) are more complex versions of mortgage-backed bonds. Although they are sold as a reasonable alternative to more conventional bonds, evaluating their risks and rewards requires more specialized skills.

Bonds with Conditions

A subordinated bond is one that will be paid after other loan obligations of the issuer have been met. **Senior** bonds are those with stronger claims. Corporations sometimes sell senior and subordinated bonds in the same issue, offering more interest and a shorter term on the subordinated ones to make them more attractive.

Floating-rate bonds promise periodic adjustments of the interest rate—to persuade you that you aren't locked into what seems like an unattractively low rate.

Convertible bonds give you the option to convert, or change, corporate bonds into company stock instead of getting a cash repayment. The terms are set at issue. They include the date the conversion can be made, and how much stock each bond can be exchanged for. The conversion option lets the issuer offer a lower initial interest rate, and makes the bond price less sensitive than conventional bonds to changes in the interest rate.

A sinking fund, established at the time a bond is issued, is a cash reserve set aside to finance periodic bond calls.

Bonds with Strings Attached

Callable bonds don't always run their full term. The issuer may **call** the bond, which means pay off the debt before the maturity date. The process is called **redemption**. The first date a bond is vulnerable to call is named at the time of issue. Call, or redemption, announcements are published regularly in The Wall Street Journal.

Issuers may want to call a bond if interest rates drop. If they pay off their outstanding bonds, they can float another bond at the lower rate. (It's the same idea as refinancing a mortgage to get a lower interest rate and make lower monthly payments.) Sometimes only part of an issue is redeemed, rather than all of it. In that case, the bonds that are called are chosen by lottery.

Callable bonds can be less attractive for investors than noncallable ones

REDEMPTION NOTICES

The following is a list of securities called for partial or complete redemption during the week ended Jan. 22. The notices are taken from advertisements appearing in editions of The Wall Street Journal and aren't meant to be definitive. Inquiries regarding specific issues should be directed to the paying agent or, if none is listed, the issuer.

CORPORATES

Fannie Mae will redeem on Feb. 4, $100 million of its 6.79% MTN issue due Feb. 4, 2002; and on Feb. 21, $200 million of its 7.8% MTN issue due Feb. 21, 2007.

MUNICIPALS

City of Wheeling will redeem on March 1, its parking revenue refunding bonds series 1978 with CUSIP number 963235 BX3 in the amount of $5,000 each, due March 1, 2002. Wesbanco Bank Wheeling is trustee.

City of Beacon Industrial Dev on Feb. 1

because an investor whose bond has been called is often faced with reinvesting the money at a lower, less-attractive rate. To protect bondholders expecting long-term steady income, call provisions usually specify that a bond can't be redeemed before a certain number of years, usually five or ten.

Popular Innovations

Zero-coupon bonds are a popular variation on the bond theme for some investors. Since **coupon**, in bond terminology, means interest, a zero-coupon by definition pays out no interest while the loan is maturing. Instead, the interest **accrues**, or builds up, and is paid in a lump sum at maturity.

You buy zero-coupon bonds at a **deep discount**, or prices far lower than par value. When the bond matures, the accrued interest and the original investment add up to the bond's par value.

Bond issuers like zeros because they have an extended period to use the money they have raised without paying periodic interest. Investors like zeros because the discounted price means you can buy more bonds with the money you have to invest, and you can buy bonds of different maturities, timed to coincide with anticipated expenses, such as college tuition bills, for example.

Zeros have two potential drawbacks. They are extremely volatile in the secondary market, so you risk losing money if you need to sell before maturity. And, unless you buy tax-exempt municipal zeros, you have to pay taxes every year on the interest you would have received had it, in fact, been paid.

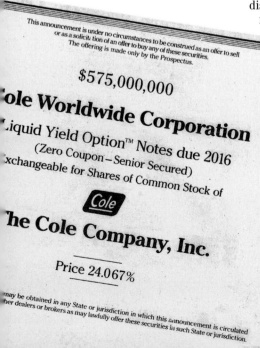

This announcement is under no circumstances to be construed as an offer to sell or as a solicitation of an offer to buy any of these securities. The offering is made only by the Prospectus.

$575,000,000

ole Worldwide Corporation

Liquid Yield Option™ Notes due 2016
(Zero Coupon – Senior Secured)
Exchangeable for Shares of Common Stock of

Cole

The Cole Company, Inc.

Price 24.067%

may be obtained in any State or jurisdiction in which this announcement is circulated from other dealers or brokers as may lawfully offer these securities in such State or jurisdiction.

Co., Inc.

Buying and Trading Bonds

Investors can buy bonds from brokers, banks or directly from certain issuers.

Newly issued bonds and those trading in the secondary market are available from stockbrokers and from some banks. Treasurys, though, are sold at issue directly to investors without any intermediary—or any commission.

The Federal Reserve Banks handle transactions in new Treasury issues—bonds, bills and notes. To buy and sell through the Federal Reserve, you establish a **Treasury Direct** account, which keeps records of the transactions and pays interest directly into your bank account. You can pick up the forms you need at most banks, call Treasury Direct at 800-943-6864 or go to the website at www.treasurydirect.gov to download some of the forms or have any that you need mailed to you. And you can handle your transactions on the phone or online.

Activity in the bond trading room is every bit as intense as a busy day on the floor of the NYSE.

THE PRICE OF BONDS
Price is one factor that may keep individuals from investing heavily in bonds. While par value of a bond is usually $1,000, bonds are often sold in bundles, or packages, that require a much larger minimum investment. The cost of bonds also limits the diversification you can achieve in your bond portfolio. As a result, many people prefer to buy bond funds (see page 107), and many of the bonds themselves are bought by large institutional investors, including fund companies.

HOW TRADING WORKS
Most already-issued bonds are traded **over the counter (OTC)**, a term that really means over the phone or by computer. Bond dealers across the country are connected via electronic display terminals that give them the latest information on prices. A broker buying a bond tries to find the dealer who is currently offering the best price and calls that dealer to negotiate a trade.

Brokerage firms also have inventories of bonds that they want to sell to clients looking for bonds of particular maturities or yields. Sometimes investors make out better buying bonds their brokers already own—or **make a market in**—as opposed to bonds the brokers have to buy from another firm.

The New York Stock Exchange and American Stock Exchange, despite their names, also list a large number of bonds. Their **bond rooms** are the scene of the same kind of brisk auction-style trading that occurs on the stock trading floor.

THE COST ISSUE
While many newly issued bonds are sold without sales expense to the buyer—because the issuer absorbs the cost—all bond trades incur sales costs. The amount you pay to buy an older bond depends on the **commission** earned by the stockbroker involved and the size of the **markup** that's added to the bond.

Markups are not officially regulated, and the total amount is not reported on confirmation orders, so charges can be excessive. A broker should reveal the markup if you ask. Or you can figure it out by finding out the current selling price of the bond and subtracting the buying price. The difference is the markup. If you check with two brokers, you may find that you would pay very different prices to buy the same bond. That means you have to be vigilant so that the cost of trading doesn't outweigh your return.

MONDAY

9 AM

T-bills offered on Thursday for Monday sale

10 AM

1 The U.S. Treasury offers 13-week and 26-week T-bills for sale every Monday.

2 Across the country, institutional investors (like pension funds and mutual funds planning to buy at least $500,000 worth of T-bills) buy up a major part of the issue by submit-

11 AM

ting competitive bids. Their bids must arrive at the Federal Reserve Bank by 1:00 p.m. Monday, the auction deadline, and state how much less than $1,000 they'd be willing to pay for each T-bill. For example, one fund might offer $980 and another $960.

NOON

3 At the same time, individual investors can submit a noncompetitive tender, or offer, through a Treasury Direct account. Investors indicate how many T-bills they want to buy and either send a check or authorize a debit for that number times $1,000. For example, someone wanting 30 bills would commit $30,000.

1 PM

— Deadline for all bids!

2 PM

4 All tenders, competitive and noncompetitive, received by the Federal Reserve before the deadline are forwarded to the Treasury Department.

5 The Treasury accepts bids, beginning with those closest to $1,000, until its quota is filled. That way, they raise the most possible revenue with the least possible debt.

3 PM

— Cut-off announcement

4 PM

6 On Monday afternoon, the Treasury announces the cut-off point, perhaps $970. News services report the information, and some bidders learn that they've bought T-bills, while others find out they bid too little.

7 The Treasury computes the average of the accepted bids

5 PM

and sells T-bills to all noncompetitive bidders for that price. It refunds to investors the difference between the $1,000 par value and the price paid. For example, if the price was $985, the refund would be $15 per bill, or $450 for 30.

8 When the bill matures, the buyers get back the full value—$1,000—of each bond they bought.

Other Bonds, Other Choices

Variety is the hallmark of the bond market—there's something for everyone.

Government agencies and government-sponsored corporations or associations issue bonds to fund specific projects or ongoing operations like mortgage lending, economic development or flood control.

Agency bonds have a double appeal for investors. They pay higher interest than Treasurys, yet they're almost as safe. They're issued by full-fledged government agencies, like the Federal Home Loan Bank or the Federal Farm Credit Bank, or by former government agencies that are now public corporations, like the Federal National Mortgage Association.

READING THE TABLES

Government agency and similar issues are reported regularly in tables that resemble those for Treasury issues. Mortgage-backed issues are included, as well as bonds sold by the World Bank, the Inter-America Development Bank and the Tennessee Valley Authority (TVA).

MORTGAGE-BACKED BONDS

Mortgage-backed bonds are among the best-known agency bonds. They're backed by pools of mortgages and issued by different organizations.

GINNIE MAES (GNMAS)

are bonds issued by the Government National Mortgage Association.

FREDDIE MACS (FHLMC)

are bonds issued by the Federal Home Loan Mortgage Corporation.

FANNIE MAES (FNMAS)

are bonds issued by the Federal National Mortgage Association.

A number of states also have mortgage loan corporations that sell bonds.

GOVERNMENT AGENCY & SIMILAR ISSUES

Thursday, February 4

Over-the-Counter mid-afternoon quotations based on large transactions, usually $1 million or more. Colons in bid-and-asked quotes represent 32nds; 101:01 means 101 1/32.

All yields are calculated to maturity, and based on the asked quote. * Callable issue, maturity date shown. For issues callable prior to maturity, yields are computed to the earliest call date for issues quoted above par, or 100, and to the maturity date for issues below par.

Source: Bear, Stearns & Co. via Street Software Technology Inc.

Rate	Mat.	Bid	Asked
7.13	3-23*	102:18	102:26
7.00	6-25	113:02	113:10
6.80	10-25	110:20	110:28

Farm Credit Fin. Asst. Co

Rate	Mat.	Bid	Asked
9.38	7-03	115:22	115:28
8.80	6-05	119:13	119:19
9.20	9-05*	107:22	107:28

Student Loan Marketing

Rate	Mat.	Bid	Asked
5.52	6-99	100:05	100:08
5.66	2-00*	100:04	100:07
5.56	3-00*	100:00	100:03
7.50	3-00	102:09	102:12
6.05	9-00	101:16	101:19
7.00	12-02	105:26	106:0
7.30	8-12	116:30	

FNMA Issues

Rate	Mat.	Bid	Asked	Yld.
8.25	12-00	105:08	105:11	5.18
5.72	1-01	101:09	101:12	4.96
5.55	1-01	100:20	100:24	5.13
5.44	1-01	100:26	100:30	4.93
5.78	1-01*	100:08	100:12	4.93
5.50	2-01	100:23	100:27	5.05
5.37	2-01	99:01	99:05	5.82
5.65	2-01*	99:02	99:06	6.08
5.41	2-01	98:08	98:12	6.27
5.36	2-01	99:00	99:04	5.82
5.63	3-01	101:02	101:06	5.01
6.16	4-01	101:21	101:25	5.27
6.63	4-01	102:		

FNMA Issues

Rate	Mat.	Bid	Asked	Yld.
6.40	12-07*	101:30	102:06	5.76
6.12	1-08*	101:10	101:18	5.72
6.41	1-08*	98:26	99:02	6.55
6.29	1-08*	100:24	101:00	5.73
6.24	1-08*	101:23	101:31	5.68
6.27	2 C8*	101:07	101:15	5.85
6.43	2-08*	99:16	99:24	6.47
6.42	2-08*	101:00		
5.75	2-08			
6.38				
6.58				

Prices are quoted as **bid** and **asked**. The 5.55 FNMA issue quoted here had a high bid of 100:20 ($1006.25). The lowest price asked was 100:24 ($1007.50). Like Treasury issues, the numbers after the colon refer to 32nds.

This bond's **yield** (**to maturity**) is 5.13%, less than the bond's stated interest rate, in part because it is trading at a premium, or above par. But the 6.41 issue due in January 2008 with bid and ask prices at a discount, or less than par, has a yield of 6.55%, slightly higher than its coupon rate of 6.41%.

U.S. SAVINGS BONDS

To many people, bonds mean the U.S. savings bonds you buy through a regular savings program at work or to use as gifts. Savings bonds differ from investment bonds in several important ways. Perhaps the most significant is that they're not marketable, which means that, while you can redeem your bonds for cash, you can't sell them to another investor. But they are alike in the sense that they pay interest on your investment principal and can be redeemed for cash at maturity. And because they're issued by the federal government, there's no danger of default.

There are three types of savings bonds: Series EE/E, Series HH/H and Series I. The EE/Es, which are available in eight denominations, are probably the best known. They resemble zero-coupons in the sense that you buy them at a discount to par and they accumulate interest so that they are worth par at maturity.

You can exchange Series EE/E bonds for four denominations of Series HH/H bonds. (You can't buy them any other way.) You pay par value and collect a fixed rate of interest on a regular basis. Series I bonds, available at face value in six denominations, are indexed for inflation, which means that the rate you earn is not guaranteed, but varies with changes in the Consumer Price Index.

You can find valuable information on how savings bonds work, the interest they pay, the way that interest is taxed and how to buy them on the World Wide Web, at www.publicdebt.treas.gov. For example, you may be able to redeem Series EE/E bonds free of any income tax if you use the proceeds to pay college tuition expenses and your income falls within a particular range.

BONDS FOR BAD TIMES

Bonds have been used throughout U.S. history to foot the cost of waging war. The first bonds the government ever authorized—in 1790—were to pay off the debts of the Revolution. And while income taxes helped pay for the Civil War and the two World Wars, **war bonds** played a big role in raising money—and popular support for the war effort.

Liberty Bonds, as World War I bonds were called, raised $16 million—an enormous sum for the time—and were traded on the New York Stock Exchange. Many people held onto their bonds after the war, for sentimental or patriotic reasons, a bonus for the government because they didn't have to be repaid.

Resolution Fund		
Rate	Mat.	B
8.13	10-19	12
8.88	7-20	13
9.38	10-20	14
8.63	1-21	1
8.63	1-30	1
8.88	4-30	1

Federal
Rate

When you buy a **savings bond**, you get a printed certificate. It's registered in your name or the name of the person you buy it for. You need that certificate to cash the bond. If you lose it, you can try to replace the lost bond by writing to The Bureau of Public Debt, Parkersburg, West Virginia 26106-1328.

A Look at the World of Bonds

	Type of bond	Par value	Maturity period
	CORPORATE BONDS Corporate bonds are readily available to investors. Companies use them rather than bank loans or new stock issues to finance expansion and other activities.	$1,000	**Short-term:** **1–5** years **Intermediate-term:** **5–10** years **Long-term:** **10–20** years
	MUNICIPAL BONDS More than one million municipal bonds have been issued by states, cities and other local governments to pay for construction and other projects.	$5,000 and up	From **1** month to **40** years
	T-BONDS AND T-NOTES These long-term debt issues of the federal government are a major source of government funding to keep operations running and to pay interest on national debt.	$1,000 (also issued in $5,000, $10,000, $100,000 and $1 million denominations)	**Bonds:** **30** years **Notes:** **2–10** years
	T-BILLS Treasury bills are the largest component of the money market—the market for short-term debt securities. The government uses them to raise money for immediate spending at lower rates than bonds or notes.	$1,000 (also issued in amounts up to $1 million)	**13** weeks **26** weeks **52** weeks
	AGENCY BONDS The most popular and well known are the bonds of mortgage associations, nicknamed **Ginnie Mae**, **Fannie Mae** and **Freddie Mac**. But many federal and state agencies also issue bonds to raise money for their operations and projects.	$1,000 to $25,000 and up	From **30** days to **20** years

BONDS

Trading details	Rated	Tax status	Call provisions	Interest and safety
Through brokers, either on an exchange or OTC	Yes	Taxable	Callable	**Riskier** than government bonds, but potentially **higher yields** than government bonds. Very little risk with highly rated bonds Usually **large minimum investment required**
Through brokers, OTC. Often, investment bankers underwrite whole issues and resell to dealers and brokers	Yes	Exempt from federal taxes Exempt from state and local taxes under certain conditions	Sometimes callable	**Lower interest rates** than comparable corporate bonds **because of tax-exemption** Especially attractive to high-tax-bracket investors, who benefit from tax-exemption feature Usually **large minimum investment required**
New issues: Through Treasury Direct **Outstanding issues**: Through brokers, OTC	Not rated, since considered risk-free	Exempt from state and local taxes	Sometimes callable	**Maximum safety**, since backed by federal government, but relatively **low** interest rates
New issues: By auction at any Federal Reserve Bank **Outstanding issues**: Through brokers, OTC	Not rated, since considered risk-free	Exempt from state and local taxes	Not callable	**Short-term investments**, with no periodic interest payments. Instead, interest consists of the difference between a discounted buying price and the par amount paid at maturity
By brokers, OTC or directly through banks	Some issues rated by some services	**Ginnie Mae**, **Fannie Mae** and **Freddie Mac** taxable **Other federal agencies** exempt from state and local taxes	Sometimes callable	Marginally **higher risk and higher interest** than Treasury bonds Usually **large minimum investment required**

Mutual Funds: Putting It Together

A mutual fund buys investments with money it gets from selling shares in the fund, and manages its portfolio to meet its financial goals.

Most investment professionals agree that it's smarter to own a variety of stocks and bonds than to gamble on the successful performance of just a few. But diversifying can be tough because buying a portfolio of individual stocks and bonds can be expensive. And knowing what to buy—and when—takes time and concentration.

Mutual funds offer one solution: When you put money into a fund, it's pooled with money from other investors to create much greater buying power than you would have investing on your own.

Since a fund can own hundreds of different securities, its success isn't dependent on how one or two holdings do. And the fund's professional managers keep constant tabs on the markets, trying to adjust the portfolio for the strongest possible performance.

How Mutual Funds Work

A LARGE NUMBER OF PEOPLE WITH MONEY TO INVEST BUY SHARES IN A MUTUAL FUND

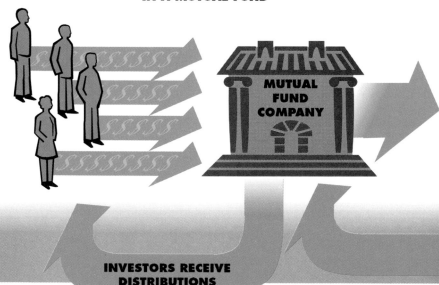

MUTUAL FUND COMPANY

INVESTORS RECEIVE DISTRIBUTIONS

PAYING OUT THE PROFITS

A mutual fund makes money in two ways: by earning dividends or interest on its investments and by selling investments that have increased in price. The fund distributes, or pays out, these profits (minus fees and expenses) to its investors.

Income distributions are paid from the income the fund earns on its investments. **Capital gain distributions** are paid from the profits from selling investments. Different funds pay their distributions on different schedules—from once a day to once a year. Many funds offer investors the option of reinvesting all or part of their distributions to buy more shares in the fund.

You pay taxes on the distributions you receive from the fund, whether the money is reinvested or paid out in cash. But if a fund loses more than it makes in any year, it can use the loss to offset future gains. Until profits equal the accumulated losses, distributions aren't taxable, although the share price may increase to reflect the profits.

HOW A MUTUAL FUND IS CREATED

A mutual fund company decides on an investment concept

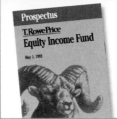

Then it issues a prospectus

Finally, it sells shares

CREATING A FUND

Mutual funds are created by investment companies (called mutual fund companies), brokerage houses and banks. The number of funds these sponsors offer varies widely, from as few as two or three to over 150. At the time of publication, there were more than 400 fund groups, offering almost 8,000 different funds.

Each new fund has a professional manager, an investment objective, and a plan, or investment program, it follows in building its portfolio. The funds are marketed to potential investors with ads in the financial press, through direct mailings and press announcements, and often with the support of registered representatives who make commissions selling them.

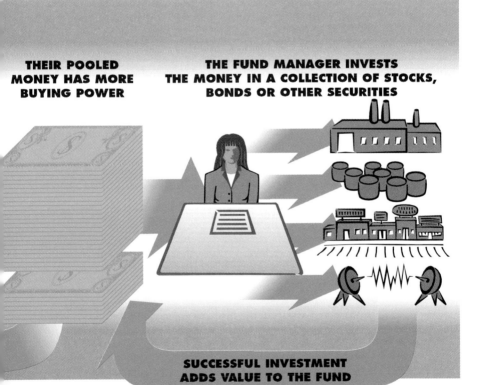

THEIR POOLED MONEY HAS MORE BUYING POWER

THE FUND MANAGER INVESTS THE MONEY IN A COLLECTION OF STOCKS, BONDS OR OTHER SECURITIES

SUCCESSFUL INVESTMENT ADDS VALUE TO THE FUND

OPEN AND CLOSED END FUNDS

Most mutual funds are **open-end funds**. That means the fund sells as many shares as investors want. As money comes in, the fund grows. If investors want to sell, the fund buys their shares back. Sometimes open-end funds are closed to new investors when they grow too large to be managed effectively—though current shareholders can continue to invest money. When a fund is closed this way, the investment company often

creates a similar fund to capitalize on investor interest.

Closed-end funds more closely resemble stocks in the way they are traded. While these funds do invest in a variety of securities, they raise money only once and offer only a fixed number of shares that are traded on an exchange (hence the name **exchange-traded** funds) or over the counter. The market price of a closed-end fund fluctuates in response to investor demand as well as to changes in the value of its holdings.

The Mutual Funds Market

Mutual funds never invest at random. Each shops for products that fit its investment strategy.

There are three main categories of mutual funds:

- **Stock funds,** also called equity funds, invest primarily in stocks
- **Bond funds** invest primarily in corporate or government bonds
- **Money market funds** make short-term investments to keep their share value fixed at $1

THE PART DIVERSITY PLAYS

Most funds diversify their holdings by buying a wide variety of investments that correspond to their category. A typical stock fund, for example, might own stock in 100 or more companies providing a range of different products and services. The charm of diversity is that losses on some stocks will often be offset—or even outweighed—by gains on others.

On the other hand, some funds are extremely focused. For example:

- **Precious metal funds** trade chiefly in mining stocks
- **Sector funds** buy shares in a particular industry, such as health care, electronics or utilities
- **High-yield bond funds** buy risky bonds to produce high income

The appeal of focused funds is that when they're doing well, the returns can be outstanding. The risk is that a change in the economy or in the sector can wipe out any gains.

FIRST MUTUAL FUND

The first investment trust, a forerunner of modern mutual funds, was put together by Robert Fleming in the 1800s. Fleming collected money from fellow Scots and traveled to the U.S., where he invested—with notable success—in growing enterprises. And he shared the profits with the other investors.

The first U.S. mutual funds, Massachusetts Investors Trust and State Street Research Investment Trust, were established in 1924 and are still doing business. But today there are over 9,500 mutual funds to choose from.

STOCK FUNDS

The name says it all: Stock funds invest in stocks. But stock fund portfolios vary, depending on the fund's investment objectives. For example, some stock funds invest in well-established companies that pay regular dividends. Others invest in younger, more growth-oriented firms or companies that have been operating below expectation for several years.

Unlike individual investors, who might buy several different types of stocks to diversify their portfolios, a fund typically concentrates in one area, like blue chips or small-company stocks. A fund's prospectus identifies its major holdings and its investment goals—though funds sometimes buy more widely to try to provide stronger returns.

LEAVE THE DETAILS TO US

ALL KINDS OF
STOCK FUNDS
- FOCUSED
- DIVERSIFIED

GLOBAL FUNDS
CAPITAL APPRECIATION FUNDS
INTER-NATIONAL FUNDS
GROWTH FUNDS
SECTOR FUNDS
FROM BLUE CHIPS TO SMALL COMPANIES

There are several different types of stock funds. A key distinction among them is that some stress growth, some income and some a combination of the two. Some funds involve more risk to capital than others because they buy stock in emerging companies. The profits on all stock fund distributions are taxable (unless held in a qualified retirement account), but no tax is due on the increased value of a fund until you sell it.

BOND FUNDS

Like bonds, bond funds provide income. Unlike bonds, however, these funds have no maturity date and no guaranteed repayment of the amount you invest, in part because the fund's holdings have different terms.

On the plus side, though, you can automatically reinvest your dividends to buy more shares. And you can buy shares in a bond fund for much less than you would need to buy a bond on your own—and get a diversified portfolio to boot. For example, you can often invest $1,000 to open a fund, and make additional purchases for smaller amounts.

Bond funds come in many varieties, with different investment goals and strategies. There are investment-grade **corporate bond funds** and riskier junk bonds often sold under the promising label of high-yield funds. You can choose long- or short-term **U.S. Treasury bond funds**, funds that combine issues with different maturities, and a variety of tax-free municipal bond funds, including some limited to a particular state.

IT'S ALL IN THE FAMILY

Mutual fund companies usually offer a variety of funds—referred to as a family of funds—to their investors. Keeping your money in the family can make it easier to transfer money between funds, but like most families, some members do better than others.

MONEY MARKET FUNDS

Money market funds invest to maintain their value at $1 a share, so that they're described as cash equivalent investments. Typically, you earn interest on the investments the fund makes. Since these funds are considered safe, some investors prefer them to stock or bond funds. But the interest the funds pay is low when interest rates are low. As an added appeal, most money market funds let investors write checks against their accounts. There's usually no charge for check-writing—although there may be a per-check minimum.

BOND FUNDS
- SAFE OR RISKY
- SHORT-TERM OR
- LONG-TERM

HIGH-YIELD TAXABLE FUNDS

INTERMEDIATE NDS

GENERAL UNICIPAL DEBT

GINNIE MAEs

TAX-FREE FUNDS

MONEY MARKET FUNDS
- TAXABLE OR TAX-FREE
- LOW RISK

SHORT-TERM MUNICIPAL

COMMERCIAL PAPER

13-WEEK T-BILLS

SHORT-TERM CORPORATE DEBT

The two main categories of bond funds are **taxable** and **tax-free**. Distributions earned on corporate and U.S. government funds (including Treasurys and agency funds) are taxed. There's no federal tax on municipal bond fund distributions, and no state or local taxes for investors who live in the municipality that issues the underlying bonds. New Yorkers, for example, can buy **triple tax-free** New York funds and keep all their earnings.

Money market funds also come in two varieties, **taxable** and **tax-free**. Taxable funds buy the best-yielding short-term corporate or government issues available, while tax-free funds are limited to buying primarily municipal debt. Taxable funds pay slightly higher dividends than tax-free funds, but investors must pay tax on any distributions they receive. In either case, the rate a fund pays is roughly the same as bank money market accounts or CDs.

Targeted Investments

Mutual funds aim at particular targets. To hit
them, the funds make certain types of investments.

INVESTMENT OBJECTIVE

Every mutual fund—stock, bond or money market—is established with a specific investment objective that fits into one of three basic goals:

- **Current income**
- **Some income and growth**
- **Future growth**

To achieve its objective, the fund invests in securities it believes will produce the results it wants. To identify those securities, a fund often does a vast amount of research, including what's known as a bottom-up style, which involves a detailed analysis of individual companies. When the objective is small-company growth or the focus is on emerging markets, the process can be more difficult because there's only limited information readily available.

In addition, each fund manager has a buying style, seeking a particular type of investment from the pool that may be appropriate for the objective. Some equity-fund managers, for example, stress **value**, which means buying stocks whose price is lower than might be expected. Other managers may be **contrarians**, buying investments that others are shunning.

THE RISK FACTOR

There is always the risk that a fund won't hit its target. Some funds are, by definition, riskier than others. For example, a fund that invests in small new companies takes the chance that some of its investments will do poorly because it believes that some, at least, will do very well.

FUNDS TAKE AIM

These charts group funds in three categories by investment objective. They also illustrate the correlation between a fund's objective and the risks it may face.

INCOME FUNDS

Kind of fund	Investment objective	Potential risks	What the fund buys
Agency bond	Income and regular return of capital	Value and return dependent on interest rates	Securities issued by U.S. government-sponsored agencies and related institutions
Corporate bond	Steady income	Interest-rate changes and inflation	Highly rated corporate bonds, with various maturities
High-yield bond	Highest current income	High-risk bonds in danger of default	Low-rated and unrated corporate and government bonds
International money market	Income and currency gains	Changes in currency values and interest rates	CDs and short-term securities
Municipal bond	Tax-free income	Interest-rate changes and inflation	Municipal bonds in various maturities
Short-/inter-mediate-term debt	Income	Small risk of loss. Less influenced by changes in interest rate	Different types of debt issues with varying maturities, depending on type of fund
U.S. Treasury bond	Steady income	Interest-rate changes and inflation	Highly rated government bonds

GROWTH AND INCOME

Kind of fund	Investment objective	Potential risks	What the fund buys
Balanced	Income and growth	Limited risk to principal. Moderate long-term growth	Part stocks and preferred stocks (usually 60%) and part bonds (40%)
Equity income	Income and growth	Limited risk to principal. Moderate long-term growth	Blue chip stocks and utilities that pay high dividends
Growth and income	Growth plus some current income	Limited risk to principal. Moderate long-term growth	Stocks that pay high dividends and provide some growth
Income	Primarily income	Limited risk of loss to principal, but less growth in strong market	Primarily bonds, but some dividend-paying stocks

GROWTH FUNDS

Kind of fund	Investment objective	Potential risks	What the fund buys
Aggressive growth, also called capital appreciation	Long-term growth	Very volatile and speculative. Risk of above-average losses to get above-average gains	Stocks of new or under-valued companies expected to increase in value
Emerging markets	Growth	Typically more volatile than other growth funds	Stocks in companies in developing countries
Equity index	Imitate the stock market	Average gains and losses for the market the index tracks	Stocks represented in the index the fund tracks
Global equity	Global growth	Gains and losses depend on stock prices and forex fluctu-ation. Some risk to principal	Stocks in various markets
Growth	Above-average growth	Can be volatile. Some risk of loss to principal to get higher gains	Stocks in mid-sized or large companies whose earnings are expected to rise quickly
International equity	International growth	Potentially volatile, based on price changes and currency fluctuation	Stocks in non-U.S. companies
Sector	Growth	Volatile funds, dependent on right market timing to produce results	Stocks in one particular industry, such as energy or transportation
Small company growth	Long-term growth	Volatile and speculative. Risk of above-average losses to get higher gains	Stocks in small companies traded on the exchanges or over the counter
Value funds	Growth	Often out of step with overall market	Stocks in companies whose prices are lower than they seem to be worth

HEDGING

International fund managers may use a practice called hedging to protect the return on their funds. That's because if a currency gains value in relation to others, investments **denominated**, or sold, in those other currencies have less value when they are converted into the stronger currency. To protect against losses that could result from that situation, mutual funds often buy futures contracts on a currency at preset exchange rates.

Funds that hedge may put up to 50% of their total assets in currency con-tracts rather than stocks or bonds. But other funds don't hedge at all, figuring that exposure to other currencies is part of the reason for investing overseas.

Focused Funds

Mutual fund companies have expanded their horizons—and the opportunities they offer to investors—by developing specialty funds.

Stock funds are the oldest and still the most popular category of mutual fund. But as investing in funds has grown increasingly popular, fund companies have responded by expanding their offerings in a effort to appeal to people with specific investment goals. Many of the newer funds have narrowly defined objectives and strategies, focusing on previously untapped market segments. Others have been added to compete with popular existing funds.

SPECIAL INVESTMENT OBJECTIVES

INDEX FUNDS

Index funds are designed to produce the same return that you would get if you owned all the stocks in a particular index—such as the S&P 500. While this diversity would be overwhelming for an individual, it's all in a day's work for an index fund. There are currently more than 140 equity-index funds—tracking almost every known index for large, mid-cap and small companies, as well as bond market indexes and several international indexes.

Index funds are popular because the performances of the major stock and bond indexes often surpass the returns that professional mutual fund money managers achieve by following a particular investment strategy. Investing in an index fund can eliminate having to decide among specific stock or bond funds. It can also provide a balance to other investments.

In certain economic cycles, however, individual fund performance can leave index funds in the dust. And as a rule, index funds that track small companies have produced spottier results than growth funds that invest directly in specific small companies.

QUANT FUNDS

These funds are named for their quantitative investment style—they aim to beat the index funds they imitate by relying on statistical analysis to decide which securities will top the benchmarks. Instead of buying all the stocks in the S&P 500, they buy selected stocks that their numbers tell them will turn a higher profit.

An **efficient market** isn't one that works quicker or smarter. Rather, it's the object of constant, intensive analysis, and the information is available to everyone almost immediately. **Inefficient markets**, conversely, aren't as widely analyzed and can offer enormous opportunity for profit to savvy fund managers who track them.

MARKET NEUTRAL FUNDS

Some newer mutual funds follow a controversial investment strategy once the realm of private hedge funds: market neutral investing, also called zero beta or long/short portfolio investing.

Market neutral funds aren't trying to beat the market, but to maintain average annual returns that are a few points above three-month U.S. Treasury bills, regardless of whether the market is going up or down. That means providing a measure of stability within your investment portfolio.

These funds use computer programs to evaluate and rank possible investments quantitatively, analyzing factors such as price/earnings ratios, yield, volatility and earnings growth. The funds then buy the top-ranking stocks and sell short the ones ranked at the bottom (see page 48).

Some market neutral funds use multiple managers in an attempt to diversify their risk. Since meeting the fund's goals depends so heavily on accurate assessments of future market movements, a manager's decisions may even be more crucial to overall return than if the fund were following a more conventional trading approach.

TAX-FREE FUNDS

Although the earnings on all stock funds and most bond funds are taxable, it's possible to invest in a variety of mutual funds that pay tax-free distributions. Tax-free income is particularly appealing to people in the highest tax brackets, since they may come out ahead at tax time, even though tax-free funds typically provide slightly lower yields than taxable funds.

The biggest tax savings occur when a person who lives in a high-tax state—like California—buys a fund that specializes in bonds issued there. The interest is free of both state and federal tax. And when a fund buys bonds issued by a municipality like New York City, the interest is triple tax-free for residents who invest in the fund.

The dilemma that many funds face is finding enough high-quality investments to meet investor demands. This can be especially hard for tax-free funds, and even harder for single state funds.

SECTOR FUNDS

Sector funds focus on the stocks of a particular industry or segment of the economy, such as technology, health care or financial services. In that sense, they are out of step with the underlying principle behind mutual funds—diversity. While a sector fund is more diversified than a single stock, there is nothing in the fund portfolio to offset a downturn in its sector.

Since sectors are highly volatile, they offer an opportunity for big profits to investors who ride the right wave. Often, though, one year's hot sector is slow the next. Health care and emerging markets are just two of the sectors that have had roller coaster rides in recent years.

Precious metal funds resemble sector funds, since all their money is invested in mining stocks and bullion—but they're more predictable. When inflation is high or there's political turmoil, precious metal funds tend to do well because they are a hedge against instability.

GREEN AND OTHER CONSCIENCE FUNDS

Mutual fund companies have also created funds to attract investors whose strong political or social commitments make them unwilling to invest in companies whose business practices are at odds with their beliefs. A green fund might avoid tobacco companies, companies with poor environmental records or those that sell certain products in underdeveloped countries. While green funds rarely make it to the top of performance charts because of the restrictions on what they can buy, many have posted above-average growth.

Unlike other specialty funds, green funds aren't treated as a special category by companies that track fund performance, such as Lipper Inc. Investors who feel strongly about where their money goes may have to do extra research to find a fund they're comfortable with. Some special interest groups sponsor or recommend particular funds.

Inside a Mutual Fund

Mutual funds operate virtually around the clock, managing their portfolios and serving their investors.

A mutual fund has two distinct yet intertwined businesses: making a profit and providing services to its clients. Each fund, or closely related group of funds, is run by one or more professional managers responsible for both its day-to-day operations and for its performance. In fact, some experts believe the success of a fund is so closely linked to the skill of its manager that they select funds based almost entirely on their managers—and lose interest when a manager leaves.

A typical fund depends on a battalion of employees, including financial analysts, accountants, traders, sales representatives and support staff. Equally crucial are the software programs, computers and other electronic equipment—and the people who keep them running—that make this kind of operation work.

Operating the Fund

Each fund buys and sells securities in a specific financial market or markets. A stock fund, for example, buys and sells shares through brokers on the exchanges, over the counter and in private transactions. Because they trade in large volumes, mutual funds are known as **institutional traders** (see page 44).

While clients may not be able to talk to a telephone representative at the fund until around 8:00 a.m. local time, reports on the fund's previous day's performance are available in the financial press and online well before then.

Every day the fund's manager and analysts digest how the markets did the day before, where the fund stands in relation to other funds and its benchmark indexes, and what economic news might affect the fund's value.

Servicing the Investor

Funds are never static. Money moves in and out constantly—in staggering amounts. In 1998, for example, $477 billion poured into mutual funds. And at the end of 1998, total assets in mutual funds had reached $5.5 trillion.

The mailroom at Fidelity Investments sends out an average of 800,000 pieces of mail per day—that's more than 200 million pieces per year.

Mail pours into mutual fund offices by the ton. Each piece must be opened, coded with an account number, and put in the right in basket. Checks are credited to the right client accounts at the day's closing price. Then they're shipped off to the bank.

Checks and confirmations from the previous day's transactions are mailed out to clients, making good on the claim that mutual funds are among the most liquid investments.

OTHER WAYS TO BUY FUNDS

One big question investors face when buying mutual funds is whether to buy directly from the fund—the process that's described here—or through a broker, bank or other financial agent. You may wonder, for example, whether professionals can identify better performing funds than you can on your own.

In fact, the evidence shows that there's very little difference in performance. However, buying through an advisor generally means paying a sales charge, which can reduce what you actually gain on the fund. That charge is offset only if you hold the fund for an extended period. On the other hand, some experts point out that if an advisor gives you the incentive to invest, it's worth the added cost.

By the time a typical fund manager leaves the office on any given day, he or she has handled millions of dollars in securities transactions.

Fund managers and analysts are always in the market for new securities that meet the fund's investment objectives. Their research staff provides up-to-the-minute price information and analysis.

Trading managers authorize buy and sell orders. Traders, looking for the best price, keep their eyes on the computer screen and their hands on the telephone. Other employees keep a running count of the fund's balance sheet.

In time to meet the press deadline, details of the fund's current value and the change from the day before are calculated by the staff and sent to the National Association of Securities Dealers (NASD).

Investors can open accounts, send checks or have money transferred into their accounts throughout the day. At the close of business, the money is invested in shares of the fund. Written confirmations follow all the telephone and electronic transactions. As a result of this follow-up documentation, the industry as a whole has high quality control.

Telephone reps keep busy answering client questions and acting on orders. Conversations are recorded to back up the actions the reps take. There are very few transactions that can't be done by phone—as long as you sign up for phone services when the account is opened. Fund transfers, however, have to go to accounts registered in the same name(s).

At most funds, customers can talk to a representative after the exchanges close, placing orders that will be acted on the next day. After the people go home, automated phone systems continue to provide details about earnings, balances and recent trades, as well as other account and performance information.

Mutual Fund Quotations

As the popularity of mutual funds has grown, so has the information about them.

As investors have put more money into mutual funds, there's been a revolution in the way that fund performance is reported. The Wall Street Journal, for example, tracks individual funds daily, monthly, quarterly and annually in different formats.

The funds themselves supply the basic information daily to the National Association of Securities Dealers (NASD), and Lipper Inc. calculates the performance, cost and rankings.

A fund must have at least 1,000 shareholders or net assets of $25 million to be listed, by NASD rules. Generally, a family of funds needs assets of $5 billion or so to stay alive. Otherwise, it's vulnerable to a takeover by a larger, more aggressive fund.

MUTUAL

NAV$ 2/28	Fund Name	Inv Obi	Total Return					Max Init Chrg	Exp Ratio
			Feb	1Yr	3Yr-R	5Yr-R	10Yr-R		
7.25	US Sht	SE	+3.9	−14.9 C	NS ..	NS ..	NS ..	0.00	1.57
	Price Funds:								
18.44	Balanced	RI	−2.2	+9.3 B	+15.4 B	+14.1 B	+13.7 A	0.00	0.81
30.63	BIChip	GR	−2.8	+18.3 C	+25.6 B	+23.6 A	NS ..	0.00	0.95
10.96	CA Bond	SS	−0.6	+5.9 A	+6.9 A	+6.5 A	+7.7 B	0.00	0.58
12.80	CapApp	CP	−2.0	−0.5 D	+10.5 D	+11.9 D	+11.9 D	0.00	0.64
17.44	CapOpp	CP	−3.6	+1.5 D	+11.9 D	NS ..	NS ..	0.00	1.35
9.62	CorpInc	AB	−2.3	−0.3 E	+6.5 C	NS ..	NS ..	0.00	0.80
21.12	DivGro	GI	−1.6	+1.6 D	+20.4 C	+19.5 C	NS ..	0.00	0.80
9.84	DvsfSmGr	SC	−9.5	−15.0 C	NS ..	NS ..	NS ..	0.00	1.25
8.95	EmgMktB	WB	+0.8	−25.9 E	+6.7 B	NS ..	NS ..	0.00	1.25
8.12	EmMktS	EM	−3.0	−27.8 C	−9.7 B	NS ..	NS ..	0.00	1.75
25.46	EqInc	EI	−0.8	+1.5 D	+16.6 C	+17.9 B	+14.4 B	0.00	0.79
33.68	EqIndex	GI	−3.1	+17.5 A	+26.5 A	+23.8 A	NS ..	0.00	0.40
21.14	Europe	EU	−1.8	+10.0 C	+20.0 C	+17.2 B	NS ..	0.00	1.05
10.50	ExtIndex r	MC	−5.1	−0.7 C	NS ..	NS ..	NS ..	0.00	NA
16.60	FinSvcs	SE	−0.9	+4.3 A	NS ..	NS ..	NS ..	0.00	1.25
10.86	FL Inter	IM	−0.8	+5.3 B	+5.3 D	+5.6 B	NS ..	0.00	0.60
17.45	ForEq	IL	−1.8	+2.8 C	+9.1 C	+7.6 B	NS ..	0.00	0.75
9.44	GNMA	MG	−0.9	+5.0 C	+6.8 B	+6.8 A	+8.4 B	0.00	0.70
11.03	GA Bond	SS	−0.7	+5.7 A	+6.8 A	+6.5 A	NS ..	0.00	0.65
9.85	GlbBond	WB	−4.2	+1.8 C	+4.5 C	+6.1 B	NS ..	0.00	1.20
14.77	GlbStk	GL	−2.1	+7.6 B	+16.4 B	NS ..	NS ..	0.00	1.20
31.69	Growth	GR	−2.7	+14.8 C	+23.2 C	+20.5 B	+17.1 C	0.00	0.75
25.69	Gr&In	GI	−0.5	+2.6 D	+17.2 D	+16.9 D	+14.2 D	0.00	0.78
15.67	HelSci	HB	−4.0	+11.2 C	+15.4 C	NS ..	NS ..	0.00	1.18
8.39	HiYield	HC	−0.2	+2.8 A	+9.9 A	+7.5 C	+8.6 D	0.00	0.81
8.58	N Inc	AB	−2.4	+2.2 E	+5.5 E	+6.1 D	+8.0 E	0.00	0.71
9.78	IntlBond	WB	−4.3	+5.9 B	+4.8 D	+6.3 B	+8.6 A	0.00	0.86
16.86	IntlDis	IL	+2.6	+4.1 B	+4.7 D	+0.7 E	+6.9 D	0.00	1.47
14.53	IntlStk	IL	−1.9	+2.7 C	+8.9 C	+7.5 B	+9.6 B	0.00	0.85
7.72	Japan					6.0 B			1.22

NAV$ 2/28	Fund Name	Inv Obi	Feb
27.83	StkIdxI	GI	−3.1
27.82	StkIdxZ	GI	−3.1
11.23	UtilityZ	UT	−2.3
17.65	GloZ	GL	−3.4
9.69	PugetSnd	SE	+1.6
16.27	Purisima TR p	MP	−3.0
	Putnam Funds Class A:		
8.74	AmGv p	LG	−2.4
9.34	AZ TE	SS	−0.8
8.92	Asia p	PR	−2.3
11.84	AABal p	MP	−3.3
10.35	AACn p	MP	−2.0
13.45	AAGr n	MP	−3.8
10.59	BalRet p	BL	−1.8
8.77	CATx p	SS	−0.6
21.90	CapApr p	CP	−5.7
7.28	CapOp p	SC	−3.1
19.28	Conv p	MP	−3.1
13.61	DvrEq p	GL	−3.8
11.28	Dvrin p	GT	−1.4
6.97	EmMkt p	EM	−0.4
15.54	EqIn p	EI	−1.4
21.64	EuGr p	EU	−2.4
9.47	FLTx	SS	−0.9
17.76	Geo p	BL	−1.7
12.64	GIGv p	WB	−2.3
12.41	GIGr p	GL	−4.3
12.87	GIGrInA p	GL	−1.8
15.14	GINtRs p	NR	+0.3
20.39	GrIn p	GI	−2.1
13.96	GrInIIA p	GI	−1.8

The **mutual fund company's name** appears first, followed by its different funds listed in alphabetical order.

r after the fund name means the fund charges a fee to redeem shares for cash. This type of charge is also known as a **back-end load**.

p after the fund name means the fund charges a fee for marketing and distribution costs, also known as **12b-1 fees**.

t after the fund name means both r and p apply: You pay back-end loads and 12b-1 fees.

NAV is the fund's **net asset value**. A fund's NAV is the dollar value of one share in the fund, and the price a fund pays you per share when you sell. It's figured by totaling the value of all the fund's holdings and dividing by the number of shares. For example, the NAV of the Price Blue Chip fund is $30.63.

A fund's NAV moves up or down to reflect market conditions, though the short-term changes are rarely dramatic. Those changes are reported for each trading day, as are year-to-date yields.

R stands for ranking. The return each fund has provided is compared with the results for other funds with the same **investment objective**. Investment objectives, expressed as a two-letter abbreviation in the column following the fund's name, identify the type or types of investments the fund makes. A chart identifying each of the 36 categories and what each buys is printed in the monthly, quarterly and annual reviews. The example highlighted here, EU, indicates a fund investing in Europe.

Total return is the percentage of gain (+) or loss (−) the fund has provided, assuming all distributions have been reinvested. This chart reports those figures for 1-, 3-, 5- and 10-year periods as well as for the previous month. An **NS** in a column indicates that the fund wasn't operating at the beginning of the period.

Here, for example, the total return on Putnam Funds' Balanced Return fund is up 4.5% over one year, and an average of 13% over three years and 12.3% over ten years.

Many mutual funds charge a **load**, or sales charge, when you buy shares. Loads are a percentage of the investment amount and may be charged when you buy, when you sell or throughout the period you own the fund. Funds that charge when you buy are often identified as Class A shares, as the Putnam Funds are here. When those charges apply, they are listed in the column labeled **maximum initial charge**. If 0.00 appears, the fund is a **no-load**.

Load charges are not included in the fund's total return, but the annual expenses you pay are figured in. The differences in return among funds with the same investment objective can be the result of the fees they charge.

FUNDS

	Total Return				Max Init Chrg	Exp Ratio	NAV$ 2/28	Fund Name	Inv Obj		Feb	1Yr	Total Return 3Yr-R	5Yr-R	10Yr-R		Max Init Chrs
Yr	3Yr-R	5Yr-R	10Yr-R														
9.5 A	NS ..	NS ..	NS ..	0.00	0.30	9.91	HiQual p	LG	−2.3	+4.1 E	+5.8 D	+6.1 C	+7.7 D	4.
9.5 A	+26.2 A	+23.6 A	NS ..	0.00	0.40	7.42	HIYTotP p	HC	−0.4	−8.5 E	NS ..	NS ..	NS ..	4.
1.4 E	NS ..	NS ..	NS ..	0.00	0.57	7.78	HIYTrll p	HC	−0.5	−4.0 D	NS ..	NS ..	NS ..	4.
1.4 B	NS ..	NS ..	NS ..	0.00	1.13	61.65	Hiln p	HB	−3.3	+11.2 C	+20.2 B	+25.2 A	+20.5 D	5.
NS ..	NS ..	NS ..	NS ..	0.00	1.13	8.12	HYAd p	HC	−0.6	−10.7 E	+3.8 C	+4.7 E	+8.8 D	4.
0.1 A	NS ..	NS ..	NS ..	0.00	1.50	10.74	HIYd p	HC	−0.6	−9.3 E	+5.5 E	+5.7 D	+9.1 C	4.
						6.75	Incm p	AB	−2.4	+1.1 E	+5.4 E	+5.9 D	+8.4 C	4.
5.3 C	+6.6 B	+6.6 B	+7.4 E	4.75	1.03	19.54	IntlGr p	IL	−2.4	+10.4 A	+17.3 A	+12.8 A	NS ..	5.
4.5 C	+5.7 D	+5.3 D	NS ..	4.75	0.99	10.96	IntGrln p	IL	−1.3	+2.1 C	NS ..	NS ..	NS ..	5.
2.8 B	−8.3 B	−4.8 A	NS ..	5.75	1.46	13.42	IntlNop p	IL	−2.9	+11.4 A	+10.7 B	NS ..	NS ..	5.
4.4 C	+13.5 B	+13.0 C	NS ..	5.75	1.22	4.92	IntUS p	SG	−1.2	+5.5 B	+6.0 A	+6.2 A	NS ..	3.
4.9 C	+10.2 D	+9.7 D	NS ..	5.75	1.39	13.88	IntVoy p	IL	−1.7	+15.9 A	+20.0 A	NS ..	NS ..	5.
4.5 B	+15.1 B	+14.5 B	NS ..	5.75	1.31	14.97	Inv p	GR	−3.6	+25.6 A	+28.6 A	+24.2 A	+19.8 A	5.
4.5 D	+13.0 D	+12.8 C	+12.3 D	5.75	1.13	9.60	MaTx p	SS	−0.6	+4.9 D	+6.3 C	+6.0 B	NS ..	4.
3.2 C	+6.3 C	+6.1 B	+7.6 B	4.75	0.77	9.28	MiTx p	SS	−0.9	+3.9 E	+6.0 D	+5.6 D	NS ..	4.
0.5 D	+19.0 C	+18.5 B	NS ..	5.75	1.03	9.19	MNTX p	SS	−0.4	+4.7 D	+5.7 D	+5.5 D	NS ..	4.
NS ..	NS ..	NS ..	NS ..	5.75	NA	9.30	Munl p	GM	−0.6	+5.1 C	+6.3 C	+6.2 B	NS ..	4.
0.3 D	+12.0 C	+12.0 C	+12.6 B	5.75	0.97	57.68	NwOp p	GR	−6.2	+12.9 C	+16.0 D	+19.8 C	NS ..	5.
3.0 A	+19.1 A	NS ..	NS ..	5.75	1.37	13.59	NwValA p	GI	−2.4	+4.4 D	+15.0 E	NS ..	NS ..	5.
4.1 E	+4.6 E	+5.2 D	+8.5 C	4.75	0.97	9.32	NJTx p	SS	−0.7	+4.4 E	+6.1 C	+5.6 D	NS ..	4.
7.0 B	−7.3 A	NS ..	NS ..	5.75	2.10	8.94	NYTx p	SS	−0.8	+4.8 D	+6.1 C	+5.3 D	+7.5 C	4.
8.9 B	+18.6 B	+18.5 A	+13.7 C	5.75	0.99			SS	−0.6	+4.9 D	+6.4 B	+6.4 A	NS ..	4.
0.9 B	+21.0 B	+18.2 A	NS ..	5.75	1.32									NS ..	5.
4.8 D	+6.0 C	+5.8 C	NS ..	4.75	0.96										5.
5.4 C	+14.9 C	+14.9 B	+13.3 A	5.75	1.00										5.
1.4 D	+3.6 D	+3.7 D	+7.1 C	4.75	1.26										5.
4.2 C	+17.8 A	+13.5 B	+12.8 A	5.75	1.18										4.
8.9 A	+3.4 A	+4.8 A	+8.0 B	5.75	1.70										4.
8.3 C	+18.7 C	+8.7 C	+15.7 B	5.75	1.20										4.
6.0 C	+13.0 C	NS ..	NS ..	5.75	0.84										4.
					0.96										

The ranking code assigns an A to funds that rank among the top 20%, a B to the next 20% and so on, with an E indicating the bottom 20%. When a fund with a higher total return gets a lower rating than a fund with a lower return, as with the one-year returns on the Price Balanced and Blue Chip funds, it is because they have different objectives.

Some funds receive similar rankings for all periods, like the Price Balanced fund, while others, like the company's Emerging Markets B, have less consistent returns and rankings.

MUTUAL FUND OBJECTIVES

Categories compiled by The Wall Street Journal, based on classifications by Lipper Inc.

STOCK FUNDS

AU Gold: Gold mines, gold-oriented mining finance houses, gold coins or bullion.

CP Capital Appreciation: Seeks rapid capital growth, often through high portfolio turnover.

EI Equity Income: Tends to favor stock with the highest dividends.

EM Emerging Markets: Emerging markets equity securities (based on economic measures such as a country's GNP per capita).

EU European Region: European markets or operations concentrated in Europe.

GI Growth & Income: Pursues both price and dividend growth. Category includes S&P 500 Index funds.

GL Global Stock: Includes small cap global. Can invest in U.S.

GR Growth: Invests in companies expecting higher than average revenue and earnings growth.

HB Health & Biotechnology: Health care, medicine and biotechnology.

IL International: Canadian; International; International Small Cap.

LT Latin America: Markets or operations concentrated in Latin America.

MC MidCap: Shares of middle-sized companies.

NR Natural Resources: Natural resources stocks.

PR Pacific Region: Japanese; Pacific Ex-Japan; Pacific Region; China Region.

SC Small Cap Growth: Stocks of lesser-known, small companies.

SE Sector: Financial Services; Real Estate; Specialty & Miscellaneous.

TK Science & Technology: Science, technology and telecommunications stocks.

UT Utility: Utility stocks.

TAXABLE BOND FUNDS

AB Long-Term: Corporate A-rated; Corporate BBB-rated.

GT General U.S. Taxable: Can invest in different types of bonds.

HC High Yield Taxable: High yield high-risk bonds.

IB Intermediate: Investment grade corporate debt of up to 10-year maturity.

IG Intermediate U.S.: U.S. Treasury and government agency debt.

LG Long-Term U.S.: U.S. Treasury; U.S. government; zero coupon.

MG Mortgage: Ginnie Mae and general mortgage; Adjustable-Rate Mortgage.

SB Short-Term: Ultrashort obligation and short, short-intermediate investment grade corporate debt.

SG Short-Term U.S.: Short-term U.S. Treasury; short, short-intermediate government funds.

WB World: Short....

It's All in the Charts

You can use a number of benchmarks and time frames to evaluate a fund's performance.

There are a number of tools you can use to evaluate how well individual mutual funds, or mutual funds in general, are performing. The Wall Street Journal regularly prints **benchmark indexes and averages** that track different categories of investments, including stocks and bonds, which are the underlying investments of mutual funds. There are also indexes tracking mutual funds grouped by investment objective.

For example, if the benchmark Standard & Poor's 500-stock index reports a gain in large-company stock performance, as it does in the example here, you can reasonably expect that a mutual fund investing in large-company stocks should also have a gain. Similarly, if you're discouraged by the performance of your small-cap stock fund, it may make you more comfortable to know that Vanguard's Small Company Index fund, which tracks the Russell 2000 (a small-cap benchmark), is reporting a loss over the last year.

MUTUAL FUND INDEXES

The performance of 21 categories of mutual funds, each with a different investment objective, is reported daily in the **Lipper Indexes**. Ten of the indexes track funds that invest in stocks and 11 track types of bond funds. Each index reports the gain (+) or loss (−) for one category of fund, based on the performance of the largest funds in that category.

The numbers in the first column indicate the combined NAVs of all the funds in the sample. That gives you a sense of which categories of fund are the largest, specifically stock growth funds and growth and income funds.

The next three columns indicate the percentage the current NAV has increased or decreased from the previous day, for the week and since December 31. These fluctuations in value are shown in percentages, which means you can compare the gains or losses of different fund categories. For example, the strongest performance here is in Emerging Markets funds, one of the smallest categories, and one that experienced significant losses the year before (though that information isn't provided in this chart).

Benchmarks for Mutual-Fund Investors

	ON A TOTAL RETURN BASIS				
	YEAR-TO-DATE	FOUR WEEKS	ONE YEAR	3 YRS (annualized)	5 YRS (annualized)
DJIA (w/divs)	+ 17.37%	+ 11.02%	+ 18.93%	+ 26.75%	+ 26.77
S&P 500 (w/divs)	+ 10.95	+ 7.19	+ 21.93	+ 30.25	+ 27.52
Small-Co. Index Fund[1]	+ 1.82	+ 11.55	− 11.95	+ 10.23	+ 14.15
Lipper Index: Europe	+ 0.08	+ 3.23	− 1.51	+ 18.93	+ 16.05
Lipper Index: Pacific	+ 17.59	+ 11.84	+ 12.79	− 7.43	− 3.09
Lipper L-T Govt[2]	− 0.65	+ 0.22	+ 5.48	+ 7.01	+ 6.70

[1]Vanguard's: tracks Russell 2000   [2]Includes government agency de

PERFORMANCE YARDSTICKS

On Fridays, the **Performance Yardstick** table provides total return information for 32 categories of funds, each with a different investment objective. This table shows how the groups of funds have performed—not only since December 31, but in various time frames over the past five years.

While it's the most recent market fluctuations that make the headlines, long-term performance is generally a far better indicator how well a category of funds is doing. For example, although Health & Biotech funds are down 0.65% from the beginning of the year, their annualized performance is up 22.31% over five years, second only to Science & Technology funds.

LIPPER INDEXES

Monday, May 3

Equity Indexes	Prelim. Close	Prev.	Wk ago	Dec. 31
Capital Appreciation ...	2487.38	+ 1.03	− 1.10	+ 11.00
Growth Fund	8579.99	+ 1.10	− 1.23	+ 8.93
Small Cap Fund	630.55	+ 0.41	− 0.38	+ 1.21
Growth & Income	7578.03	+ 1.70	+ 1.76	+ 10.58
Equity Income Fd	3959.37	+ 1.67	+ 2.46	+ 8.99
Science and Tech Fd ...	831.63	+ 0.12	− 4.42	+ 13.00
International Fund	725.90	+ 0.29	+ 1.30	+ 6.30
Gold Fund	79.05	+ 1.65	+ 8.67	+ 11.30
Balanced Fund	4497.78	+ 0.09	+ 0.44	+ 5.97
Emerging Markets	75.46	+ 1.12	+ 3.27	+ 24.32
Bond Indexes				
Corp A-Rated Debt	800.91	− 0.01	− 0.38	− 0.41
US Government	302.64	− 0.01	− 0.38	− 0.86
GNMA	329.43	− 0.00	− 0.10	+ 1.00
High Current Yield.....	811.66	− 0.00	+ 0.18	+ 5.83
Intmdt Inv Grade	221.71	− 0.00	− 0.33	− 0.08
Short Inv Grade	201.52	+ 0.05	− 0.01	+ 1.36
General Muni Debt......	579.21	− 0.02	+ 0.09	+ 0.79
High Yield Municipal ..	281.84	− 0.02	+ 0.01	+ 1.16
Short Municipal	122.70	− 0.02	+ 0.01	+ 1.10
Global Income	210.80	− 0.06	+ 0.01	− 0.75
International Income...	138.63	− 0.16	− 0.06	− 2.75

Indexes are based on the largest funds within the same investment objective and do not include multiple share classes of similar funds. The Yardsticks table, appearing with Friday's listings, includes all funds with the same objective. Source: Lipper Inc. The Lipper Funds Inc. are not affiliated with Lipper Inc.

Ranges for investment companies, with daily price data supplied by the National Association of Securities Dealers and performance and cost calculations by Lipper Inc. The NASD requires a mutual fund to have at least 1,000 shareholders and net assets of $25 million before being listed. NAV-Net Asset Value. Detailed explanatory notes appear elsewhere on this page.

Performance Yardsticks
How Fund Categories Stack Up

Benchm

INVESTMENT OBJECTIVE	ON A TOTAL RETURN BASIS				
	YEAR-TO-DATE	FOUR WEEKS	ONE YEAR	3 YRS (annualized)	5 YRS (annualized)
Capital Appreciation	+ 10.03%	+ 8.70%	+ 14.77%	+ 17.75%	+ 17.47%
Growth	+ 9.15	+ 7.00	+ 16.47	+ 23.51	+ 22.22
Small-Cap Stock	− 0.23	+ 10.30	− 12.80	+ 8.31	+ 13.82
Mid-Cap Stock	+ 5.17	+ 9.91	+ 3.01	+ 14.82	+ 17.62
Growth & Income	+ 8.42	+ 7.55	+ 11.10	+ 22.86	+ 21.70
Equity Income	+ 6.50	+ 7.42	+ 6.23	+ 19.68	+ 18.93
Global (inc U.S.)	+ 6.35	+ 6.63	+ 2.54	+ 13.06	+ 13.15
International (non U.S.)	+ 4.64	+ 5.00	− 0.39	+ 9.09	+ 8.46
European Region	− 0.52	+ 3.10	− 3.77	+ 17.18	+ 15.64
Latin America	+ 23.37	+ 18.15	− 26.56	+ 1.49	− 0.46
Pacific Region	+ 19.10	+ 13.82	+ 11.35	− 8.46	− 4.23
Emerging Markets	+ 18.07	+ 13.07	− 20.67	− 6.12	− 3.56
Science & Technology	+ 23.55	+ 11.64	+ 52.14	+ 27.99	+ 27.10
Health & Biotech	− 0.65	+ 1.60	+ 9.73	+ 14.75	+ 22.31
Natural Resources	+ 18.87	+ 13.45	− 16.27	+ 2.32	
Gold	+ 3.95	+ 5.67	− 23.91		
Utility	+ 2.63	+ 4.08	+ 10.90		
Balanced	+ 4.87	+ 4.66	+ 9.14		
Intermediate Corp. Debt	+ 0.02	+ 0.31	+ 5.67		
Intermediate Govt	− 0.41	+ 0.24	+ 5.86		
Long-Term Govt.	− 1.16	+ 0.16	+ 5.6		
High-Yield Taxable					

DJIA (w/divs)
S&P 500 (w/divs
Small-Co. Index
Lipper Index: Eu
Lipper Index: Pa
Lipper L-T Gov

'Vanguard's:

LEADER
Fidelity
Fidelity
Amer
Va

PERFORMANCE GRAPHS

Every weekday, a feature called the **Fund Performance Derby** provides a snapshot of the 12-month performance of a particular type of fund in relation to a relevant benchmark, when one exists, and to the performance of one or more related but different categories of fund.

Growth funds, for example, are presented in relation to the S&P 500, whose performance it closely resembles, and to small-cap funds, which are also growth funds but buy stock in smaller companies than the funds described simply as growth.

This visual information helps put a category's performance into perspective, giving you a sense of its overall movement. And it can help you evaluate where individual funds within the category fall: Is their performance stronger, weaker or about the same as the overall average?

THE EFFECT OF FEES

Performance figures for the funds include all asset-based fees the fund charges for management and other expenses. The higher the fees a specific fund charges, the more difficult it may be for its performance to equal or surpass the results for other funds in that category.

You can get a sense of the relative expense of each fund in The Wall Street Journal's regular mutual fund reviews. That information is provided in the final column of information for each fund, under the heading Expense ratio. Experts point out that even half a percentage point can make a significant difference over time.

The information is most relevant when you compare two funds with the same or similar investment objectives. For example, index funds typically have low fees, and international equity funds have high ones.

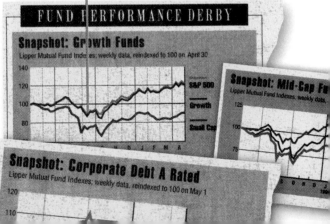

FUND PERFORMANCE DERBY

Snapshot: Growth Funds
Lipper Mutual Fund Indexes, weekly data, reindexed to 100 on April 30

S&P 500
Growth
Small Cap

Snapshot: Mid-Cap Fu
Lipper Mutual Fund Indexes, weekly data,

Snapshot: Corporate Debt A Rated
Lipper Mutual Fund Indexes, weekly data, reindexed to 100 on May 1

Tracking Fund Performance

There are several formulas for measuring mutual fund performance. The bottom line is whether the fund is meeting your investment goals.

Whether a mutual fund aims for current income, long-term growth or a combination of the two, there are three ways to track its performance and judge whether or not it is profitable. Investors can evaluate a fund by:

- Following changes in share price, or **net asset value (NAV)**
- Figuring **yield**
- Calculating **total return**

You can compare a fund's performance to similar funds offered by different companies, or you can evaluate the fund in relation to other ways the money could have been invested—stocks or bonds, for example.

Because return is figured differently for each type of investment, there isn't a simple formula for comparing funds to individual securities.

NAV CHANGE

$$\frac{\text{Value of fund}}{\text{Number of shares}} = \text{NAV}$$

for example

$$\frac{\$52,500,000}{3,500,000} = \$15$$

A fund's **NAV** is the dollar value of one share of the fund's stock. It's figured by dividing the current value of the fund by the number of its outstanding shares. A fund's NAV increases when the value of its holdings increases. For example, if a share of a stock fund costs $15 today and $9 a year ago, it means the value of its holdings increased about 66% per share, and you could sell at a profit.

YIELD

$$\frac{\text{Distribution per share}}{\text{Price per share}} = \text{Yield (\%)}$$

for example

$$\frac{\$.58}{\$10.00} = 5.8\,\%$$

Yield measures the amount of income a fund provides as a percentage of its NAV. A long-term bond fund with an NAV of $10 paying a 58-cent income distribution per share provides a 5.8% yield. You can compare the yield on a mutual fund with the current yield on comparable investments to decide which is providing a stronger return. Bond fund performance, for example, is often tracked in relation to individual bonds (see pages 86-87), or bond indexes.

TOTAL RETURN

$$\frac{\text{Change in value + dividends}}{\text{Cost of initial investment}} = \frac{\text{Total}}{\text{Return (\%)}}$$

for example

$$\frac{\$1,250}{\$8,000} = 15.6\%$$

A fund's **total return** is the annual amount your mutual fund investment changes in value plus the distributions the fund pays on that investment. It's typically reported as **percentage return**, figured by dividing the dollar value of the total return by the amount of the initial investment. For example, an $8,000 investment with a one-year total return of $1,250 ($1,000 increase in value plus $250 in reinvested distributions) has an annual percentage return of 15.6%.

WATCHING RETURN

The most accurate measure of a mutual fund's past and current performance is its **total return**, or its increase in value plus its reinvested distributions. Total return is reported for several time periods, typically for as long as the fund has been in operation. When the figure is for periods longer than a year, the number is annualized, or converted to an annual figure by dividing the total return over the period by the number of years.

While there's no guarantee that a fund's future performance will equal its current or past record, many experts point to a strong total return history as one reasonable basis on which to make an investment decision.

Among the key factors that influence total return are the direction of the overall market or markets in which the fund is invested, the performance of the fund's portfolio of investments, and the fund's fees and expenses.

Mutual Fund Scorecard/Growth

INVESTMENT OBJECTIVE: Capital growth without regard for income; usually characterized by moderate portfolio turnover. Bull/Bear ratings are figured over the latest two rising and two falling market cycles

ASSETS MAR. 31 (in millions)	PAST PERFORMANCE BULL MKTS	BEAR MKTS	FUND NAME	TOTAL RETURN¹ IN PERIOD ENDING APRIL 29 4 WEEKS	52 WEEKS	5 YEARS*
TOP 15 PERFORMERS						
35.0	**	**	Grand Prix Fund	−0.60%	111.27%	**%
1.9	**	**	Thurlow Growth²	7.51	96.39	**
8.2	**	**	Millennium Growth²	2.69	77.10	**
5.9	**	**	Nich-App:Lg Cp Gr;I²ʾ⁴	4.30	68.04	**
20.1	**	**	Pilgrim:Lg Cp Gr;B²ʾ⁴	4.10	65.77	**
250.8	**	**	WM:Growth;A⁴	4.22	65.10	29.03
251.5	**	**	Excelsior:Large Cap Grow²	0.28	63.42	**
87.7	**	**	Excelsior Inst:Opt Gr;In²ʾ⁴ʾ⁵	−1.80	62.75	**
BOTTOM 10 PERFORMERS						
0.4	**	**	Pauze:Tombstone;A³ʾ⁴	24.19%	−44.81%	**
0.1	**	**	Hudson Investors Fund²	−0.26	−37.46	**
41.6	**	**	Texas Cap:Value & Growth³	4.73	−35.25	**
1569.5	Med	Med	Merrill Growth Fund;B²ʾ⁴	−4.03	−33.06	6.43
	**	**	Lighthouse Cont			
10.6	**	**	Reserve Prv:Blue Chp;R²ʾ⁴	1.09	48.22	**
AVG. FOR CATEGORY				2.74%	15.31%	21.07%
NUMBER OF FUNDS				1169	1022	385

KEEPING SCORE

Every weekday, The Wall Street Journal publishes a **Mutual Fund Scorecard** highlighting a particular category of fund from among the 32 categories it covers. The Scorecard provides performance statistics for the top 15 and bottom 10 performers in the category, ranked by their total return over the past 52 weeks, as well as the average returns for the category and the number of funds it includes. In this case, that's currently 1,169 funds—147 more than a year ago.

The chart reports each fund's assets, or the amount it is investing. The size of a fund can have a major impact on its performance record, since the larger a fund grows, the more difficult it can be to trade enough shares rapidly enough to take advantage of changes in the marketplace.

You can also gauge the funds' performance in the two most recent up and down—or bull and bear—cycles, if the funds have been in operation long enough to have that kind of history.

The growth funds featured in this example invest in stocks expected to provide significant increase in value but little, if any, current income. The top-ranking fund, the Grand Prix, had a total return more than double the fund that was ranked fifteenth over the past year, though it is down over the past four weeks. And like most of the funds in the category, it has a short track record.

In contrast, the funds with the weakest records have all had a negative return—a loss—over the year, though some have done well in the past few weeks.

The Prospectus

The prospectus provides a detailed roadmap of a fund—covering everything from its objective and fees to its portfolio holdings and manager.

Mutual funds are tightly regulated by the Securities and Exchange Commission (SEC). The SEC requires all mutual funds to publish a prospectus and issue a copy to potential investors before they buy or with the confirmation of an initial investment. The prospectus must explain the fund's objectives, management, fees and past performance, and provide details of its operation.

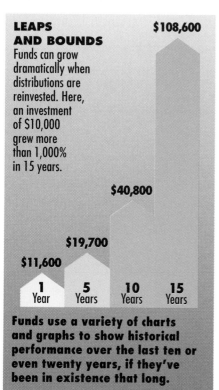

LEAPS AND BOUNDS

$108,600

Funds can grow dramatically when distributions are reinvested. Here, an investment of $10,000 grew more than 1,000% in 15 years.

$40,800

$19,700

$11,600

| 1 Year | 5 Years | 10 Years | 15 Years |

Funds use a variety of charts and graphs to show historical performance over the last ten or even twenty years, if they've been in existence that long.

A FUND'S OPERATIONS

A fund's prospectus explains the programs and policies the fund's management uses to achieve its investment goals.

As an investor, you have the right to vote on changes a fund proposes in its underlying financial policies, including the amount of money it can **leverage**, or borrow to make additional investments. Since mutual fund investors are actually shareholders of the fund, you vote in the same way corporate shareholders do, either in person at the annual meeting, by proxy or online. And you vote on major issues, not on day-to-day matters like the fee structure.

FEES

A summary of fees and expenses usually appears near the beginning of the prospectus. The fees can range anywhere from a low of 0.2% up to 8.5%, with bond and index funds at the bottom and international equity and emerging market funds at the top.

Here are the types of fees you're likely to run into:

Sales charges, also known as loads, are levied by some, but not all, funds. The charges are typically figured as a percentage of the amount you invest. **Front-end loads**, charged at the time you purchase your shares, are the most common. Or you may pay a **back-end load**, also known as a contingent deferred sales charge, when you sell shares during the first few years after purchase. A third type, known as a **level load**, has no front- or back-end charges but imposes annual fees each year you own the fund.

When a fund offers you a choice of when to pay the sales charge, it typically identifies front-end loads as Class A shares, back-end loads as Class B shares and level-loads as Class C shares.

Redemption charges are a type of back-end load some fund companies charge on certain of their funds to discourage frequent in-and-out trading.

Marketing fees (called **12b-1 fees**) cover marketing and advertising expenses, and are sometimes used to pay employee bonuses. About half of the mutual funds charge these fees.

Exchange fees can apply when money is shifted from one fund to another within the same mutual fund company.

PORTFOLIO TURNOVER RATE

All open-end mutual funds trade securities regularly—some more regularly than others. A fund's **portfolio turnover rate** reveals how much buying and selling is going on. The range can be enormous, with some funds turning over more than 100% annually. In general, high turnovers mean higher stockbroker expenses. That means the fund needs higher returns to offset the cost.

THE NUTS AND BOLTS

The prospectus also tells you how to buy and sell shares in the fund, as well as how to use all the fund's services.

Minimum investments exist for most funds. A higher amount is required for opening an account than for adding to it. Sometimes the minimum initial investment is as low as $500, sometimes as high as several thousand dollars.

Investment options let you buy online, over the phone, by mail, through a broker or with automatic direct deposit.

Reinvestment options let you decide what to do with the money you earn. You can plow your distributions back into the fund, take the money in cash or some combination of the two.

Exchange services let you transfer money from one fund to another.

Redemption options provide lots of ways for you to get your money out of the fund. They include checks, wire transfers, electronic transfers and automatic withdrawal plans.

Check-writing privileges let you use checks to redeem your holdings or pay your bills. However, redeeming stock and bond funds by check has tax consequences, since there's always a profit or loss on the investment. Money market funds are the only ones that really work like checking accounts.

AND THE GADGETS

Most funds have automated telephone services that provide 24-hour information on every detail of an account. By using a series of codes, you can find out a fund's balance, current yield, price and dividends. The same information is available through several different computer programs. And as the digital revolution expands, the information options will undoubtedly follow suit.

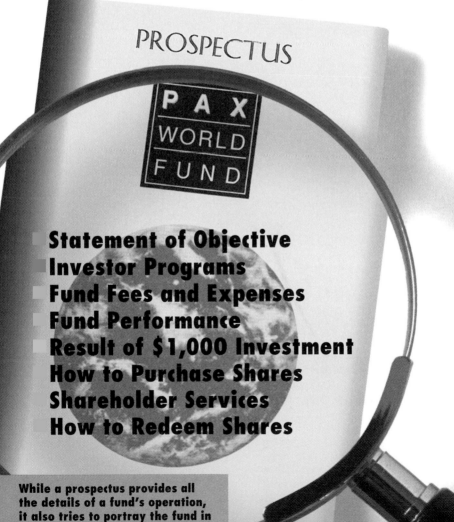

PROSPECTUS

PAX
WORLD
FUND

■ **Statement of Objective**
■ **Investor Programs**
■ **Fund Fees and Expenses**
■ **Fund Performance**
■ **Result of $1,000 Investment**
■ **How to Purchase Shares**
■ **Shareholder Services**
■ **How to Redeem Shares**

While a prospectus provides all the details of a fund's operation, it also tries to portray the fund in the best possible terms. Smart investors carefully sift through all the information.

International Funds

If someone needed to invent a reason for the existence of mutual funds, investing abroad might be the best one.

The number of mutual funds that invest in overseas markets has multiplied rapidly over the past ten years. In addition to diversification, professional management and ease of investing, overseas funds give even small investors access to markets they couldn't enter on their own. There are overseas stock funds, bond funds and money market funds to appeal to a variety of interests. While they're often referred to generically as international funds, there are actually four specific categories of funds: **international**, **global**, **regional** and **country**.

INTERNATIONAL FUNDS

Also known as **overseas funds**, international funds invest exclusively in stock or bond markets outside the U.S. By spreading investments throughout the world, these funds balance risk by owning securities not only in mature, slow-growing economies but also in the more volatile economies of emerging nations.

GLOBAL FUNDS

Also called **world funds**, these funds include U.S. stocks or bonds in their portfolios as well as those from other countries. The manager moves the assets around, depending on which markets are doing best at the time. That means that the percentage invested in U.S. stocks can wary widely, depending on their performance in comparison with others around the world.

Despite what the name suggests, global funds often invest up to 75% of their assets in U.S. companies.

REGIONAL FUNDS

These funds focus on a particular geographic area, like the Pacific Rim, Latin America or Europe. Many mutual fund companies that began by offering international or global funds have added regional funds to capitalize on the growing interest in overseas investing and on the strength of particular parts of the world economy.

Like the more broad-based funds, regional funds invest in several different countries so that even if one market is in the doldrums, the others may be booming.

Regional funds tend to focus on groups of smaller countries or emerging markets, where one country may not issue enough securities to make a single country fund viable.

EUROPE

THE RISK OVERSEAS

When you put money into overseas funds, you don't have to deal directly with currency fluctuations or calculating foreign taxes—they're handled by the fund. But the value of any fund that invests in other countries is directly affected not only by market conditions but by exchange rates.

Overseas **bond funds** are less dependable than U.S. funds as income producers because changes in the dollar's value directly affect the fund's earnings. If a bond fund is earning high interest, but the country's currency is weak against the dollar, the yield is less. For example, if a fund earns £100 when £1 equals $2, the yield is $200. But if the pound drops in value, and £1 equals $1.50, the yield is only $150.

Equity funds are somewhat less vulnerable to currency fluctuation because they profit from capital gains. So if international markets are paying high dividends, a U.S. investor can make money, especially when the dollar is weak. However, if the dollar strengthened by 10% during a year that an overseas stock fund gained 10%, there would be no profit. And if the dollar strengthened by 20%—which may happen as part of the regular ebb and flow of international markets—you would actually have a loss of 10%.

COUNTRY FUNDS

These funds allow you to concentrate your investments in a single overseas country—even countries whose markets are closed to individual investors who aren't citizens. When a fund does well, other funds are set up for the same country, so that there may be many funds all investing in the same country. Many single-country funds are closed-end funds that are traded through a broker once they have been established.

By buying stocks and bonds in a single country, you can reap the benefits of a healthy, well-established economy, or profit from the rapid economic growth as emerging markets start to industrialize or expand their export markets. The risk of investing in emerging country funds, however, is that their value may be eroded in the event of political or economic turmoil.

Closed-end funds that buy big blocks of shares in a country's industries can influence share prices and sometimes corporate policy—just as institutional investors do when they buy U.S. stocks.

GERMANY

INTERNATIONAL INDEX FUNDS

Like other index funds, international index funds attempt to produce the results you would get if you owned all the stocks in a particular index. The Morgan Stanley Capital International Europe, Australasia, Far East Index (EAFE), for example, follows around 1,000 stocks from around the world.

International index funds are an easy way to start investing in overseas markets. And they generally have smaller sales charges than other types of funds that invest abroad. But, particularly in more volatile markets, index funds may not produce results as strong as those funds run by managers who are constantly monitoring their holdings.

Futures and Options

Futures and options are complex and volatile but also useful investments.

FUTURES ARE OBLIGATIONS TO BUY OR SELL a specific commodity—such as corn, gold or Treasury bonds—on a specific day for a preset price.

(Calendar note: JUNE — pchs'd gold options (June 1); Gold options expire must trade or let go! (June 16); WHEAT FUTURES EXPIRE—trade or they're mine! (June 24))

OPTIONS ARE THE RIGHT TO BUY OR SELL a specific item—such as stocks, precious metals or Treasury bonds—for a preset price during a specified period of time.

DERIVATIVE INVESTMENTS

One reason futures and options are complex is that they're **derivative** investments. Instead of representing shares of ownership—like stocks—or the promise of loan repayment—like bonds—each futures contract and option is once or twice removed from an underlying product. A feeder cattle futures contract, for instance, is a bet on the way cattle prices will move. What happens to the cattle itself interests ranchers and meat packers but not most of the investors who buy the contract. One step further removed, an option on the feeder cattle futures contract interests only investors who want to speculate on the direction of cattle prices, not those who buy or sell the cattle.

REDUCING THE RISK

For some, futures and options can be ways to reduce risk. Farmers who commit themselves to sell grain at a good price are protected if prices drop. Investors who sell options on stock they own can offset some of their losses if the market collapses.

Most investors trade futures and options to take risk because the possibility of a big loss is offset by the opportunity for a huge gain. But individual investors are usually small players in the futures and options markets because the stakes are high and the returns are unpredictable.

LEVERAGE ENHANCES RISK

Leverage, in financial terms, means using a small amount of money to make an investment of much greater value. You can buy a **futures contract** worth thousands of dollars with an initial investment of about 10% of the total value. For example, if you buy a gold contract worth $35,000 (when gold is $350 an ounce) you would put up about $3,500.

That's your **good faith deposit** and gives you leverage over 100 ounces of gold.

A $3,500 INVESTMENT

BUYS A $35,000 CONTRACT

100oz. GOLD

|← LEVERAGE →|
OF
10 to 1

When Leverage Works

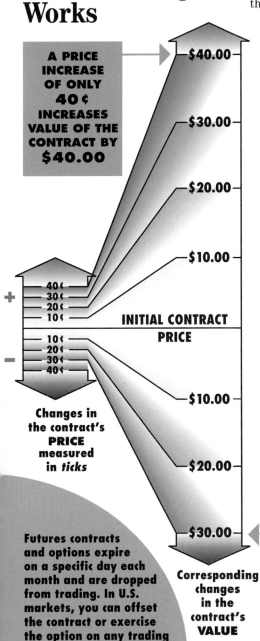

A PRICE INCREASE OF ONLY 40 ¢ INCREASES VALUE OF THE CONTRACT BY $40.00

$40.00

$30.00

$20.00

$10.00

40¢
30¢
20¢
10¢

+

INITIAL CONTRACT PRICE

−

10¢
20¢
30¢
40¢

$10.00

Changes in the contract's PRICE measured in *ticks*

$20.00

$30.00

Futures contracts and options expire on a specific day each month and are dropped from trading. In U.S. markets, you can offset the contract or exercise the option on any trading day before it expires.

Corresponding changes in the contract's VALUE

With a commodity as volatile as gold, price swings of $100 within the lifespan of the contract are entirely possible. So, if the price went up $100, to $450 an ounce, the value of your investment would jump $10,000—almost a 300% gain on your $3,500. Every time the price of an ounce of gold gained ten cents, the value of the contract would increase by $10, as the illustration to the left shows.

But, of course, the opposite can happen. If the price fell and the value of your investment dropped 300%, it could cost you more than $10,000—sometimes a lot more—to make good on the loss. So, while leverage makes the initial commitment easy, the way derivative investing works means you could have major losses.

CREATED TO EXPIRE

While futures and options are deals for the future, the future they're talking about isn't very far away. Futures contracts on grains and other food sources generally expire within a year, though it is possible to find contracts on certain financial futures—like Eurodollars—that last five years.

Options normally expire within a year or less. But **Long-term Equity Anticipation Securities (LEAPS)**, linked to stocks or stock indexes, can trade for up to 36 months.

When Leverage Hurts

A PRICE DECREASE OF ONLY 30 ¢ DECREASES VALUE OF THE CONTRACT BY $30.00

Commodities

Modern life depends on raw materials—the products that keep people and businesses going. Anticipating what they'll cost fuels the futures market.

Commodities are raw materials: the wheat in bread, the silver in earrings, the oil in gasoline and a thousand other products. Most producers and users buy and sell commodities in the **cash market**, commonly known as the **spot market** because the full cash price is paid on the spot.

DETERMINING CASH PRICES

Commodity prices are based on **supply and demand**. If a commodity is plentiful, its price will be low. If it's hard to come by, the price will be high.

Supply and demand for many commodities move in fairly predictable seasonal cycles. Tomatoes are cheapest in the summer when they're plentiful (and most flavorful), and most expensive in the winter when they're out of season. Soup manufacturers plan their production season to take advantage of the highest-quality tomatoes at the lowest prices.

But it doesn't always work that way. If a drought wipes out the Midwest's wheat crop, cash prices for wheat surge because bakers buy up what's available to avoid a short-term crunch. Or if political turmoil in the Middle East threatens the oil supply, prices at the gas pumps jump in anticipation of supply problems.

MINIMIZING FUTURE RISK

Since people don't know when such disasters will occur, they can't plan for them. That's why **futures contracts** were invented—to help businesses minimize risk. A baker with a futures contract to buy wheat for $3.20 a bushel is protected if the spot price jumps to $3.70—at least for that purchase.

Farmers, loggers and other commodity producers can only estimate the demand for their products and try to plan accordingly. But they can get stung by too much supply and too little demand—or the reverse. Similarly, manufacturers have to take orders for future delivery without knowing the cost of the raw materials they will need to make their products. That's why they buy futures contracts in the products they make or use: to smooth out the unexpected price bumps.

What's in a Contract and What Can Affect Its Price

PRICES RISE WHEN

Bad weather ruins U.S. wheat crop

WHAT THE CONTRACT IS FOR AND WHAT IT COSTS

ONE WHEAT CONTRACT IS 5,000 BUSHELS

If wheat is $3.20 a bushel, one contract is worth **$16,000**

PRICES FALL WHEN

Russia has bumper crop of wheat

CASH PRICES AS CLUES

The derivative markets watch cash prices closely. The price of a futures contract for next month, or five months from now, is based on today's prices, seasonal expectations, anticipated changes in the weather, the political scene and dozens of other factors, including what the market will bear.

The fluctuation in cash prices provides clues to what consumers can expect to pay in the marketplace for products made from the raw materials.

FINANCIAL COMMODITIES

Though we don't think of dollars or yen or Treasury bonds as commodities, they really are. Money is the raw material of trade, both domestic and international. What the interest rate will be next summer, or what the dollar will be worth against the euro, concerns people whose businesses depend on the money supply, or on what imported materials will cost. They use futures to hedge against sudden changes in rates or currency values.

However, institutional traders, rather than individuals, do the bulk of financial futures trading, both on futures exchanges and in private, over-the-counter transactions.

While the same forces of supply and demand affect the shopper in the supermarket or the driver at the gas pumps, the futures market doesn't deal in five pounds of sugar or ten gallons of gas. Efficiency demands that commodities be sold in large quantities.

Mideast turmoil causes oil shortage

Insects ravage cane crops

Pound gains in value against dollar

ONE GASOLINE CONTRACT IS 42,000 GALLONS

If gasoline is 54.93¢ a gallon, one contract is worth
$23,071

ONE SUGAR CONTRACT IS 112,000 POUNDS

If sugar is 21.33¢ per pound, one contract is worth
$ 23,890

ONE STERLING CONTRACT IS 62,500 POUNDS

If a pound is selling at $1.5050, one contract is worth
$94,062.50

Oil producers increase output

Health fad causes drop in sugar consumption

Falling interest rates in U.K. lower pound's appeal

CASH PRICES

GRAINS AND FEEDS

	Wed	Tues	Yr.Ago
Barley, top-quality Mpls., bu	2.00- 55	2.00- 50	2.22½
Bran, wheat middlings, KC ton	69.-71.0	67.-69.0	63.00
Corn, No. 2 yel. Cent. Ill. bu	bp2.17	2.21	2.20½
Corn Gluten Feed, Midwest, ton ..	66.-89.0	c66.-89.0	100.00
Cottonseed Meal,			
Clksdle, Miss. ton	185.-190.	190.-192½	157.50
Hominy Feed, Cent. Ill. ton	58.00	60.00	71.00
Meat-Bonemeal, 50% pro. Ill. ton.	230.00	230.-235.	220.00
Oats, No. 2 milling, Mpls., bu	1.49¾-64¾	153¼-66¼	1.57
Sorghum, (Milo) No. 2 Gulf cwt ...	4.30	4.37	4.2¢
Soybean Meal,			
Cent. Ill., 44% protein-ton	195.-197.	197½-201½	
Soybean Meal,			
Cent. Ill., 48% protein-ton	208.-211.	211½-21?¢	
Soybeans, No. 1 yel Cent.-Ill. bu ..	bp6.47		
Wheat,			
Spring 14%-pro Mpls			

As the chart shows, the price range for bran increased Wednesday from the level on Tuesday—and both are higher than last year's price. So cereal lovers might reasonably expect to pay more for raisin bran next fall. But the other prices illustrate that the cash market in each product operates independently of the others.

The Futures Exchanges

Futures are traded on exchanges that offer markets in everything from pork bellies to stock indexes.

Futures contracts linked to a range of commodities and financial products are traded on nine futures exchanges in the U.S., on exchanges in Europe and Asia, and in hundreds of private, over-the-counter transactions arranged for specific clients through banks, brokerage firms and other financial institutions.

Typically, exchange-traded contracts are traded only on the exchange that issues them, and attract both individual and institutional investors. Private contracts, on the other hand, are almost always commercial arrangements.

HOW TRADING WORKS

Orders sent to the floor of a U.S. exchange are filled by **open outcry**. That means every order to buy or sell is called out publicly, in an auction process called **price discovery**. It also means that the trading process can be boisterous.

Increasingly, however, buying and selling is handled by electronic trading systems developed by the exchanges, in part to keep their products competitive with those on overseas markets where electronic, continuous trading is already well established.

Sometimes an exchange's electronic system operates side-by-side with the open outcry session, but the computer-based systems are also open for business virtually around the clock. The Project A trading system at the Chicago Board of Trade, for example, is open 22 hours a day and handles its greatest volume in the early morning hours, when there's no open outcry.

THE COST OF TRADING

Exchange traders charge their clients commissions to execute their orders. Unlike the commissions on stock transactions, one for buying and another for selling, futures brokers charge only once, called a **round-turn commission**, to open and close a position. Commissions and other fees are typically higher than stock trades, often 18% or more of the cost of the transaction, instead of 2% or less.

MARKET REGULATION

The Commodities Futures Trading Commission (CFTC) is the federal watchdog agency responsible for monitoring the activity on the various exchanges. It does for futures trading what the SEC does for stock transactions. The exchanges themselves also scrutinize trading and enforce regulations through the **National Futures Association (NFA)**.

Exchanges provide speedy clearing of trades, an accurate record of prices, trading limits to prevent excessive price fluctuations both for floor and electronic transactions, and a system to assure that an investor's obligations to buy or sell are met. However, since over-the-counter trading isn't regulated, those protections can't be guaranteed.

Where the Exchanges Are

The U.S. futures exchanges whose trading is reported in The Wall Street Journal are located in four different cities. Each one specializes in particular commodities.

CHICAGO

CBT Chicago Board of Trade: grains, Treasury bonds and notes, precious metals, financial indexes

CME Chicago Mercantile Exchange: meat and livestock, currency

MCE MidAmerica Commodity Exchange: financial futures, currency, livestock, grain, precious metals

KANSAS CITY

KC Kansas City Board of Trade: grains, livestock and meats, food and fiber, stock indexes

MINNEAPOLIS

MPLS Minneapolis Grain Exchange

NEW YORK

CTN, NYFE, FINEX New York Cotton Exchange and its divisions New York Futures Exchange and Financial Instrument Exchange: cotton, orange juice, foreign currency, Treasurys, stock indexes

CSCE Coffee, Sugar and Cocoa Exchange: coffee, sugar and cocoa

NYM, CMX-COMEX New York Mercantile Exchange and its division Commodity Exchange: financial futures, precious metals, copper

How They Work

Exchange floors are divided into pits where the actual trading occurs. To impose some order, each commodity is usually traded in one specific area on the floor, although pits for soybeans, gold and even stock index futures may stand side-by-side. **Options** on the futures contracts (see page 147) always trade in an area next to the corresponding futures trading area.

A **trading pit** is shaped like a ring and tiered into three or four levels. During heavy activity, traders jockey for position to see over the heads of the traders in front of them. Some pits are divided into sections so several different commodities can be traded at the same time.

Trades are recorded on **trading cards**, which create a written record of the details of a transaction, or they're keyed into a hand-held computer. Using these records, the exchange's **clearing house** has the responsibility to guarantee that an agreement between a buyer and a seller is fulfilled. The trading cards are picked up by pit reporters, who time-stamp them and send the information, via computer, to the clearing house.

Brokerage firm traders and some individual members, called **locals**, can work on the trading floor. While all market players have indirect access to the trading floor through a broker, only members of the exchange can actually trade on the floor.

Large **electronic display boards** circle the trading floor. They're constantly updated with new trade data, which is simultaneously sent out to the rest of the world by quote machine.

Trading Futures Contracts

You don't need to invest much to enter a futures contract, but you need nerve—and luck—to ride this financial roller coaster.

To trade futures, you give an order to buy or sell a commodity on a particular date in the future—such as October wheat, December pork bellies, or June Eurodollars. The price is determined in trading on the exchange where there's a market in that commodity.

The cost of the contract is what the commodity will be worth if it is delivered. But the price of buying the contract is only a fraction (2% to 10%, depending on who the client is) of that total. It's paid as a good faith deposit, called the **initial margin**. For example, a contract for 5,000 bushels of wheat is $17,500 if wheat is $3.50 a bushel. The initial margin required would be about $1,750.

AFTER THE ORDER

When an order is filled, the contract typically goes into a pool at the exchange's clearing house with all the other filled orders. Buyers and sellers are anonymously paired. Since contracts are traded aggressively, the pairing process is always in motion.

Since the price of a contract changes continually throughout the day, the value of your account changes, too. At the end of each trading day, the clearing house moves money either in or out of its members' accounts, depending on the shifting worth of the contracts. The process is called **marking to market**. The financial effect on a portfolio is often dramatic, as shown below.

Winning and Losing with a Futures Contract

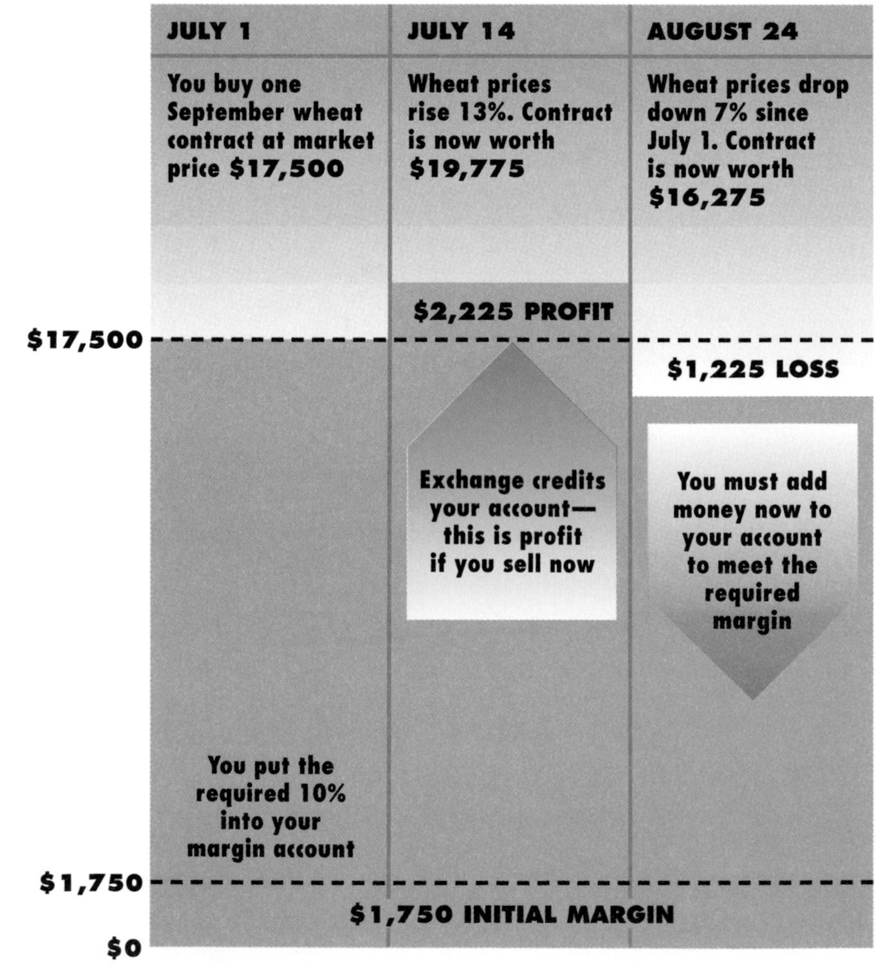

JULY 1	JULY 14	AUGUST 24
You buy one September wheat contract at market price $17,500	Wheat prices rise 13%. Contract is now worth $19,775	Wheat prices drop down 7% since July 1. Contract is now worth $16,275
	$2,225 PROFIT	
		$1,225 LOSS
	Exchange credits your account— this is profit if you sell now	You must add money now to your account to meet the required margin

$17,500

You put the required 10% into your margin account

$1,750

$1,750 INITIAL MARGIN

$0

THE LANGUAGE OF FUTURES

Futures trading involves contracts that cancel, or offset, each other: For every buy there's a sell and vice versa. The language of futures trading reflects this phenomenon.

To Enter the Market	Which Means	To Leave the Market	Which Means
GO LONG	ENTER A FUTURES CONTRACT TO **BUY**	**GO SHORT**	ENTER A FUTURES CONTRACT TO **SELL**
GO SHORT	ENTER A FUTURES CONTRACT TO **SELL**	**GO LONG**	ENTER A FUTURES CONTRACT TO **BUY**

MEETING THE MARGIN

Your margin level must be kept constant, in part to reassure the exchange that the terms of the contract will be met. If an account is down at the end of the day, it has to be brought up to the required margin level. For example, if wheat slipped from $3.50 to $3.25 a bushel, a 7% drop, the account value would drop by $1,225 (the decrease of 25 cents a bushel times 5,000 bushels). When that happens, you must add money to your account to bring it up to the required minimum.

Similarly, if the price of wheat dropped again the next day—perhaps on news of a bumper crop in Russia—the same thing would happen again. The original margin required could grow quickly to many thousands of dollars while the underlying value of the commodity continued to fall.

PROTECTING THE PRICE

The exchanges do have a mechanism, called **price limits**, to protect investors in a fast-moving market. If a contract price moves up or down to the pre-established price limit, the market locks up or locks down, and doesn't open for trading again until the price gets to an acceptable level.

In reality the lock-limit system often means that investors sustain huge losses or benefit from comparable gains because they are unable to sell a contract until the price has stabilized at the underlying commodity's new level. A suddenly devalued currency, for example, could send futures contracts on that currency into a tailspin. And when the dust clears, the value of the contract would probably be significantly lower than it had been when trading began.

> **When you go short, it's because you expect a contract's price to drop, or you're hedging a bet that it will rise. It's related to selling a stock short—which you do for similar reasons.**

LEAVING THE MARKET

Fewer than 2% of all futures contracts actually result in the transfer of goods. The remaining contracts have been **offset**, or neutralized, with a contract that carries the opposite obligation.

For example, if you buy a September wheat contract at $3.50 per bushel with a $1,750 margin payment, you expect the price to go up.

If the price of the contract climbs to $3.80 after a storm-plagued July week devastates the wheat crop, your account is credited with $1,500, and you're ahead of the game. You then sell a September wheat contract, which cancels your obligation to buy, and use your profit (minus commissions and other expenses) to invest in a different futures contract.

But it can work the other way, too. If prices drop and you're losing money, you may sell an offsetting contract at the best price you can get to cancel your obligation and get out of the market before your losses are any greater. Statistics suggest that between 75% and 90% of all futures traders lose money in a given year.

REDUCING TRADING RISKS

The strategy called **spread trading** is one of the techniques used by futures traders to reduce the risk of losing large sums of money from a sudden shudder in the market, though it also limits rewards.

Basically, it means buying one contract and selling another for the same commodity at the same time. One contract will usually make money, and the other one will lose. The key to ending up with a profit is getting the **spread**, or the difference between the two contracts' prices, to work in your favor. For example, if you lose money on a contract to sell but make money on a contract to buy, the difference between those prices is the spread. If it's five cents in your favor, you'd make $250 on the contract. If it's five cents against you, the $250 would be your loss.

Hedgers and Speculators

Futures have the reputation of being a game for high-risk speculators. But they perform the important function of stabilizing prices.

There are two distinct classes of players in the futures markets.

Hedgers are interested in the commodities. They can be producers, like farmers, mining companies, foresters and oil drillers. Or they can be users, like bakers, paper mills, jewelers and oil distributors. In general, producers sell futures contracts while users buy them.

Speculators, on the other hand, trade futures strictly to make money. If you trade futures but never use the commodity itself, you are a speculator. Speculators may either buy or sell contracts, depending on which way they think the market is going in a particular commodity.

HEDGER'S FARMSTAND

CORN *ALWAYS* **58¢** PER LB.

HOW HEDGERS USE THE MARKET

Hedgers are interested in protecting themselves against price changes that will undercut their profit. For example, a textile company may want to hedge against rising cotton prices as a result of boll weevil infestation. In August, the company buys 100 December cotton futures, representing five million pounds of cotton at 58 cents a pound.

During the fall, the cotton crop is infested and the prices shoot up. The December contract now trades at 68 cents. But the textile maker has hedged against exactly this situation. In December it can take delivery of cotton at 58 cents a pound, 10 cents less than the market price, and save $500,000 (10 cents times 5 million pounds).

Or the company can sell the futures contracts for 10 cents a pound more than it paid for them and use the profit to offset the higher price it will have to pay for cotton in the cash market. In either case, there's no nasty surprise in added commodity costs because the cash price and the futures price cancel each other out.

HOW SPECULATORS USE THE MARKET

Speculators hope to make money in the futures market by betting on price moves. A speculator may load up on orange juice futures in November, for instance, betting that if a freeze sets in and damages the Florida orange crop, prices of orange juice and the futures contracts based on them will soar.

If the speculators are right, and the winter is tough, the contracts on orange juice will be worth more than they paid. The speculators can sell their contracts at a profit. If they're wrong, and there's a bumper crop, the bottom will fall out of the market, and the speculators will be squeezed dry by falling prices.

costs in the event of a freeze, and orange farmers couldn't earn enough money in a good year to pay their production costs.

Speculators also keep the market active. If only those who produced or used the commodities were trading, there would not be enough activity to keep trading going. Buy and sell orders would be paired slowly, erasing the protection that hedgers get when the market responds quickly to changes in the cash market.

SPECULATORS ARE INDISPENSABLE

Speculators are crucial to the success of the futures market because they complete a symbiotic relationship between those wishing to avoid risk and those willing to take it.

Since hedgers, in planning ahead, want to avoid risk in what is undeniably a risky business, others have to be willing to accept it. Unless some speculators are willing to bet that orange juice prices will rise while others bet that prices will fall, an orange juice producer could not protect against dramatically increased

INFLUENCES ON FUTURES CONTRACT PRICES

The price of a futures contract is influenced by natural and political events (see page 126), but it's also affected by the economic news that the government releases, the length of time the contract has to run and by what speculators are doing and saying.

Virtually every day of every month, the government releases economic data, sells Treasury bills, or creates new policies that influence the price of futures contracts for both natural and financial commodities. News on new home sales, for example, directly influences the price of lumber futures, as hedgers and speculators try to pin the rise or fall of lumber sales to what the construction industry will be ordering.

If a producer agrees to hold a commodity for future delivery, the contract will reflect storage, insurance and other carrying costs to cover daily expenses until delivery. Generally, the further away the delivery date, the greater the carrying costs. Even so, prices rarely go up regularly in consecutive months. When the prices do increase this way, the relationship is called a **contango**.

Speculation also influences a commodity's price. Sudden demand for a contract—sparked by rumor, inside information or other factors—can drive its price sky-high. Or the reverse can happen when rumors or events make investors scramble to sell.

HEDGER'S WAY
THROUGH ROAD

- Avoid risk
- Protect against price changes

SPECULATOR'S LEAP
SCENIC OVERLOOK

- Accept risk
- Bet on large profits from price rises

Investing in futures and options is different from investing from stocks, bonds and mutual funds because futures and options markets are **zero sum markets**. That means for every dollar somebody makes (before commissions), somebody else loses a dollar. Put bluntly, that means that any gain is at somebody else's expense.

How Futures Work

Though they have different goals, hedgers and speculators are in the market together. What happens to the price of a contract affects them all.

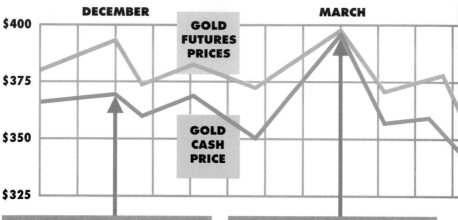

DECEMBER

GOLD IS $370 AN OUNCE IN THE CASH MARKET AND $385 FOR THE JUNE CONTRACT

In December, the price of gold in the cash market—what a buyer would pay for immediate delivery—is $15 less than the price of the June contract.

PRODUCERS (HEDGERS)

Gold producers hedge by selling futures contracts.

The gold producers sell June futures contracts because they won't have gold ready for delivery until then.

Earned in December sale $385

USERS (HEDGERS)

Gold users hedge by buying futures contracts.

The gold users buy June futures contracts because that's when they need the gold.

Cost of December buy   – $385

SPECULATORS

Speculators buy gold futures contracts if they think the price is going up.

Cost of December buy   – $385

MARCH

GOLD IS $395 AN OUNCE IN THE CASH MARKET. THE JUNE CONTRACT IS SELLING FOR $398

In March, the price of gold has gone up to $395 in the cash market. The June futures contract is selling for $398. The hedgers wait for the expiration date. Speculators sell offsetting contracts, thinking price has hit the top.

PRODUCERS (HEDGERS)

The producers can't sell their gold because it isn't ready yet.

BUYERS (HEDGERS)

This upswing in the cash price is exactly what the buyers were trying to protect themselves against.

SPECULATORS

The speculators sell, thinking gold has reached its peak. One clue is that the contract price is so close to the cash price. If speculators thought higher prices in the cash market were likely in the near future, they would be willing to pay higher prices for futures contracts.

This time the speculators made money in the market if they sold in March when the contract price reached its peak.

Price from March sell $398
Cost of December buy   –   385
Profit on trade $ 13

> Note that this example doesn't include commissions or other costs that would result from trading futures contracts, and it assumes that everyone bought one option at the same price.

JUNE

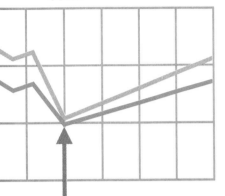

The oldest futures contracts date back to 17th-century Japan, when **rice tickets** provided landlords who collected rents in rice with a steady secondary income source. They sold warehouse receipts for their stored rice, giving the holder the right to a specific quantity of rice, of a specific quality, on a specific date in the future.

The merchants who paid for the tickets could cash them in at the appointed time or sell them at a profit to someone else. Like futures contracts today, the tickets themselves had no real worth, but they represented a way to make money on the underlying commodity—the rice.

JUNE

CONTRACTS EXPIRE WHEN GOLD IS $350 AN OUNCE IN THE CASH MARKET AND $352 IN THE FUTURES MARKET

In June, when the contract expires, both the producers and the users equalize their profit or loss in the futures market through offsetting trades in the cash market.

PRODUCERS (HEDGERS)

Because the price of the gold futures contract had dropped, the producers made money on the offsetting trade.

Earned in December sale	**$385**
Cost of June buy	**– 352**
Result of trade (profit)	**$ 33**

Even though producers had to sell their gold in the cash market for less than the anticipated price, the profit from their futures trades gave them the expected level of profit.

Earned in cash market	**$350**
Futures profit	**+ 33**
Gross profit	**$383**

USERS (HEDGERS)

THE GOLD USERS

The users lost money on the futures contracts because it cost more to sell the offsetting contacts than they had paid to buy.

Earned in June sell	**$352**
Cost of December buy	**– $385**
Result of trade (loss)	**– $ 33**

Since it cost the users less to buy gold in the cash market than they had expected, the total cost was what they anticipated.

Cost in cash market	**$350**
Cost of futures trade	**+ 33**
Actual cost of gold	**$383**

In any given futures contract, the profit or loss of the hedgers could be reversed, depending on the rise or fall of the futures price. In the end, however, their profit or loss in the futures trade would be offset by profit or loss in the cash market. The speculators could lose as frequently—maybe more frequently—than they gained, depending on changing prices and the timing with which they entered and left the market.

CORNERING THE MARKET

Some commodities traders aren't satisfied with the money they can make by betting on price fluctuations. They'd rather control prices by engineering a financial **corner**, or monopoly on the commodity itself. Frederick Phillipse has the dubious distinction of introducing the technique in North America. In 1666, he successfullly cornered the market on wampum—Native American money—by burying several barrels of it. Fur traders had to pay his prices to carry on their business.

Reading Futures Tables

For futures traders, daily price reports chronicle the changing value of their accounts. For others, they're a glimpse at future prices.

The tables reporting on futures markets show opening and closing prices, price history and volume of sales every trading day. Because the futures markets reflect current political and economic conditions, the charts also provide interesting commentary on the state of the economy and the way people feel it's headed.

Open is the opening price for sugar on the previous trading day. Depending on what's happened in the world overnight, the opening price may not be the same as the closing price the day before. Since prices are in cents per pound, the 22.37 means sugar opened for sale at 22.37 cents per pound. Multiplying this

amount by 112,000 pounds (the number of pounds in the contract) equals $25,054.40 per contract.

High, low and **settle** report the contract's highest, lowest and closing prices for the previous trading day. Taken together, they're a good indication of the commodity's market **volatility** during the trading day. Here the

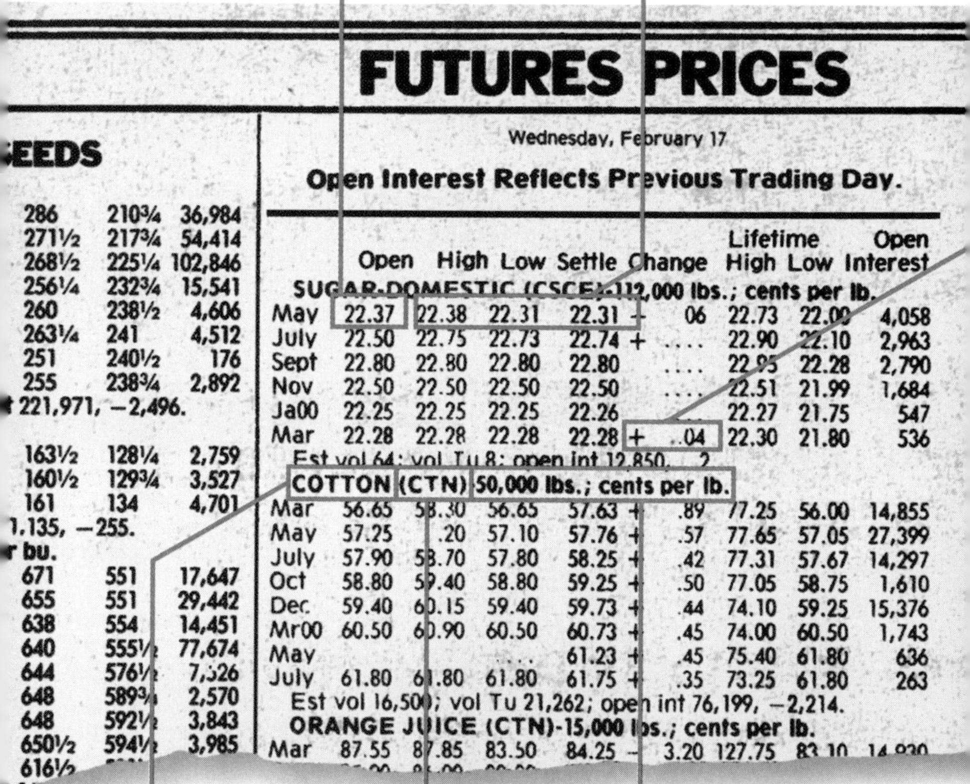

FUTURES PRICES

Wednesday, February 17

Open Interest Reflects Previous Trading Day.

SEEDS

286	210¾	36,984
271½	217¾	54,414
268½	225¼	102,846
256¼	232¾	15,541
260	238½	4,606
263¼	241	4,512
251	240½	176
255	238¾	2,892
221,971, −2,496.		
163½	128¼	2,759
160½	129¾	3,527
161	134	4,701
1,135, −255.		
r bu.		
671	551	17,647
655	551	29,442
638	554	14,451
640	555½	77,674
644	576½	7,326
648	589¾	2,570
648	592½	3,843
650½	594½	3,985
616½		

	Open	High	Low	Settle	Change	Lifetime High	Low	Open Interest
SUGAR-DOMESTIC (CSCE)-112,000 lbs.; cents per lb.								
May	22.37	22.38	22.31	22.31	− 06	22.73	22.00	4,058
July	22.50	22.75	22.73	22.74	+	22.90	22.10	2,963
Sept	22.80	22.80	22.80	22.80	....	22.95	22.28	2,790
Nov	22.50	22.50	22.50	22.50	....	22.51	21.99	1,684
Ja00	22.25	22.25	22.25	22.26		22.27	21.75	547
Mar	22.28	22.28	22.28	22.28	+ .04	22.30	21.80	536
Est vol 64; vol Tu 8; open int 12,850. 2								
COTTON (CTN) 50,000 lbs.; cents per lb.								
Mar	56.65	58.30	56.65	57.63	+ .89	77.25	56.00	14,855
May	57.25	.20	57.10	57.76	+ .57	77.65	57.05	27,399
July	57.90	58.70	57.80	58.25	+ .42	77.31	57.67	14,297
Oct	58.80	59.40	58.80	59.25	+ .50	77.05	58.75	1,610
Dec	59.40	60.15	59.40	59.73	+ .44	74.10	59.25	15,376
Mr00	60.50	60.90	60.50	60.73	+ .45	74.00	60.50	1,743
May				61.23	+ .45	75.40	61.80	636
July	61.80	61.80	61.80	61.75	+ .35	73.25	61.80	263
Est vol 16,500; vol Tu 21,262; open int 76,199, −2,214.								
ORANGE JUICE (CTN)-15,000 lbs.; cents per lb.								
Mar	87.55	87.85	83.50	84.25	− 3.20	127.75	83.10	14,930

The **product** is listed alphabetically within its particular grouping. Cotton is listed under the heading Foods & Fibers. Generally, detailed information is given in these charts for the most actively traded futures contracts. Activity for additional contracts is summarized at the end of the column under the heading Other Futures.

The **exchange** on which a particular contract is traded appears. Here CTN is The New York Cotton Exchange. Some commodities, like wheat and corn, trade on more than one exchange. The exchange whose activity is watched most closely is the one that is shown.

The **size of each contract** reflects the bulk

trading unit used during the normal course of commercial business. One cotton contract covers the rights to 50,000 pounds of cotton. The **price per unit** is expressed in either dollars or cents per unit, depending on the commodity. Here, it's cents per pound. To find the total cost of the contract, multiply the price per unit by opening price of a sugar contract was close to the high of 22.38. The contract settled at its closing price of 22.31 cents, down 0.06 cents from the closing price the previous day.

Change compares the closing price given here with the previous closing price. A plus (+) indicates prices ended higher and a minus (–) means that prices ended lower. In this case, sugar for March 2000 delivery settled 0.04 cents higher than the previous day.

The **month of the**

contract is the month in which it expires. Mr00 indicates this contract will expire on the third Friday of March 2000. When the expiration date arrives, the contract is dropped from the table.

The expiration cycles for each commodity usually correspond with activity in that commodity. For example, trading in grains follows the cycle of planting, harvesting and exporting.

Lifetime highs and **lows** show volatility over the lifetime of a particular contract. Prices for heating oil #2 have been more

volatile than sugar prices—meaning the investment risks are higher, but the chances of making a lot of money are also higher.

Open interest reports the total number of outstanding contracts—that is, those that have not been cancelled by offsetting trades. Generally, the further away the expiration date, the smaller the open interest because there's not much trading activity. In the case of grains and oilseed, however, there is increased activity in the months the new crop will be harvested.

	Open	High	Low	Settle	Change	Lifetime High	Lifetime Low	Open Interest
HEATING OIL NO. 2 (NYM) 42,000 gal.; $ per gal.								
Mar	.2950	.3010	.2920	.2984	+ .0032	.5830	.2920	37,713
Apr	.3020	.3065	.2990	.3047	+ .0036	.5900	.2965	29,223
May	.3075	.3130	.3060	.3112	+ .0036	.5330	.3040	15,102
June	.3140	.3195	.3130	.3177	+ .0036	.5300	.3115	14,029
July	.3245	.3290	.3230	.3262	+ .0036	.5290	.3220	12,047
Oct	.3515	.3580	.3515	.3542	+ .0031	.5200	.3510	5,089
Dec	.3690	.3750	.3690	.3712	+ .0031	.5275	.3680	12,279
Ja00	.3750	.3780	.3745	.3772	+ .0031	.5170	.3700	11,855
Feb	.3765	.3795	.3760	.3777	+ .0031	.4960	.3750	1,908
Mar	.3765	.3775	.3760	.3772	+ .0031	.5060	.3760	665

Est vol na; vol Tue 44,727; open int 162,748, + 1,956.

	Open	High	Low	Settle
GASOLINE-NY Unleaded (NYM)) 42,000 gal.; $ per gal.				
Mar	.3280	.3375	.3255	.3
Apr	.3620	.3675	.3580	.3
May	.3760	.3805	.3730	.3
June	.3850	.3885	3830	.3
July	.3935	.3955	.3910	.3
Aug	.3970	.3970	.3950	.3
Sept	.3950	.4000	.3950	.3
Oct	.3925	.3930	.3890	.3

Est vol na; vol Tue 33,162; c

	Open	High
SHORT STERLIN		
Mar	94.66	94.70
June	94.93	94.98
Sept	95.05	95.07
Dec	94.85	94.87
Mr00	95.03	95.06
June	95.03	95.06
Sept	94.97	95.00
Dec	94.85	94.88
Mr01	94.86	94.89
June	94.88	94.89
Sept	94.86	94.88
Dec	94.86	94.86

COMMODITY INDEXES

Several commodity indexes track futures markets and reflect the performance of commodities as an asset class, parallel to the way stock indexes reflect what's happening on the stock markets. For example, when the indexes are mixed as they are here in comparison to last year, it can indicate volatile commodity prices.

The newest index, the Dow Jones-AIG Commodity Index, is weighted by trading liquidity and includes 20 commodities from eight major sectors. The unweighted Bridge/CRB index includes 17 commodities, and the Goldman Sachs Commodity Index, which includes 22 commodities, is weighted by worldwide production volume.

the number of units. The July cotton contract closed at $29,125 (50,000 times 58.25 cents).

There are also cumulative daily figures for all the contracts in each commodity combined. The volume for heating oil no. 2 was 44,727 trades, leaving an open interest of 162,748. The + 1,956 shows the increase in the open interest. Those contracts can be cancelled by offsetting trades.

COMMODITY INDEXES

Wednesday, February 17

	Close	Net Chg.	Yr. Ago
Dow Jones-AIG Futures	74.621	+ .076	108.728
Dow Jones Spot	111.65	+ 0.37	132.36
Reuter United Kingdom	1421.5	– 10.9	1717.8
C R B BRIDGE Futures	184.17	– 0.16	229.61

Financial Futures

Stocks, bonds and currencies are the commodities of the investment business.

Just as dramatic changes in the price of wheat affect farmers, bakers and ultimately the consumer, so changes in interest rates, the future value of currencies and the direction of the stock market send ripples—and sometimes waves—though the financial community.

With the creation of a market in financial futures, traders, like pension fund and mutual fund investment managers and securities firms that rely on financial commodities, can protect themselves against the unexpected. They're the **hedgers** of the financial futures market.

Financial Futures in Action

THE HEDGERS

Mutual fund that owns S&P 500 stocks	**Hedges by taking a sell position** to protect against falling stock prices	**If stock stays strong**, gets out of market by buying offsetting contract **If stock prices drop**, offsets losses by selling contract at profit
Mutual fund that plans future purchase of U.S. Treasury bonds	**Hedges by taking a buy position** to protect against bond price increases if interest rates fall	**If rates stay high**, sells offsetting contract to neutralize position **If rates drop** and prices increase, fund's price is protected by being locked in

THE SPECULATORS

Speculators gamble on price changes	**Buy when they think prices are low** **Sell when they think prices are high**	**Sell when they think prices are high** **Buy when they think prices are low**

KEEPING MARKETS LIQUID

As in other futures markets, **speculators** keep the markets active by constant trading. Speculators buy or sell futures contracts depending on which way they think the market is going. World politics, trading patterns and the economy are the unpredictable factors in these markets. Rumor, too, plays a major role.

Financial speculators are no more interested in taking delivery of $100,000 of Treasury bonds than grain speculators are in 5,000 bushels of wheat. What they're interested in is making money. So at what seems to be a good time, they offset the contract they own by purchasing an opposing one, and take their profits or cut their losses.

For example, the September contract on the **British pound**, which closed here at 1.5056, was as low as $1.3980 and as high as $1.5800. If a speculator bought at the low and sold at the high, the gain (before commissions and other charges) would have been 18 cents per pound, or $11,250 on a contract worth £62,500.

CURRENCY

	Open	High	Low	Settle	Change	Lifetime High	Low	Open Interest
BRITISH POUND (CME)—62,500 pds.; $ per pound								
Sept	1.4880	1.5070	1.4826	1.5056	+ .0190	1.5800	1.3980	32,026
Dec	1.4830	1.4980	1.4770	1.4968	+ .0188	1.5670	1.3930	444
Est vol 16,304; vol Mon 14,125; open int 32,507, −2,398.								
SWISS FRANC (CME)—125,000 francs; $ per franc								
Sept	.6625	.6670	.6603	.6654	+ .0042	.7100	.6380	3
Dec	.6630	.6645	.6585	.6624	.0041	.7050	6	
Est vol 25,217								

WHAT'S BEING TRADED

The financial futures contracts in the marketplace are always in flux. Like other commodities, they trade on specific exchanges, where they're often among the most actively traded products. The Chicago Board of Trade's U.S. Treasury Bond interest rate contract, and Chicago Mercantile Exchange's Eurodollar interest rate contract, are good examples.

The contracts divide, roughly, into three general categories:

- **Currencies**
- **Stock indexes**
- **Interest rates**

Currency trading has the longest history in the futures market, dating back to the 1970s. Interest rate futures began trading in 1975, and stock index futures trading was added in 1982.

Reflecting the international scope of financial futures trading, many of the contracts tracked in The Wall Street Journal are traded on overseas exchanges, including the London International Financial Futures Exchange (LIFFE), the Sydney Futures Exchange (SFE), and the Singapore International Monetary Exchange (SIMEX).

ARBITRAGE: MANEUVERING THE MARKETS

Indexes, and futures contracts on those indexes, don't move in lockstep. When they are out of sync, the index futures contract price moves either higher or lower than the index itself. Traders can make a lot of money by simultaneously buying the one that's less expensive and selling the more expensive. This technique is known as **arbitrage**, and the chief tool is a very sophisticated computer program following the shifts in price.

Often, the price difference is only a fraction of a dollar. But arbitragers trade huge numbers of contracts at the same time, so the results are significant—if the timing is right. And since many arbitragers are making the same decisions at the same time, their buying and selling can produce changes in the markets in which they trade.

NO DELIVERY PLANNED
Most financial futures contracts are offset before their expiration date, just as contracts on other commodities are. But if an investor takes delivery, it's the cash value of the contract.

INDEX

DJ INDUSTRIAL AVERAGE (CBOT)-$10 times average

	Open	High	Low	Settle	Chg	High	Low	Open Interest
Mar	9570	9630	9490	9575	1	9760	7220	17,416
June	9665	9705	9570	9655	....	9810	7670	1,406
Sept	9737	9780	9660	9738	+ 1	9891	7875	905
Dec	9820	9860	9745	9823	+ 3	9974	7987	864
Dc00	....							

Est vol 16,000; vol /
Idx prl: High 9611.3
S&P 500 INDEX (C

INTEREST RATE

TREASURY BONDS (CBT)-$100,000; pts 32nds of 100%

	Open	High	Low	Settle	Change	Lifetime High	Low	Open Interest
Mar	123-21	123-31	121-23	122-26	— 29	134-26	103-04	515,524
June	123-07	123-10	122-03	122-11	— 29	134-02	110-07	286,223
Sept	122-23	122-24	121-24	121-29	— 29	131-06	115-11	8,620
Dec	121-11	121-18	121-09	121-09	— 29	128-28	118-07	3,299

Est vol 605,000; vol Mn 332,760; open int 813,616, —31,514.
TREASURY BONDS (MCE)-$50,000
Mar 123-20 123-25 122-17 122-24

READING THE FINANCIAL FUTURES CHARTS

The details of financial futures trading are recorded daily.

The value of an index contract is calculated differently from other futures contracts. That's because an index is two steps removed from the commodity. Instead of dollars per yen or tons of soybeans per dollar, U.S. indexes are valued by multiplying a fixed dollar amount times the current value of the index. A DJIA contract, for example, is valued at $10 times its current value.

In other words, if you took delivery of a March DJIA contract at the value, or settle price, shown in this example, it would be worth $95,750, or $10 times 9575.

Interest rate futures contracts also differ somewhat from other contracts. Their value is figured as percentage points, or in the case of U.S. and U.K. bonds, in 32nds to correspond to the way changes in value are measured in the bonds themselves (see page 94). For U.S. Treasury notes and bonds, and for Eurodollars, the tables report current yield rather than lifetime highs and lows.

A World of Options

Options are opportunities to make buy and sell decisions—if the market takes the right turns.

Holding an option gives you the right to buy or sell a specific investment at a set price within a preset time period. But there's no obligation **to exercise the option**, and actually buy or sell, before it expires.

The particular item that an option deals with—stock, index, Treasury bond, currency or futures contract—is called the **underlying investment**. If the stock or futures markets move in the direction an investor thinks they will, exercising the option can mean a healthy profit.

Options are traded on stock or commodity exchanges at a specific **strike (or exercise) price**, which is the dollar amount you'll pay or receive if the trade takes place. The strike price is set by the exchange. The market price rises or falls depending on the performance of the underlying investment on which the option is based.

BUYING OPTIONS

Buying options is a way to capitalize on changes in the market price. If you buy **call** options, you are betting that the price of the underlying investment is going up. Conversely, if you buy **put** options, you think the price is going down.

With either type of buy option, your potential loss is limited to the **premium**, or dollar amount, you pay to buy the option. That's known in the securities industry as a limited, predetermined risk.

SELLING OPTIONS

The biggest difference between buying options and selling them is the nature of your commitment. Buyers have no obligation to do anything. They can simply let the option expire. Sellers, on the other hand, are required to go through with a trade if the party they sold the option to (by **writing a put** or **writing a call**) wants to exercise the option.

WRITING COVERED CALLS

The most basic form of option trading is **writing covered stock calls**, and it's the first type of option trading most people do. It means you sell the right to some other party to buy stocks that you already own for a specific price. The key is that you own them—that's what makes the call covered.

NAKED—BEARING IT ALL

The greatest risk in options trading is **writing naked calls**. That means you sell an option that allows someone to buy something from you that you don't already own. In a typical worst-case example, you'd write a naked stock call. The price of the underlying stock would hit the strike price, the option would be exercised and you'd have to buy the shares at the market price in order to sell them at the agreed-on price. Your cost—and loss—could be thousands of dollars.

THREE WAYS TO BUY OPTIONS

Investor buys ten call options (1,000 shares) on stock X

Price: $55/share

Strike price: 60

Premium: $750

1. **HOLD TO MATURITY AND TRADE AT THE STRIKE PRICE**

2. **TRADE FOR PROFIT BEFORE OPTION EXPIRES**

3. **LET THE OPTION EXPIRE**

TWO WAYS TO SELL OPTIONS

Investor owns 1,000 shares of stock X

Price: $55/share

Investor owns no shares of stock X

1. **WRITE TEN COVERED CALLS**
Strike price: 60
Collect premium $750

2. **WRITE TEN NAKED CALLS**
Strike price: 60
Collect premium $750

THE LANGUAGE OF OPTIONS

In the specialized language of options, all transactions are either puts or calls. A put is the right to sell and a call is the right to buy.

	CALL	PUT
BUY	The right to buy the underlying item at the strike price until the expiration date	The right to sell the underlying item at the strike price until the expiration date
SELL	Selling the right to buy the underlying item from you at the strike price until the expiration date. Known as **writing a call**	Selling the right to sell the underlying item to you until the expiration date. Known as **writing a put**

TRADE OR EXERCISE

Like futures contracts, options can be sold for a profit before the expiration date or neutralized with an offsetting order. Unlike most futures contracts, though, options are frequently exercised when the underlying item reaches the strike price. That's because part of the appeal of options, and stock options in particular, is that they can be converted into real investments even though the options themselves are derivatives.

THE OPTIONS KEEP CHANGING

The underlying investments on which options are available keep growing. At the time of publication, five types of exchange-listed options are generally traded:

- Individual stocks
- Stock and bond market indexes
- Currencies
- Treasury bills and bonds
- Futures contracts

IF STOCK PRICE RISES TO 65
Trade option at strike price of 60

$5,000 from trade
− $750 premium
$4,250 PROFIT

IF STOCK PRICE RISES TO 60
Trade option at strike price of 60

$0,000 from trade
− $750 premium
$750 LOSS

IF STOCK PRICE RISES TO 62
Trade option before expiration at strike price of 60

$2,000 from trade
− $750 premium
$1,250 PROFIT

IF STOCK PRICE RISES TO 60½
Trade option before expiration at strike price of 60

$500 from trade
− $750 premium
$250 LOSS

IF STOCK PRICE DROPS TO 45
There are no takers for an option with a 60 strike price

less your premium only
$750 LOSS

IF STOCK PRICE RISES TO 57
No takers—options expire

keep the premium
$750 PROFIT

IF STOCK PRICE RISES TO 60
Buy 10 calls to cancel obligation and prevent losing stocks

$750 premium collected
− $750 premium on offsetting calls
BREAK EVEN

IF STOCK PRICE RISES TO 57
No takers—options expire

keep the premium
$750 PROFIT

IF STOCK PRICE RISES TO 65
Option is exercised. You must buy 1,000 shares at $65 to sell at $60

$750 premium
− $5,000 loss on transaction
$4,250 LOSS

Stock Options Tables

Successful stock option trading requires lots of attention to detail—including information on what's happening in the marketplace.

The price of a stock option is closely tied to the current market price of the underlying stock. In fact, the relationship between the two is so central to the way an option trades that it's described using a special vocabulary.

An **in the money option** means the market price is higher than the strike price of a call option and lower than the strike price of a put option. An **at the money option** means that the market price and the strike price are the same. With an **out of the money option**, the spread between the market price and the strike price is large enough to make it unlikely that the option will be exercised, especially if it's due to expire shortly. A **deep out of the money option**, or DOOM, has a strike price so far from the market price that there's little trading.

In fact, the strike prices of the most actively traded options are quite close to the underlying stock's market price, except when there's been a dramatic, recent change. That's because the exchanges establish the strike prices to reflect analysts' evaluations of the stock and the market in general.

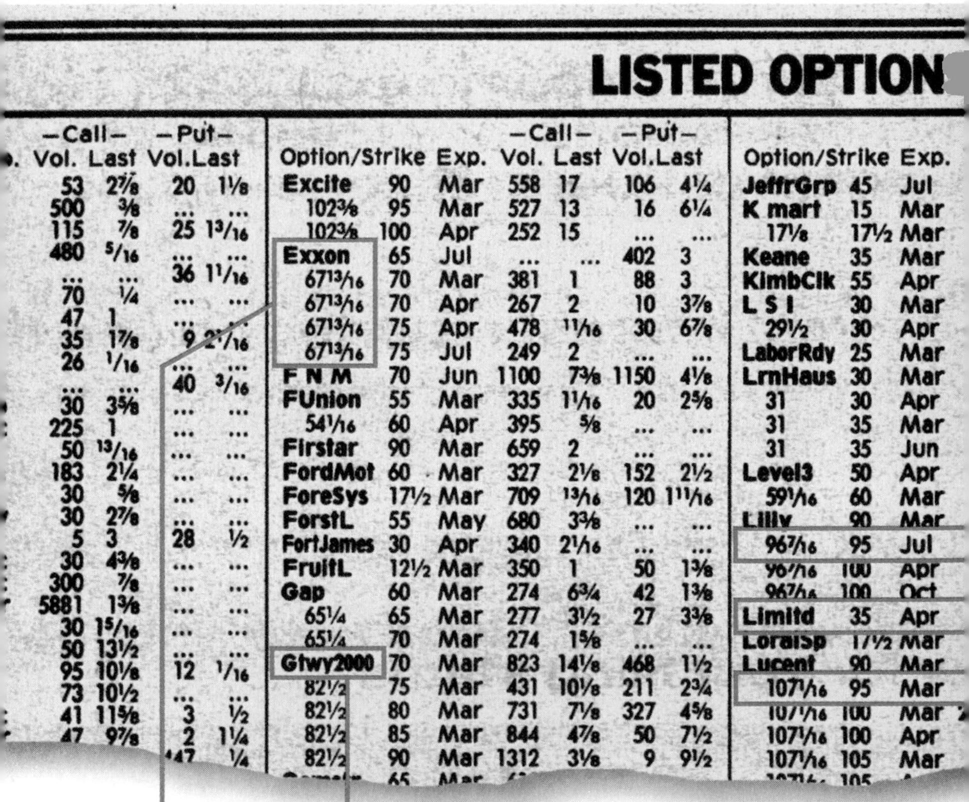

LISTED OPTION

.	Vol.	Last	Vol.	Last	Option/Strike		Exp.	Vol.	Last	Vol.	Last	Option/Strike		Exp.
	53	2⅞	20	1⅛	Excite	90	Mar	558	17	106	4¼	JeffrGrp	45	Jul
	500	⅜	...	...		102⅜	95	Mar	527	13	16	6¼	K mart	15	Mar
	115	⅞	25	1³/₁₆		102⅜	100	Apr	252	15	...	...		17⅛	17½	Mar
	480	⁵/₁₆	...	...	Exxon	65	Jul	...	...	402	3	Keane	35	Mar
	...	...	36	1¹¹/₁₆		67¹³/₁₆	70	Mar	381	1	88	3	KimbClk	55	Apr
	70	¼	...	...		67¹³/₁₆	70	Apr	267	2	10	3⅞	L S I	30	Mar
	47	1	...	...		67¹³/₁₆	75	Apr	478	¹¹/₁₆	30	6⅞		29½	30	Apr
	35	1⅞	9	2⁷/₁₆		67¹³/₁₆	75	Jul	249	2	...	...	LaborRdy	25	Mar
	26	¹/₁₆	...	...	F N M	70	Jun	1100	7⅜	1150	4⅛	LrnHaus	30	Mar
	...	...	40	³/₁₆	FUnion	55	Mar	335	1¹/₁₆	20	2⅝		31	30	Apr
	30	3⅝	...	...		54¹/₁₆	60	Apr	395	⅝	...	...		31	35	Mar
	225	1	...	...	Firstar	90	Mar	659	2	...	...		31	35	Jun
	50	¹³/₁₆	...	...	FordMot	60	Mar	327	2⅛	152	2½	Level3	50	Apr
	183	2¼	...	...	ForeSys	17½	Mar	709	¹³/₁₆	120	1¹¹/₁₆		59¹/₁₆	60	Mar
	30	⅝	...	...	ForstL	55	May	680	3⅜	...	...	Lilly	90	Mar
	30	2⅞	...	...	FortJames	30	Apr	340	2¹/₁₆	...	...		96⁷/₁₆	95	Jul
	5	3	28	½	FruitL	12½	Mar	350	1	50	1⅜		96⁷/₁₆	100	Apr
	30	4⅜	...	...	Gap	60	Mar	274	6¾	42	1⅜		96⁷/₁₆	100	Oct
	300	⅞	...	...		65¼	65	Mar	277	3½	27	3⅜	Limitd	35	Apr
	5881	1⅜	...	...		65¼	70	Mar	274	1⅝	...	...	LoralSp	17½	Mar
	50	13½	...	...	Gtwy2000	70	Mar	823	14⅛	468	1½	Lucent	90	Mar
	95	10⅛	12	¹/₁₆		82½	75	Mar	431	10⅛	211	2¾		107¹/₁₆	95	Mar
	73	10½	...	...		82½	80	Mar	731	7⅛	327	4⅝		107¹/₁₆	100	Mar
	41	11⅜	3	½		82½	85	Mar	844	4⅞	50	7½		107¹/₁₆	100	Apr
	47	9⅞	2	1¼		82½	90	Mar	1312	3⅛	9	9½		107¹/₁₆	105	Apr
			↑47	¼		65	Mar						107¼	105	

The **number** repeated in the first column is the current market price of the underlying stock. The relationship between the current price and the strike price is one factor affecting how actively the option is traded. In this example, for instance, Exxon sold for 67¹³/₁₆ a share at the end of the previous trading day,

and the most actively traded put option had a strike price of 65.

The **name** of the stock being optioned is often abbreviated and in alphabetical order. Some names, like Excite and Gap, are easily recognized. Others, like Gtwy2000, may need deciphering. (It's Gateway, the computer company.)

The abbreviations are often, but not always, the same ones that are used in the stock tables.

Information about the most actively traded options and LEAPS, or long-term options, is given separately at the beginning and the end of the regular listed options columns.

OPTION PRICES

Option prices are quoted in whole numbers and fractions that represent a dollar amount. To convert a whole number and a fraction to an option price, multiply both the whole number and the fraction by 100 and add the results.

for example

$$2\tfrac{5}{8} = (2 \times 100) + (\tfrac{5}{8} \times 100)$$
$$= (200) + (0.625 \times 100)$$
$$= 200 + 62.50$$
$$2\tfrac{5}{8} = \$262.50$$

This chart gives the decimal equivalent of the fractions:

$\tfrac{1}{16}$	=	0.0625
$\tfrac{1}{8}$	=	0.125
$\tfrac{3}{16}$	=	0.1875
$\tfrac{1}{4}$	=	0.250
$\tfrac{5}{16}$	=	0.3125
$\tfrac{3}{8}$	=	0.375
$\tfrac{7}{16}$	=	0.4375
$\tfrac{1}{2}$	=	0.5
$\tfrac{9}{16}$	=	0.5625
$\tfrac{5}{8}$	=	0.625
$\tfrac{11}{16}$	=	0.6875
$\tfrac{3}{4}$	=	0.750
$\tfrac{13}{16}$	=	0.8125
$\tfrac{7}{8}$	=	0.875
$\tfrac{15}{16}$	=	0.9375

expires on the third Friday of the month that's named. The strike price is the dollar amount a trade would cost if the option were exercised. For example, a Lucent March 95 means that anytime up to the third Friday in March, an option holder could buy 100 shares of Lucent stock for $95 a share.

Often the same month appears several times with different strike prices, but with the groupings by price rather than date.

For example, Merck has options at 75, 80 and 85, all of the 80s are together, and so on.

A list of options beginning with the closest **expiration date** and lowest **strike price** appears after the name of the company. The option

QUOTATIONS

Put Vol.	Last	Option/Strike		Exp.	Call Vol.	Last	Put Vol.	Last	Option/Strike		Exp.	Call Vol.	Last
	...	$83^{15}/16$	90	Apr	280	$2\tfrac{7}{8}$	...	...	ParkPl	$7\tfrac{1}{2}$	Mar	320	1
30	$\tfrac{1}{4}$	$83^{15}/16$	90	Jun	1872	$5\tfrac{3}{8}$	7	$9\tfrac{3}{8}$	$7^{15}/16$	$7\tfrac{1}{2}$	Apr	1100	$1^{3}/16$
38	$1\tfrac{1}{8}$	MarshMcL	65	Jul	6	$9^{7}8$	250	$2\tfrac{7}{8}$	Paychex	40	Mar	19	$3\tfrac{5}{8}$
514	$4\tfrac{1}{2}$	$72^{5}/16$	70	Jul	450	$7\tfrac{1}{8}$	...	...	Peoplesoft	20	Mar	759	2
...	...	Mastec	25	Oct	500	$5\tfrac{3}{8}$	...	...		21	$22\tfrac{1}{2}$	Mar	645	$\tfrac{3}{4}$
54	$2\tfrac{1}{4}$	Mattel	25	Apr	42	$3\tfrac{5}{8}$	292	$1\tfrac{5}{8}$	PepsiCo	40	Mar	347	1
2	$3\tfrac{1}{8}$	$26\tfrac{7}{8}$	$27\tfrac{1}{2}$	Mar	305	$1^{3}/16$	...	...	Pfizer	130	Mar	360	$6\tfrac{3}{4}$
...	...	$26\tfrac{7}{8}$	$27\tfrac{1}{2}$	Apr	41	2	1166	$2\tfrac{3}{4}$	$133^{13}/16$	130	Jun	1096	$13\tfrac{1}{4}$
465	$2\tfrac{1}{2}$	McDln	$17\tfrac{1}{2}$	Aug	..	...	500	2	$133^{13}/16$	135	Mar	650	$3\tfrac{3}{4}$
251	$4\tfrac{1}{2}$	Mc Don	85	Mar	368	$3\tfrac{1}{2}$	49	$2\tfrac{7}{8}$	$133^{13}/16$	140	Mar	442	$1\tfrac{5}{8}$
580	$5\tfrac{7}{8}$	$85^{11}/16$	90	Jun	391	$5\tfrac{1}{8}$	...	...	PharMer	5	Apr	...	...
250	$9\tfrac{1}{4}$	McKess	75	Mar	243	$1\tfrac{5}{8}$	...	...	PharUpj	50	Apr	404	$5\tfrac{7}{8}$
1500	$2^{1}/16$	Medimun	55	Mar	917	$4\tfrac{1}{4}$	10	$2\tfrac{3}{8}$	Ph Mor	$37\tfrac{1}{2}$	Jun	...	...
45	$4\tfrac{1}{2}$	Medtrn	75	May	...	...	260	$4\tfrac{3}{8}$	$40^{13}/16$	40	Mar	219	$1^{13}/16$
48	$1\tfrac{1}{4}$		77	80	Mar	2172	2	...	...	$40^{13}/16$	40	Jun	301	$3\tfrac{3}{4}$
...	...	Merck	75	Mar	139	$6\tfrac{7}{8}$	394	$\tfrac{3}{4}$	$40^{13}/16$	45	Mar	949	$\tfrac{1}{4}$
70	$6\tfrac{7}{8}$		81	75	Apr	222	$7\tfrac{7}{8}$	299	$1^{13}/16$	$40^{13}/16$	45	Jun	309	$1\tfrac{5}{8}$
1	$11\tfrac{1}{4}$		81	80	Mar	277	$3\tfrac{3}{8}$	419	2	$40^{13}/16$	60	Jun	2060	$\tfrac{1}{8}$
500	$1^{9}/16$		81	80	Apr	2216	$4\tfrac{3}{4}$	345	$3\tfrac{3}{8}$	Pohangir	$17\tfrac{1}{2}$	May	300	$\tfrac{1}{2}$
615	$\tfrac{1}{2}$		81	85	Mar	504	$1\tfrac{1}{16}$	42	$5\tfrac{1}{4}$	Polar	20	Mar	431	$3\tfrac{3}{8}$
1107	$^{11}/16$		81	85	Apr	552	$2\tfrac{3}{8}$	55	$6\tfrac{1}{8}$		22	$22\tfrac{1}{2}$	Mar	302	$1\tfrac{5}{8}$
395	$1^{3}/16$		81	8										

Call options—options to buy—are reported separately from **put options**—options to sell. Sometimes calls and puts are traded on the same option, and sometimes only one or the other is being traded. When that happens, dashes appear in the appropriate column, as they do for the Lilly July 95 and Limited April 35 contracts. When volume and price are similar for both calls and puts, they are often offsetting trades.

Volume reports the number of trades during the previous trading day. The number is unofficial but gives a sense of the activity in each option. Generally, trading increases as the expiration date gets closer if the strike price is in the money. For example, there's much more action in the Mattel March $27\tfrac{1}{2}$ option than in the April option at the same price.

Last is the closing price for the option on the previous trading day. In this case, the Pfizer June 130 call closed at $13\tfrac{1}{4}$, or $1,325 for an option on 100 shares at $130. Generally, the higher the price, the greater the profit the trader expects to make—like the people buying this call option.

Using Options

Options can work for both conservative and speculative investors.

Individual investors use options for a variety of reasons. Conservative investors, for example, might buy or sell options to help protect the value of their portfolios against falling prices, to lock in a favorable purchase price or to get some immediate income. Speculative traders like the **leverage**, or opportunity to have a potentially larger gain than they could achieve by owning the underlying investment. Of course, they could have larger losses, too, but that's the risk they're willing to take.

THE COST OF AN OPTION
Options are attractive because they cost less than actually buying the underlying stocks, Treasury notes or other investments they're based on, though commissions may add significantly to the price.

An option's **premium**, or nonrefundable price, depends on several factors, including the type of underlying investment, its price, its volatility, the current interest rates and the time remaining before the option expires. Because premiums fluctuate, traders can make profits or have losses very quickly.

INVESTMENT STRATEGIES
You can use options conservatively to increase your income or to limit your risk.

The most popular income-producing strategy is selling **covered calls**. You write call options on a share-for-share basis against stocks you own. If someone exercises the calls, you meet your obligation to sell by handing over your stocks. The goals of covered calls are to provide some protection if the stock price falls, establish a selling price above the current market price or increase your income in a **sideways market**, when prices move up and down within a very small range.

Writing **cash-secured puts** is another income-oriented approach. You sell a put for each 100 shares of stock an investor is

The Following Rules of Thumb

The greater the difference between the strike price and the actual current price of the item, the cheaper the premium because there is less chance that the option will be exercised.

The closer the expiration date of an in the money option, the more *volume*, or trading activity, there tends to be.

Option/Strike		Exp.	Call Vol.	Last	Put Vol.	Last
Citigroup	50	Feb	270	3⅜	379	⅛
53¹⁄₁₆	60	Feb	561	¹⁄₁₆	280	6⅝
53¹⁄₁₆	60					
Coke	65					
64⁵⁄₁₆	65					
ColtTel	80					
CmpUSA	12½					
11¹⁄₁₆	15					

Option/Strike		Exp.	Call Vol.	Last	Put Vol.	Last
DellCptr	45	May	286	38	34	⅞
81⁹⁄₁₆	70	Aug	105	21⅝	1590	9⅝
81⁹⁄₁₆	75	Mar	1251	10⅞	3520	3¾
81⁹⁄₁₆	80	Feb	7241	3	10044	1⁵⁄₁₆
81⁹⁄₁₆	80	Aug	900	17⅞	817	14¼
81⁹⁄₁₆	85	Feb	9291	¾	7138	4

When Citigroup is trading in February at 53³⁄₁₆, a February 50 call option costs $337.50 (3⅜), but a February 60 is only $6.25 (¹⁄₁₆).

When Dell Computer is trading at 81⁹⁄₁₆ in February, February 80 options are trading far more frequently than August 80 options.

willing to buy at a specific price. Then, as security, you invest an equivalent amount in U.S. Treasury bills or a money market account. If the put is exercised, you liquidate that investment and use the cash to buy the stock.

TRADING TECHNIQUES
You can trade options in more complex ways to hedge your investments. With a **straddle**, you buy a call and a put on the same underlying investment at the same strike price. A straddle costs more than an individual option but has the potential of making money whether the underlying price goes up or down.

If you use a **strangle**, you buy a call and a put on the same underlying invest-ment with different strike prices equally out of the money. A strangle costs less than a straddle, but the value of the underlying investment has to change much more for the strangle to make a profit.

Spread trading means that you buy or sell two options on the same underlying investment with different strike prices. If you are forced to buy or sell the underlying investment because someone exercises an option you sold, you can meet your obligation by exercising an option you bought.

TAKE THE LEAP
Long-term stock options, actually **Long-term Equity Anticipation Securities (LEAPS)** have expiration dates of up to three years. Because they last longer than other options, they are considered less risky. That's true in part because the price of the stock or stock index has much longer to perform as expected. It's also true that the money saved in buying an option instead of the stock itself can be invested elsewhere. Of course, options don't pay dividends.

The risk with LEAPS, as with all options, is that the underlying stock or index must still perform as expected, and the decision to trade, exercise or let the option expire still has to be made within the option's lifespan.

Usually Apply to Options

The more time there is until expiration, the larger the premium because the chance of reaching the strike price is greater and the carrying costs are more.

Call and put options move in opposition. Call options rise in value as the underlying market prices go up. Put options rise in value as market prices go down.

Option/Strike		Exp.	–Call– Vol. Last		–Put– Vol. Last	
81⁹⁄₁₆	100	Mar	4937	1¹¹⁄₁₆	2148	19½
81⁹⁄₁₆	100	May	1930	6	251	23⅝
81⁹⁄₁₆	100					
81⁹⁄₁₆	105					
81⁹⁄₁₆	105					
81⁹⁄₁₆	105					
81⁹⁄₁₆	110					
81⁹⁄₁₆	110					
81⁹⁄₁₆	110					
81⁹⁄₁₆	110					
81⁹⁄₁₆	115					
81⁹⁄₁₆	115					

Option/Strike		Exp.	–Call– Vol. Last		–Put– Vol. Last	
Cisco	25	Mar	1097	¾	...	...
95⅛	90	Feb	328	5½	810	⅜
95⅛	90	Mar	135	9¾	630	4
95⅛	90	Apr	449	12¼		

In February, when the price of Dell stock is 81⁹⁄₁₆, a March 100 call option costs $168.75 (1¹¹⁄₁₆), but a May 100 call is $600 (6).

In February, when Cisco is trading at 95⅛, a February 90 call option is trading at $550 (5½), but a February 90 put option is trading at $37.50 (⅜).

Options Trading

Options are a growth industry: new ways to speculate on what the future holds crop up regularly.

Options, like futures contracts, have historically been bought and sold on exchange trading floors, using the auction-style system known as **open outcry**. In fact, the sometimes rough-and-tumble activity on four exchanges—the Chicago Board of Trade, the American Stock Exchange, the Pacific Exchange and the Philadelphia Exchange—has accounted for more than 97% of all options trading in the U.S. And while some options are multiple-listed, many have traded on only one exchange.

But the winds of electronic change, which have revolutionized stock trading in recent years, are stirring up options trading as well. An electronic options exchange listing all of the most active options is likely to increase competition and reduce transaction costs for broker-dealers and ultimately for their clients, just as online brokerage firms have reduced the costs of stock trading for individual investors.

OPTIONS ON STOCK INDEXES

Buying **put options** on stock indexes is a way for you to hedge your stock portfolio against sharp drops in the market. It gives you the right to sell your options at a profit if the market falls. The money realized on the sale will—hopefully—cover the losses in your portfolio resulting from the falling market.

For this technique to work, though, your options have to be on the index that most closely tracks the kind of stocks you own. And you have to own enough options to offset the total value of your portfolio. Since options cost money and expire quickly, using this kind of insurance regularly can take a big bite out of any profits the portfolio itself produces.

Speculators use index options to gamble on shifts in market direction. Like other methods of high-risk investing, this one offers the chance of making a big killing if you get it right. Otherwise there wouldn't be any takers. But the risks of getting the price and the timing right are magnified by the short lifespan of index options.

A complicating factor is that indexes don't always move in the same direction as the markets they track. When indexes are out of kilter, there are big profits to be made, too—often by the arbitrage traders with computer programs fine-tuned enough to take advantage of the movements.

RANGES FOR UNDERLYING INDEXES

Wednesday, March 10

	High	Low	Close	Net Chg.	From Dec. 31	% Chg.	Strike	
							Jun	1
							Mar	1
							Mar	1
DJ Indus (DJX)	97.76	96.76	97.73	+ 0.79	+ 5.92	+ 6.5	Mar	1
DJ Trans (DTX)	331.02	328.40	329.00	− 1.09	+ 14.07	+ 4.5	Mar	1
DJ Util (DUX)	300.22	294.92	298.63	+ 3.62	− 13.67	− 4.4	Apr	
S&P 100 (OEX)	644.67	638.46	644.40	+ 3.47	+ 40.37	+ 6.7	Apr	

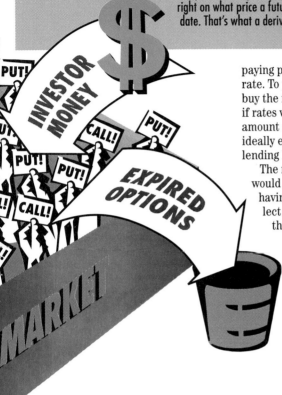

paying products to earn the higher market rate. To protect itself, the company would buy the rate cap for the assurance that if rates went up, the seller would pay the amount specified in the agreement—ideally enough to offset the insurer's lending losses.

The rate cap seller, probably a bank, would be willing to take the chance on having to pay up because it would collect the **premium**, or fee, for selling the protection.

OPTIONS ON CURRENCY
Institutional investors with large overseas holdings sometimes hedge their portfolios by buying options on the currencies of countries where their money is invested. Since the investment's value depends on the relationship between the dollar and the other currency, using options can equalize sudden shifts in value.

For example, if the value of the British pound lost ground against the dollar, U.S. investments in British companies would be worth less than they were when the pound was strong. But an option to buy pounds at the lower price could be sold at a profit, making up for some of the loss in investment value.

WHAT THE OPTIONS ARE
You can buy or sell options on stock and bond indexes, on interest rates, on currencies or on futures contracts.

If you're in the options markets to help protect your other investments from the effect of changing values, you're considered a **hedger**, in the same way that a rancher who buys a futures contract is a hedger. If you're in the market hoping to profit by changes in the financial markets that other investors don't seem to be expecting—a rapid rise in interest rates or the falling value of the dollar, for example—you're considered a **speculator**.

OPTIONS ON INTEREST RATES
Options on interest rates are actually options on bonds issued by the U.S. Treasury or by governments in other countries. Bondholders can hedge their investments by using interest rate options, just as stockholders can hedge by using index options. Interest rate options are intended to offset any loss in value between the purchase date of the option and the date the bond matures. If the money from the maturing bond has to be reinvested at a lower rate, the profit from trading the option can make up for some of the loss, provided that the cost of the option doesn't eat it up.

A related derivatives investment, known as **an interest rate cap**, can provide similar protection when interest rates increase.

An insurance company, for example, might anticipate that its policyholders would take the opportunity to borrow against their policies at below-market rates and invest the money in interest-

Tracking Other Options

There's a brisk business in a wide range of options on indexes and futures.

As the variety of options available in the marketplace has increased, so have the number of tables providing information about current trades. All options tables provide the same basic information, including the strike price, the expiration date and the current price of the option.

But there are some differences. The sales unit for each option is based on the item being optioned—100 shares of stock, 44,000 pounds of feeder cattle, $50,000 Australian dollars. So are the expiration dates, which in some cases follow a regular pattern and in other cases are random.

INDEX OPTIONS TRADING

Like stock options, index options are closely tied to the underlying item—in this case, various stock indexes. In fact, the ranges of the underlying indexes are printed in The Wall Street Journal accompanying the details of the trading.

Index options have a short time-frame and a broad range of prices. That's because they're so volatile. Trying to predict with any precision where an index will be is even more difficult than with most other options. The further in the future, the more difficult it becomes.

INDEX OPTIONS TRADING

Open Int.	Strike		Vol.	Close	Net Chg.	Open Int.	Strike		Vol.	Close	Net Chg.	Open Int.	Strik
							Mar	96 c	19	2¼	+ 1/16	8,320	
							Mar	96 p	5	5⅛	+ ⅛	1,035	
		CHICAGO					Jun	96 p	4	7⅜	+ ½	780	Call
							Feb	97 c	60	⅜	+ ⅛	1,429	Put
		DJ INDUS AVG(DJX)					Feb	97 p	4	4⅝	+ 1	801	
23	Jun	68 p	60	⅞	− ⅞	693	Mar	97 c	5	1⅝	− ⅛	28	Se
140	Mar	76 p	300	¼	− ¼	2,610	Mar	97 p	4	5¾	+ ¾	28	Ju
1	Mar	80 p	11	¾	+ 3/16	10,879	Feb	98 p	55	5⅜	+ ⅛	154	A
70	Jun	80 p	10	2½	+ ⅛	6,557	Mar	98 c	2	1¼	− ⅜	72	J
25	Feb	84 p	415	¼	...	1,204	Feb	100 c	150	1/16	− 1/16	1,955	A
127	Mar	84 p	10	1 3/16	+ 3/16	6,773	Feb	100 p	40	7¼	+ 1	199	J
102	Jun	84 p	2	3¼	+ ⅜	1,614	Mar	100 c	30	11/16	− 3/16	6,907	
39	Feb	86 c	2	7⅜	+ ¾	404	Mar	100 p	8	7½	+ ⅝	6,784	
2	Feb	8..	40	5..	¼	448	Feb	104 p	10	11¼	− ⅜	201	
							Jun	104 c	700	2	...	655	
								108 c	18	1/16	− 1/16		

The **index** on which the options are offered is listed. You can buy options on a wide variety of indexes, from the Dow Jones Industrial Average (DJX) to the much broader Russell 2000, for the U.S. market. Or you can choose indexes that track specific industries or stock markets in other countries or around the world.

The **exchange** on which the index options are traded is shown first.

The **strike** column shows the expiration date, followed by strike price and whether the option is a put (p) or a call (c). In this example of DJX index option trading, the puts predominate at the lower end (68-84) of the price scale, suggesting that those traders think the market is headed down. At the upper end (98-108), calls increase, suggesting that some traders think the market is going up.

Volume reports the number of trades during the previous trading day. In index option trading, the heaviest volume is usually in options closest to expiration—in this case, February and March.

Close is the closing price of the option at the end of the previous day's trading. As with stock options, prices are given in whole numbers and in fractions. (To get the actual price you multiply the number by 100, since each option is for 100 shares.) For example, the February 98 put is trading at 5⅜, or $537.50.

Net change is the difference between the price reported here and the closing price two trading days ago. When the two are alike, all the outstanding options have been neutralized by opposing trades.

FUTURES OPTIONS PRICES

Futures options trading includes agricultural products, other raw materials, and financial commodities like international currencies and interest rates.

The **futures contract** on which the option is based, the exchange on which it is traded, the number of units in the contract and the price units by which the price of the commodity is figured are shown. In this example, the futures contract is on soybeans traded on the Chicago Board of Trade. Each contract is for 5,000 bushels and the price is quoted in cents per bushel, so that 575 means $5.75 a bushel.

Industry group is a grouping of similar commodities traded on various exchanges. They include options on futures contracts in agricultural products, oil, livestock, currency, interest rates, and stock and bond indexes.

Puts gives the dates of the put options available in each commodity. Prices for puts and calls move in the opposite direction because they reflect the price movement of the underlying commodity. When calls are selling for more, puts are selling for less, as they are for feeder cattle here.

FUTURES OPTIONS PRICES

AGRICULTURAL

SOYBEANS (CBT)
5,000 bu.; cents per bu.

Strike Price	Calls—Settle			Puts—Settle		
	Aug	Sep	Nov	Aug	Sep	Nov
575	45½	51¾	57½	2¾	6¾	10½
600	28½	36	43	10½	16⅝	21⅝
625	18	27½	33¼	25	32	37
650	12⅜	22½	26½	44	51½	54
675	8⅛	17½	21¼	....	....	74
700	6	14⅝	18¼	....	....	96½

Est vol 15,000 Mon 14,310 calls 5,-945 puts
Op int Mon 109,516 calls 41,064 puts

SOYBEAN MEAL (CBT)
100 tons; $ per ton

Strike Price	Calls—Settle			Puts—Settle		
	Aug	Sep	Oct	Aug	Sep	Oct
185	10.50	12.45	13.25	1.25	3.25	3.70
190	7.50	9.75	10.50	3.25	5.25	5.95
195	5.50	8.00	9.00	6.00	...	9.50
200	4.00	6.60	7.50	....	...	12.90
210	2.20	4.75	5.50	....	19.75	20.80
220	1.40	3.60	4.50	....	...	...

Est vol 1,300 Mon 1,585 calls 951 puts
Op int Mon 16,262 calls 8,144 puts

SOYBEAN OIL (CBT)
60,000 lbs.; cents per lb.

Strike Price	Calls—Settle			Puts—Settle		
	Aug	Sep	Oct	Aug	Sep	Oct
2100	1.430	1.700	....	.250	.400	.460
2150	1.080	1.430	....	.400	.640	....
2200	.800	1.220	1.400	.650	.9?0	...
2250	.650	1.050	...	..		
2300	.500	.920	1.0??			
2350						

CATTLE-FEEDER (CME)
44,000 lbs.; cents per lb.

Strike Price	Calls—Settle			Puts—Settle		
	Aug	Sep	Oct	Aug	Sep	Oct
82	4.85	4.10	3.92	0.32	0.60	0.75
84	3.00	2.50	2.47	0.47	1.00	1.30
86	1.60	1.25	1.37	1.05	1.75	2.20
88	0.70	0.55	0.65	2.10	....	....
90	0.22	0.20	....	3.57	....	....
92	0.17					

Est vol 278 Mon 40 calls 167 puts
Op int Mon 1,853 calls 7,340 puts

CATTLE-LIVE (CME)
40,000 lbs.; cents per lb.

Strike Price	Calls—Settle			Puts—Settle		
	Jly	Aug	Oct	Jly	Aug	Oct
70	....	3.57	....	....	0.17	0.47
72	....	1.97	2.70	0.07	0.55	0.95
74	....	0.75	1.52	0.75	1.32	1.75
76	0.05	0.20	0.72	....	2.75	2.92
78	....	0.05	0.32	....	....	4.50
80	....	....	0.12	....	....	....

Est vol 1,787 Mon 179 calls 5?
Op int Mon 12,902

HOGS—LIVE (C?)
40,000 lbs.; ...

Strike Price
44
46
48
50
52
54

Strike price is the price at which the option owner may buy or sell the corresponding futures contract by exercising the option. Each commodity has options covering a range of prices that increase in a regular sequence (200/210/220).

Calls gives the dates of the call options currently available on this commodity. In this example, options on soybean futures contracts are available for August, September and November.

Settle shows that the exchange has adjusted the price to reflect market values at the end of trading. Because futures contracts and the options on those contracts may not trade at the same pace, the exchange will adjust an option's price to coincide with its futures price at the end of the day.

So the settle price for the August 575 option is 45½ (45½¢) a bushel, or $2,275. The futures contract itself is worth $28,750.

Estimated volume reports the number of trades on the previous trading day, separated into puts and calls.

Open interest shows the number of outstanding options contracts, broken out by puts and calls, that have not been offset by an opposite transaction.

INDEX

BOOKS FROM LIGHTBULB PRESS

Lightbulb Press books are available in bookstores everywhere. Visit us on the World Wide Web at www.lightbulbpress.com. Contact us at (917) 256-4900 for information on quantity discounts.

THE WALL STREET JOURNAL GUIDE TO UNDERSTANDING MONEY & INVESTING

by Kenneth M. Morris and Virginia B. Morris

The ideal introduction to investing—and the perfect reference for the experienced investor. Over 1,000,000 copies sold.

Stocks • Bonds • Mutual Funds • Indexes • Risk/Return • Tracking Performance • Evaluating Companies • Investing Online

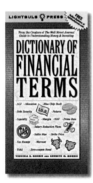

DICTIONARY OF FINANCIAL TERMS

by Virginia B. Morris and Kenneth M. Morris

The most important investing terms people hear and read every day—explained in language everyone can understand. Free online updates at www.lightbulbpress.com.

Hundreds of Definitions • Financial Acronyms • The Difference between Markets and Exchanges • Reading a Stock Ticker • Tracking the Markets

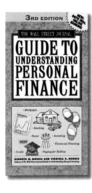

THE WALL STREET JOURNAL GUIDE TO UNDERSTANDING PERSONAL FINANCE

by Kenneth M. Morris and Virginia B. Morris

The basics of personal finance—and the pitfalls to avoid along the way in everyday financial life.

Bank Accounts • Credit Cards • Mortgages • Financial Planning • College Education • Investing • Online Banking • Taxes • Planning for Retirement

A WOMAN'S GUIDE TO INVESTING

by Virginia B. Morris and Kenneth M. Morris
Introduction by Bridget A. Macaskill

The essential information—and inspiration—women of all ages need to manage their financial lives.

Setting Financial Goals • Making Smart Investment Decisions • Choosing a Financial Advisor • Investing with and without a Partner • Dealing with the Expected and Unexpected

USER'S GUIDE TO THE INFORMATION AGE

by Kenneth M. Morris
Introduction by David C. Nagel

The bits and bytes behind the technologies that are changing everyday life in the 21st century.

Using Computers • Surfing the Internet • Connecting with Cell Phones • Enjoying Smart Appliances • Managing Online Accounts • Living in the Electronic Age

CREATING RETIREMENT INCOME

by Virginia B. Morris
Introduction by Mark J. Mackey

An in-depth look at building and managing retirement income—with a special focus on the role annuities play in an overall retirement plan.

Asset Accumulation • Income Streams • Withdrawal Options • Rollovers • Diversified Portfolios • Variable Annuities

THE WALL STREET JOURNAL GUIDE TO PLANNING YOUR FINANCIAL FUTURE

by Kenneth M. Morris, Alan M. Siegel
and Virginia B. Morris

An all-inclusive guide to retiring in comfort, including the information you need to make smart long-term decisions.

Investment Strategies • Salary Reduction Plans • Social Security • Insurance • Pension Plans • Long-term Care • Estate Planning

THE WALL STREET JOURNAL GUIDE TO UNDERSTANDING MONEY & INVESTING IN ASIA

by Kenneth M. Morris, Alan M. Siegel
and Beverly Larson

A comprehensive overview of financial markets in the Asian-Pacific region and beyond.

Stocks • Bonds • Mutual Funds • Indexes • Risk/Return • Tracking Performance • Changing Currency Values

GUIDE TO CHOOSING, SERVING & ENJOYING WINE

by Allen R. Balik and Virginia B. Morris
Foreword by R. Michael Mondavi

A sparkling guide that uncorks the myths about choosing, serving and enjoying wine and includes tips from famous winemakers and restaurateurs.

Ordering Wine in a Restaurant • Matching Wine with Food • Tasting and Judging Wines • Entertaining Guests at Home • Starting a Wine Collection

ORDER FORM

TITLES FROM LIGHTBULB PRESS

Available in bookstores everywhere or directly from Lightbulb Press.
Bulk discounts are available. Contact our sales department at 917-256-4900
for more information.

TITLE	PRICE	QUANTITY	SUBTOTAL
The Wall Street Journal Guide to Planning Your Financial Future: The Easy-to-Read Guide to Planning for Retirement ISBN: 0-684-85724-3	$15.95	_____	_____
The Wall Street Journal Guide to Understanding Money & Investing ISBN: 0-684-86902-0	$15.95	_____	_____
The Asian Wall Street Journal Guide to Understanding Money & Investing in Asia ISBN: 0-684-84650-0	$14.95	_____	_____
The Wall Street Journal Guide to Understanding Personal Finance ISBN: 0-7432-0391-7	$15.95	_____	_____
A Woman's Guide to Investing ISBN: 0-07-134524-8	$14.95	_____	_____
Creating Retirement Income ISBN: 0-07-134525-6	$14.95	_____	_____
Dictionary of Financial Terms ISBN: 0-07-135903-6	$14.95	_____	_____
Guide to Choosing, Serving and Enjoying Wine ISBN: 0-07-135905-2	$14.95	_____	_____
User's Guide to the Information Age ISBN: 0-07-134947-2	$14.95	_____	_____

Sub total _____

Tax (NY only) _____

Shipping* _____

TOTAL DUE _____

* $4 shipping for orders sent to addresses in the Continental US. Actual shipping
charges will apply for 4 or more copies (call for cost). Sorry, no international orders.

SHIPPING INFORMATION

Name _____

Address _____ Apt. _____

City _____ State ___ Zip _____

Daytime phone _____

BILLING INFORMATION
(for credit card orders only)

Name _____

Address _____ Apt. _____

City _____ State ___ Zip _____

Daytime phone _____

___ AmEx ___ MasterCard ___ Visa

Account number_____

Expiration date _____

WITH A CREDIT CARD
Call 800-581-9884.

ON THE INTERNET
Visit our website at **www.lightbulbpress.com**.

BY MAIL
Complete this form and send it with a **money order** payable to **Lightbulb Press** for the total due to the address shown below. Checks or cash cannot be accepted.

BY FAX
Complete this form, include your credit card information, and fax it to the number shown below.

LIGHTBULB PRESS, INC.
112 Madison Avenue
New York, NY 10016
www.lightbulbpress.com
Phone 917-256-4900
Fax   917-256-4949